OECD Pensions Outlook 2024

IMPROVING ASSET-BACKED PENSIONS FOR BETTER RETIREMENT OUTCOMES AND MORE RESILIENT PENSION SYSTEMS

OECD
BETTER POLICIES FOR BETTER LIVES

Please cite this publication as:
OECD (2024), *OECD Pensions Outlook 2024: Improving Asset-backed Pensions for Better Retirement Outcomes and More Resilient Pension Systems*, OECD Publishing, Paris, https://doi.org/10.1787/51510909-en.

ISBN 978-92-64-93427-6 (print)
ISBN 978-92-64-58835-6 (PDF)
ISBN 978-92-64-61954-8 (HTML)
ISBN 978-92-64-97017-5 (epub)

OECD Pensions Outlook
ISSN 2313-7630 (print)
ISSN 2313-7649 (online)

Photo credits: Cover © Thinkstock – simoningate.

Corrigenda to OECD publications may be found at: https://www.oecd.org/en/publications/support/corrigenda.html.

Preface

Over the past two decades, asset-backed pensions have become a key pillar of retirement systems, with assets more than tripling to over USD 56 trillion in 2023. These pensions diversify resources for financing retirement and complement pay-as-you-go systems, enhancing resilience to economic shocks and demographic challenges. Their robust design, regulation, and supervision are important for delivering strong retirement outcomes.

The 2024 *OECD Pensions Outlook* provides a valuable resource for policymakers, regulators, and stakeholders, providing comprehensive analysis and forward-looking guidance on ensuring pensions continue to serve as a cornerstone of financial security in retirement. Specifically, this edition examines how to extend the coverage of asset-backed pensions, looking at how employers, particularly smaller ones, and the self-employed, can be better integrated in these systems, and how financial incentives can be used to promote enrolment and contributions.

The report also analyses how investment strategies can balance sustainability and risk, deliver long-term value for savers, and ensure that pensions are resilient to market volatility. In particular, it highlights the importance of longevity protection and innovative approaches to providing retirement income, such as options for pooling risks and leveraging home equity. The report elaborates on the importance of financial education and raising awareness, as individuals need clear guidance to plan effectively for retirement. For example, digital tools, such as pension dashboards, are important to empower savers and foster awareness.

These insights and recommendations aim to support policymakers in strengthening pension systems and meeting the evolving needs of society. Enhancing the design and governance of asset-backed pensions can foster more inclusive and resilient systems, secure better outcomes for individuals and contribute to sustainable economic growth and innovation.

Mathias Cormann,

OECD Secretary-General

Foreword

The *OECD Pensions Outlook* analyses pension policy issues in OECD member countries and partner economies, addressing all pension arrangements, private and public, in which assets back retirement income. It covers their design, regulation and supervision, as well as their role in complementing other components of the pension system. The objective is to offer policy guidance to improve retirement outcomes.

This seventh edition focuses on improving inclusiveness, financial incentives, the role of equity investments, the retirement phase, and communication to help individuals plan their retirement. It discusses how pension arrangements pooling multiple employers can help to improve access to asset-backed pensions, making them more inclusive. It examines how the design of financial incentives for retirement savings in OECD countries aligns with the OECD recommendations aimed at maximising their impact on enrolment and contributions. It assesses the importance of investing in equities to reach better retirement outcomes. The edition also looks at how the design of the payout phase can better meet financial needs in retirement, including through the use of home equity release products. Finally, it discusses the development of individual pension dashboards to improve communication and assist people in better planning for retirement.

This report was prepared by the Insurance and Pensions Unit within the Capital Markets and Financial Institutions Division of the OECD Directorate for Financial and Enterprise Affairs. It benefited from the review and contributions of national government delegates, particularly delegates to the OECD Insurance and Private Pensions Committee and to the Working Party on Private Pensions, as well as members of the International Organisation of Pension Supervisors (IOPS). The views expressed do not necessarily correspond to those of the national authorities concerned.

The editorial team was led by Pablo Antolin who provided detailed comments on all the chapters. Chapter 1 was prepared by Pablo Antolin, Chapters 2, 3 and 4 by Stéphanie Payet, and Chapters 5, 6 and 7 by Jessica Mosher. Editorial and communication support was provided by Eva Abbott, Liv Gudmundson and Tom Dannequin of the Directorate for Financial and Enterprise Affairs. Serdar Çelik and Romain Despalins provided useful comments and suggestions.

The OECD gratefully acknowledges the comments and financial support from Barnett Waddingham and MBWL International, Chile's insurance and pension regulatory authorities, the European Federation of Asset Managers, and Standard Life, part of Phoenix Group.

Table of contents

FIGURES

TABLES

Executive summary

The last two decades have seen significant growth in pension assets. In advanced economies, pension assets have nearly doubled as a share of GDP to an average of 55%, exceeding 100% of GDP in eight countries. This global trend is not limited to advanced economies. Many of today's emerging and developing economies also have pension funds with hundreds of billions of US dollars in assets. The growth in pension assets has been supported by policy initiatives aimed at diversifying retirement financing sources to create more resilient pension systems and improving retirement outcomes for individuals. Over half of the working-age population participates in asset-backed pension systems in most OECD countries.

With total assets over USD 56 trillion, pension funds are also the largest investors in global capital markets, including public equity and debt markets as well as emerging private capital markets. At the end of 2023, they owned nearly one-fifth of global public equity market capitalisation.

Given their growing economic and financial importance, it is critical to understand how to improve the design of asset-backed pension systems, promote their inclusiveness and examine the role of equity investments in their growth and performance.

Asset-backed pension systems should be inclusive and not exclude employees not covered by collective agreements and the self-employed.

Pension arrangements pooling multiple employers can promote inclusiveness by encouraging and facilitating employer provision of asset-backed pension plans, especially among small employers. Combining multi-employer arrangements set up by employer and employees' representatives through collective agreements with those set up by financial institutions will provide access to all types of employers and workers. The former can cover a wide range of employers, including small employers, and employees across sectors and industries, but they tend to exclude employees not covered by collective agreements and the self-employed. Those set up by financial institutions and by associations of self-employed workers may fill this gap.

Financial incentives have improved, but tax rules remain complex and the parameters for financial incentives are not always regularly updated.

With asset-backed pensions playing an increasingly important role in retirement, many OECD countries have in the last decade increased the value of financial incentives for retirement savings. However, tax rules remain complex in many countries, and tend to favour middle- and high-income earners. On the other hand, the importance of non-tax incentives such as matching contributions and subsidies favouring middle to low-income earners are gaining ground. Many countries fail to update income thresholds and contribution limits for tax relief, which may reduce the attractiveness of financial incentives over time.

Investments in equities lead to better retirement outcomes, although market volatility increases risks close to retirement.

Investments in equities represent a significant share of the portfolio of defined contribution (DC) pensions and have been rising steadily over the past 20 years. Equity investments account for more than 40% in 13 out of 38 countries, while they are less than 20% in only 7 countries. This positive trend, as investing in equities leads to better retirement outcomes, comes with more volatile outcomes for individuals and societies. It makes pension benefits sensitive to equity market downturns, potentially when individuals are close to retirement, and tends to work better over long investment periods. However, the regulatory framework should avoid default investment strategies that are too conservative, like fixed income only strategies, because of low returns. Moreover, it should allow providers to offer life-cycle investment strategies. The ideal level and profile of equity exposure is country specific.

The design of the retirement phase of defined contribution pensions should consider their role within the broader pension system, as well as the financial needs and risks they are intended to address in retirement.

Policy makers should ensure that essential spending needs are met, allow retirees to set aside a portion of their retirement savings to cover unexpected expenses and permit flexibility to meet discretionary spending needs, while encouraging options that provide a regular income.

Policy makers should establish default options carefully, ensuring that they are unlikely to cause undue harm. They should also promote awareness and education about the payout options available, and encourage the development and use of digital tools to help individuals understand and access these options at retirement. Additionally, policy makers should leverage behavioural insights to nudge individuals towards appropriate payout options, encourage and facilitate the provision and uptake of personalised guidance, and monitor and support the development of digital solutions for personalised advice.

Home equity release products can improve homeowners' financial resources during retirement, but they require adequate consumer protection and must overcome numerous supply side challenges.

Home equity products allow retirees who own their homes to increase their financial resources in retirement. However, policy makers need to ensure that the regulatory framework for these products guarantees their suitability and provides controls for the potential risks to homeowners, while also considering the need for providers to manage their own risk exposures.

Communication to individuals can be improved using individual pension dashboards if they are carefully designed and operated.

Pension dashboards facilitate individuals' access to information about their pensions and their expected future retirement income, especially when their purpose and functionality are clearly defined and coherent. Dashboards should include content relevant and useful for individuals to plan and should present information in a way that is easily understandable and effective in engaging users.

The development of dashboards should involve different stakeholders, ensure the accuracy and security of the data provided, and promote awareness and use of the platform. Their development is a long process that requires improvements over time, as well as regular monitoring of usage and retirement outcomes. This calls for clear objectives with a timeline of milestones, and measurable metrics to assess the impact of the dashboard given its objectives.

1 Assessment and recommendations

This chapter provides an overview of the main issues, policy options and recommendations presented in the report. It begins by examining how the use of multi-employer pension plans and financial incentives can increase access, participation, and contributions to asset-backed pensions. It also looks at the advantages of investing in equity markets to improve retirement income outcomes. Looking at the payout phase, it discusses how improving its design can help meet financial needs in retirement, and how well-designed home equity release products can help people to optimise the use of their financial resources in retirement. Finally, the chapter explores countries' experiences in developing individual pension dashboards to assist people in better planning for their retirement.

1.1. Asset-backed pensions are contributing to the diversification of retirement financing and strengthening multi-pillar pension systems, but they require sound regulation and supervision and good design to improve retirement outcomes.

Asset-backed pension plans, in which savings for retirement are invested and earn a return and assets accumulated help finance retirement, have led to a diversification of the sources to finance retirement. The amount of assets earmarked for retirement (Figure 1.1) and the proportion of the working age population participating in asset-backed pensions (Figure 1.2) have grown in the last two decades (OECD, 2023[1]). By complementing pay-as-you-go public pensions, these asset-backed pensions have contributed to the development of multi-pillar pension systems, a key OECD recommendation (OECD, 2016[2]).

Figure 1.1. Assets earmarked for retirement in selected jurisdictions

As a percentage of GDP

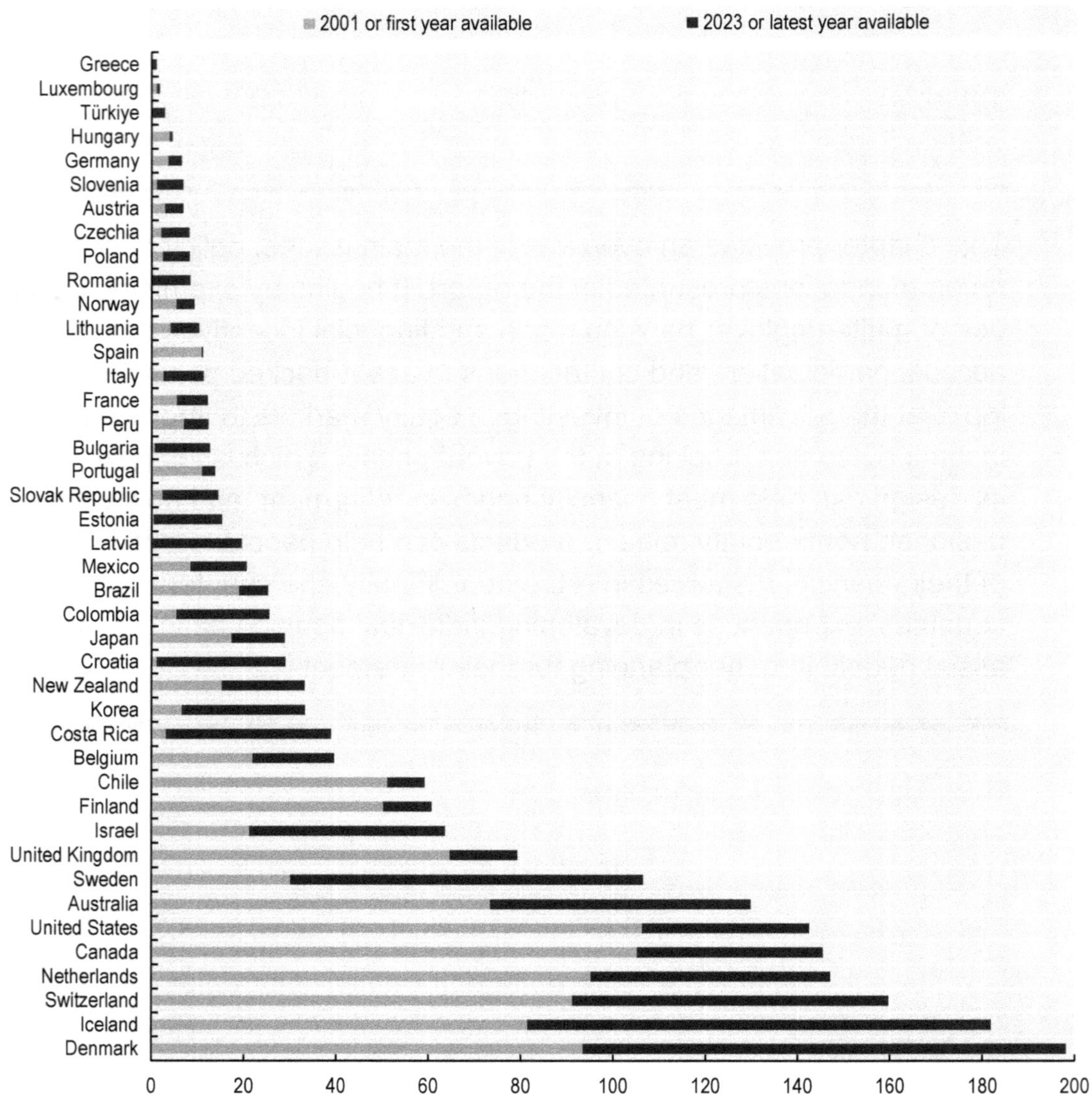

Note: Data is for 2001 for all countries except Belgium (2005), Brazil (2014), Croatia (2002), Estonia (2002), Finland (2011), France (2006), Greece (2007), Korea (2002), Lithuania (2010), Luxembourg (2005), Mexico (2005), Romania (2007), the Slovak Republic (2006), Slovenia (2003), Spain (2002) and Türkiye (2004). Data is for 2023 for all countries except Belgium (2020). The OECD Pension Markets in Focus 2024 provides detailed country-specific notes and information on the plans covered by the data.
Source: OECD (2024), *Pension Markets in Focus 2024*, OECD Publishing, Paris, https://doi.org/10.1787/b11473d3-en.

Figure 1.2. Proportion of the working-age population participating in asset-backed pensions

As a percentage of the working-age population

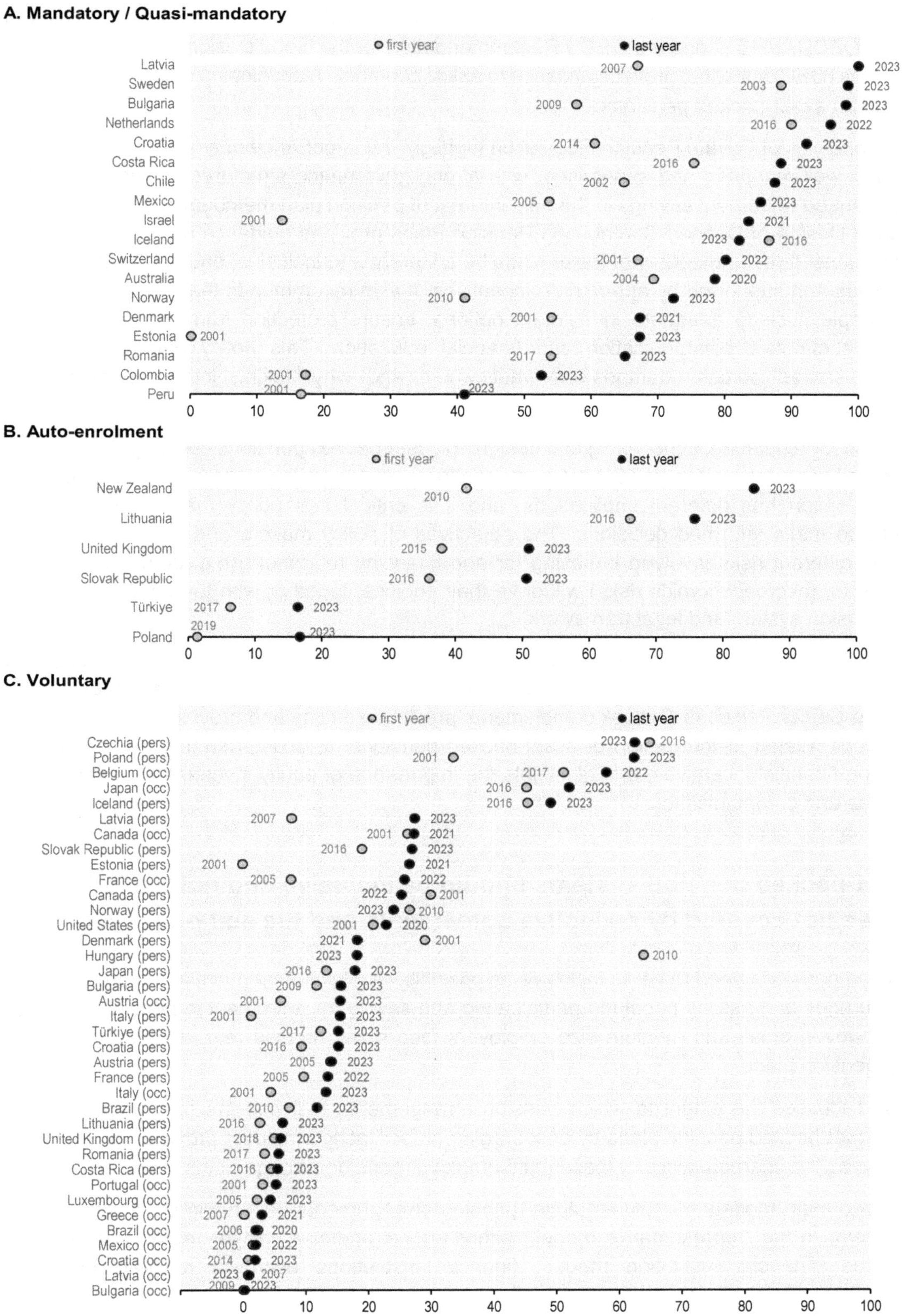

Note: See the OECD Pension Markets in Focus 2024 for details.

Source: OECD (2024), *Pension Markets in Focus 2024*, OECD Publishing, Paris, https://doi.org/10.1787/b11473d3-en.

Asset-backed pensions that are well regulated, supervised and designed, can help deliver better retirement outcomes. Policy makers need to consider the many potential challenges before introducing or reforming asset-backed pensions, during the implementation phase of the reform, and when trying to maintain or strengthen existing asset-backed pensions (OECD, 2022[3]). The OECD Core Principles of Private Pension Regulation (OECD, 2016[4]) and the OECD Recommendation for the Good Design of Defined Contribution Pension Plans (OECD, 2022[5]) provide guidance to assist countries in developing a framework to introduce and strengthen asset-backed pensions.

The Core Principles of Private Pension Regulation highlight the importance of ensuring that asset-backed pensions are well regulated and supervised, with strong governance structures to ensure that pension providers manage retirement savings in the best interest of pension plan members. The Recommendation for the Good Design of Defined Contribution Pension Plans provides guidance on how to design asset-backed pensions. It recommends that these plans be coherent and inclusive, and contributions are in line with objectives and supported by appropriate incentives. It also recommends that they should offer good value to people, include adequate investment options, ensure protection from longevity risk and are supported by effective communication and financial education. This policy guidance is based on experiences shared across countries on what works and why, taking into account the specific characteristics of each country.

Policy options for regulating, supervising and designing asset-backed pensions can vary depending on the objectives and associated risks. OECD recommendations provide policy makers with a range of options. Each policy option has different implications, and it is critical that policy makers understand these implications to make informed decisions. The objectives of policy makers and how they would like to address the different risks involved in saving for and financing retirement (e.g. demographic, financial, labour markets, macroeconomics risks) will drive their choices, together with the characteristics of their country's pension system and legal framework.

The OECD is currently developing guidance to support policy makers in implementing the Recommendation for the Good Design of Defined Contribution Pension Plans. In this context, the current edition of the *OECD Pensions Outlook* complements previous editions and provides policy messages for a set of issues related to the design of asset-backed pensions. It focuses on improving inclusiveness, strengthening financial incentives, and highlights the importance of equity investments, the design of the payout phase and communication.

1.2. Asset-backed pension systems should be inclusive and not exclude employees not covered by collective agreements and the self-employed.

Asset-backed pensions need to be as inclusive as possible. Involving employers in the provision of these plans encourages and assists people in participating and saving for retirement in pension plans (OECD, 2022[6]). However, small and medium size employers face many hurdles (e.g. administrative, costs) in setting up pension plans.

Chapter 2 discusses the extent to which pension arrangements that pool multiple employers improve access to asset-backed pension plans by encouraging or facilitating employer provision of pension plans. It also analyses the characteristics of these multi-employer pension arrangements.

There are two main models of multi-employer pension arrangements depending on which stakeholders establish them. In the "representative model", either worker and/or employer representatives establish them. In the "financial institution model", financial institutions establish multi-employer pension arrangements.

Under the representative model, a multi-employer pension arrangement for employees requires a collective bargaining agreement at the level of the firm, the industry or sector, or at the national level. The governing body comprises employer and employee representatives, but the management may be delegated to a financial institution. Only employers in certain industries or sectors covered by a collective bargaining agreement have access to the arrangement and participation is usually mandatory for employers. Membership is also usually restricted to certain employees depending on their union membership, industry or sector. Onboarding into the arrangement is automatic for employers covered by a collective agreement or requires simple adherence to the plan in case of voluntary participation. The self-employed tend to be excluded as agreements between employees and employers are not binding for them. However, some arrangements specifically target these workers.

Under the financial institution model, a multi-employer pension arrangement can cover different employers without any kind of pre-existing relationship. The governing body comprises financial professionals, although a mix governance structure with employer and employee representatives exists in some countries. The employer is usually responsible for selecting the financial institution for its pension plan. Nevertheless, at the firm level, this model may require a consultation or an agreement with employee representatives. The arrangement provides unrestricted access to all employers, but some providers may refuse to cover selected employers (e.g. small employers). Onboarding into the arrangement requires the employer to select and sign a contract with the provider of the arrangement. The self-employed may be able to join the arrangement on a voluntary basis.

Multi-employer pension arrangements have advantages over single-employer arrangements. For example, they may encourage a broader range of employers to offer a pension plan to their employees, in particular small employers. They also bring challenges. Table 1.1 shows that these advantages and challenges vary depending on the model.

Table 1.1. Main advantages and challenges of multi-employer pension arrangements

<table>
<tr><th></th><th>Representative model</th><th>Financial institution model</th></tr>
<tr><td rowspan="7">Advantages</td><td colspan="2">Reduce costs through economies of scale</td></tr>
<tr><td colspan="2">Reduce the administrative burden on employers</td></tr>
<tr><td colspan="2">Improve plan governance</td></tr>
<tr><td colspan="2">Provide more diverse investment opportunities</td></tr>
<tr><td>Improve portability</td><td></td></tr>
<tr><td>Can be run by non-for-profit institutions</td><td></td></tr>
<tr><td>Can fit the needs of workers in the industry</td><td></td></tr>
<tr><td rowspan="10">Challenges</td><td colspan="2">Provide fewer options to employers to tailor the plan to their needs</td></tr>
<tr><td colspan="2">May not prevent unequal participation rates across different types of workers when participation is voluntary</td></tr>
<tr><td colspan="2">Governing body less representative of specific employers and employees</td></tr>
<tr><td>Employers can be negatively affected by the behaviour of other participating employers</td><td></td></tr>
<tr><td>Exclude employees outside collective agreements</td><td></td></tr>
<tr><td>Contribution rates may be low</td><td></td></tr>
<tr><td>Members of the governing body may lack sufficient skills and knowledge</td><td></td></tr>
<tr><td></td><td>Economies of scale may not be passed on to employers and plan members</td></tr>
<tr><td></td><td>Small employers may be excluded, charged higher prices or provided with fewer options</td></tr>
<tr><td></td><td>Transition may be complex</td></tr>
</table>

Countries contemplating multi-employer provision of asset-backed pension plans may consider introducing a mix of different models, so that they complement each other to provide access to all types of employers and workers. On the one hand, while multi-employer pension arrangements established by employer and employee representatives through collective agreements can cover a wide range of employers and employees across sectors and industries, they tend to exclude employees not covered by collective agreements as well as the self-employed. Multi-employer pension arrangements established by financial institutions and by associations of self-employed workers may fill that gap. On the other hand, multi-employer pension arrangements established by financial institutions can cover a wide range of unrelated employers but may not serve well the needs of small employers. Multi-employer pension arrangements established through collective agreements in industries with many small employers could better serve the needs of small employers.

1.3. Financial incentives have improved, but tax rules remain complex and the parameters for financial incentives are not always regularly updated.

The design of financial incentives for retirement savings in asset-backed pensions should aim to maximise their impact on enrolment and contributions. Financial incentives are a useful tool for promoting savings for retirement and they seem to have been effective at increasing retirement savings and helping individuals to diversify their sources to finance retirement income (OECD, 2018[7]). Tax rules should be straightforward, stable, and common to all asset-backed plans as complex tax incentive structures and frequent changes may reduce the positive impact of tax incentives on retirement savings by hindering the ability of individuals to plan. Their design should at least make all income groups neutral between consuming and saving. Identifying the retirement savings needs and capabilities of different population groups could help to improve the design of incentives. In addition, non-tax incentives, for example matching contributions and fixed nominal subsidies, could help low-income earners save. Moreover, tax-deductibility ceilings for contributions should be updated regularly and consider factors beyond price inflation (e.g. when wages grow faster than inflation) to reduce the likelihood that individuals will reach the contribution ceiling and reduce their contributions.

Chapter 3 describes and compares the design of financial incentives for retirement savings across OECD countries. It also analyses recent trends in the design of financial incentives and assesses the extent to which countries follow OECD policy guidelines (OECD, 2018[7]). Overall, the design of financial incentives is in line with the OECD good practice.[1] However, tax rules remain complex in many countries and the parameters for financial incentives are not always updated regularly.

Most OECD countries provide individuals with financial incentives to encourage savings for retirement in asset-backed pension plans. Nearly all OECD countries provide tax incentives by applying a different tax treatment to retirement savings compared to other forms of savings, with the “Exempt-Exempt-Taxed” (“EET”) tax regime being the most common (Figure 1.3). In most cases, the tax treatment of retirement savings is likely to provide most individuals with an incentive to save rather than to consume. Moreover, some countries provide non-tax financial incentives in the form of matching contributions and fixed nominal subsidies, either as a complement to or a substitute for tax incentives. Since 2015, many countries have increased the value of financial incentives for retirement savings to increase the role that asset-backed pension plans are expected to play in financing retirement income.

Figure 1.3. Overview of the tax treatment of retirement savings in OECD countries, 2023

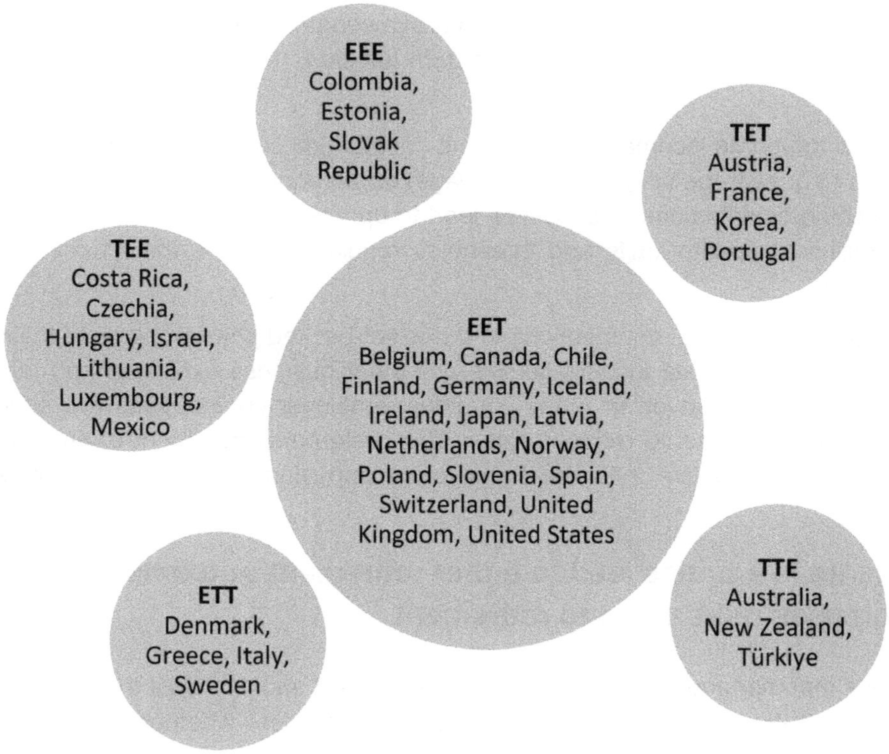

Note: Main asset-backed pension plan in each country. "E" stands for exempt and "T" for taxed for contributions, investment income and pension benefits, respectively. Countries offering tax credits on contributions are considered as taxing contributions when the tax credit does not cover the full amount of tax paid on those contributions for some individuals. The tax treatment of an annuity is assumed when different tax treatments apply to different types of retirement income payments.

Source: OECD (2023[8]), Annual survey on financial incentives for retirement savings, https://www.oecd.org/en/publications/annual-survey-on-financial-incentives-for-retirement-savings_2154cc08-en.html.

Yet, tax rules for retirement savings remain complex in many countries. Tax rules tend to vary depending on the type of pension plan, the voluntary or mandatory nature of the plan, and who pays the contributions. Even in countries where only one tax treatment generally applies to all retirement savings, differences may exist in tax-deductibility limits, tax rates or tax credit levels. Moreover, frequent changes to tax rules have occurred in some countries over the past decade, potentially deterring individuals from saving in asset-backed pension plans, as changes make people uncertain about the tax treatment that may apply to them in the future given the long-term nature of saving for retirement.

The tax treatment of retirement savings tends to favour middle and high-income earners in most OECD countries. Tax relief on contributions can take the form of a tax exemption, a tax deduction, a tax credit or a reduced tax rate. As most countries have progressive personal income tax systems, all these forms of tax relief, except tax credits, favour higher earners as they have higher marginal tax rates. By contrast, tax credits provide the same tax relief on contributions to all individuals and can even be set at a higher level for lower earners. In all OECD countries that use tax credits, these credits are non-refundable. This means individuals with a tax liability lower than the value of the tax credit can only partially benefit from it.

Matching contributions provide the same incentive to all individuals as a proportion of earnings. However, state matching contributions tend to be capped, thereby reducing the value of the incentive for higher earners. Additionally, some countries use matching contributions to target specific groups of workers, in particular low earners. Finally, fixed nominal subsidies favour low earners as the fixed amount represents a higher share of their income.

Countries generally tax pension benefits and apply the same tax treatment across all types of retirement income payments (e.g. annuities, drawdowns, lump sums). A minority of countries use the tax system to either encourage people to take their pension benefits in a certain form or to discourage early withdrawals. Among the countries exempting pension benefits from taxation, most restrict how and when individuals can take money out.

Many countries fail to update income thresholds and contribution limits for tax relief purposes in line with inflation or wages (e.g. average wage, minimum wage) on an annual basis. Moreover, countries offering government matching contributions or subsidies tend to update the maximum entitlements, at best, only discretionally. Failing to update limits and thresholds regularly reduces the attractiveness of financial incentives over time.

From an employer's perspective, contributions to the asset-backed pension plans of their employees are always deductible from corporate income tax like any other business expenses and rarely benefit from additional tax incentives. However, in many countries, employer contributions are exempt from social security contributions or subject to reduced rates. This preferential treatment of employer contributions makes them a more cost-effective option for employers than paying the same amount as salary.

1.4. Investments in equities lead to better retirement outcomes, although market volatility increases risks close to retirement.

Pension providers that manage people's savings for retirement should invest them in the best interest of members to achieve better retirement outcomes. Chapter 4 assesses whether investing in equity markets leads to better retirement income outcomes for members of defined contribution pension plans. First, it looks at the current practices and trends in equity investments in defined contribution schemes across a wide range of countries. Second, the chapter looks at whether investing in equities provides better outcomes using three complementary analyses. It assesses whether investing in equities provides higher average investment performance by examining the investment of actual pension funds, higher levels of assets accumulated at retirement using historical returns, and higher replacement rates considering capital, labour market and longevity risks using stochastic modelling.

Chapter 4 shows that equity investments represent a significant share of the portfolio of defined contribution pensions and that this share has been rising steadily over the past 20 years. In 2022, the total equity exposure of the schemes assessed including public and private equities, represented more than 40% of total investment in 13 out of 38 OECD countries. By contrast, total equity exposure represented less than 20% of total investment in only 7 countries. Average equity exposures tend to be lower in jurisdictions that cap equity investment. Moreover, there has been a general upward trend in the equity exposure of defined contribution pension schemes in many jurisdictions, with an increase of more than 20 percentage points between 2001 and 2022 in 5 OECD countries (Figure 1.4).

Figure 1.4. Evolution of equity exposure in defined contribution pension schemes

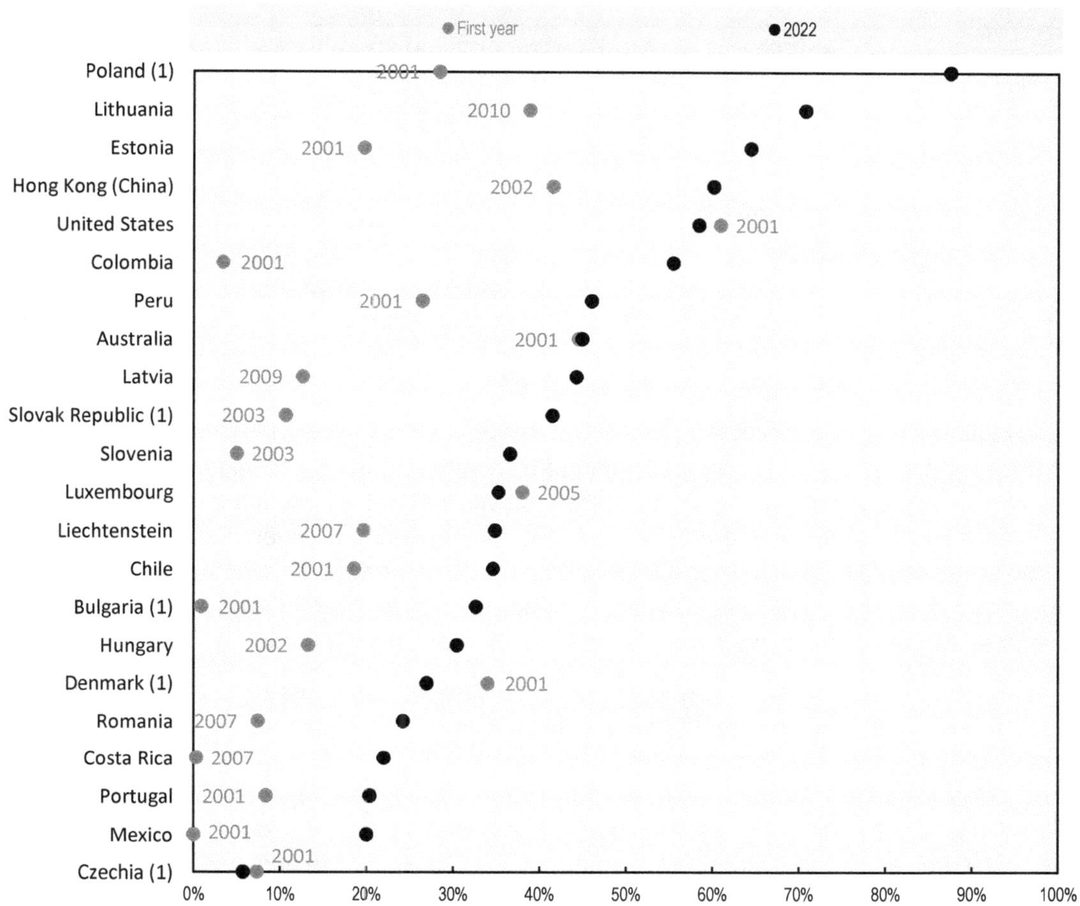

Note: 1. Equity exposure also includes investments in collective investment schemes as the look-through into different asset classes is not available.
Source: OECD Global Pension Statistics and US Federal Reserve.

Investing in equity markets leads to better retirement income outcomes for members of defined contribution pension plans. The analysis shows that higher investments in equity usually bring higher average performance when comparing defined contribution pension funds having different levels of equity exposure within countries or within pension entities. Still, diversification in terms of asset classes and geographical coverage plays a role in investment performance for a given equity exposure. Beyond investment returns, what matters to members is the total assets they will have accumulated by the time they retire and the pension benefits they will receive during retirement. Using historical returns on selected asset classes, the chapter shows that over 80% of cohorts across 19 OECD countries would have accumulated more assets at retirement had they invested at least part of their retirement savings for 40 years in a mix of domestic and foreign equities instead of only investing in domestic fixed income securities (government bonds plus cash and deposits). The analysis incorporating uncertainty using stochastic modelling shows a probability between 87% and 91% of getting a higher replacement rate when investing in equities compared to only investing in fixed income when considering a lifelong annuity for the payout phase (Table 1.2). The range depends on the investment strategy.

Table 1.2. Pairwise comparisons of the probability of obtaining a higher replacement rate with different investment strategies, lifelong annuity

	Fixed income	Equity	60/40 portfolio	Life cycle 10 years	Life cycle 20 years
Fixed income		87%	90%	90%	91%
Equity	13%		19%	24%	22%
60/40 portfolio	10%	81%		61%	41%
Life cycle 10 years	10%	76%	39%		24%
Life cycle 20 years	9%	78%	59%	76%	

Note: The table compares the probabilities to obtain a higher replacement rate with each investment strategy compared to the others. For example, the second column shows that the equity portfolio would produce a higher replacement rate with a probability of 87% when compared to the fixed-income portfolio, 81% when compared to the 60/40 portfolio, and so on. In contrast, the first column shows that the fixed-income portfolio would produce a higher replacement rate than the other strategies with a probability of no more than 13%.

However, investing in equities comes with certain caveats. First, achieving better retirement income outcomes from investing in equities requires saving for retirement for long periods, either by starting early or delaying retirement. Cohorts saving for 20 years instead of 40 would accumulate less in all investment strategies, with a much larger difference for portfolios fully invested in diversified equities compared to other investment strategies. Over longer contribution periods, the effect of compounded returns becomes more pronounced. Still, even with only 20 years of contributions, at least 69% of cohorts across countries would have been better off investing in equities than in domestic fixed income.

The second caveat is that investing in equities leads to volatile outcomes for individuals and societies. Case studies suggest that defined contribution pension schemes with higher equity exposures have usually faced more volatile annual investment returns over the past 7 to 21 years. Additionally, the volatility of replacement rates increases with equity investments, and, during the payout phase, yearly benefits are also more volatile when retirement savings remain invested in equities rather than in fixed income. Individuals therefore face more uncertainty regarding their level of pension benefits when investing in equities, complicating financial planning in retirement. Higher uncertainty and volatility also occur at societal level, as successive cohorts of individuals are more likely to accumulate different levels of assets at retirement when savings are invested in equities instead of domestic fixed income. Volatile equity returns imply that two individuals born just one year apart could end up with large differences in accumulated assets at retirement despite having the exact same earnings history, contribution rate and investment strategy. Even though such differences could be seen as unfair and hard to understand, they should be nuanced by the fact that both individuals would in general be better-off with a portfolio invested in equities than with any other investment strategy.

The final caveat is that investing in equities makes pension benefits sensitive to any equity market downturns that occur when people are close to retirement. For example, the stochastic model shows that if individuals buy a life annuity at retirement, the median replacement rate of the equity portfolio declines from 39% for all simulations to 31% for simulations with a fall in equity markets of at least 10% in the year just before retirement. Life-cycle investment strategies can mitigate that risk by maintaining a high exposure to equities during the first part of the accumulation phase and reducing it gradually as the retirement date approaches. The analysis from the stochastic model shows that, while the equity portfolio outperforms life-cycle strategies in terms of replacement rates in more than 75% of the cases, life-cycle strategies produce higher replacement rates than the equity portfolio with a probability between 40% and 50% when there is a fall in equity markets the year just before retirement. The attractiveness of the life-cycle strategies compared to the equity portfolio diminishes when the equity market fall happens further away from the year of retirement, as there is more time for a market rebound before retirement.

A common approach to address these caveats is to offer conservative investment strategies, but they provide only moderate protection to members of defined contribution pension plans. Chapter 4 shows that although retirement income outcomes are less volatile with a fixed-income portfolio than with investment strategies with some equity exposure, most people are likely to be worse-off with portfolios only invested in fixed income and would forego significant pension benefits.

There are important trade-offs when investing in equities during the payout phase. The level of equity investment in the payout phase affects the comparison between regular drawdowns and lifelong annuities. The analysis from the stochastic model shows that, when equity exposure does not exceed 20% during the payout phase, people would be better-off taking a lifelong annuity than taking regular drawdowns in at least 75% of the cases. By contrast, there is a 60% probability of getting higher replacement rates when staying invested fully in equities during the payout phase and taking regular drawdowns instead of buying a lifelong annuity at retirement. Therefore, if individuals value flexibility and take regular drawdowns, large investments in equities would increase expected benefits. However, this comes at the cost of higher volatility of benefits and the risk of outliving one's resources, which are risks that lifelong annuities address. Moreover, if individuals take regular drawdowns and withdraw too little during the payout phase or pass away early, they may leave a bequest to their heirs.

Based on this analysis, Chapter 4 presents a set of recommendations for policy makers:

- Pension regulators should avoid setting frameworks that lead to default investment strategies that are too conservative as equity investments tend to bring better retirement income outcomes. Individuals investing their retirement savings in the default option tend to stay in the default even though it may not match their level of risk tolerance (OECD, 2018[9]). While high exposures to government bonds and low equity investments in the default option may not penalise plan members in the short term in countries where government bonds provide high returns, lack of investment diversification may increase the concentration risk. Economic developments may also reduce future expected returns from government bonds, thereby affecting accumulated assets and pension benefits in the long run.
- Countries where defined contribution schemes invest mostly in fixed income should assess the appropriateness of their investment regulations. Investment limits for equity investments may be binding for defined contribution schemes in some countries. Countries should ensure that their investment regulations are not constraining equity investments in a way that could reduce risk-adjusted returns.
- Pension regulators should allow providers to offer life-cycle investment strategies to alleviate the risk of large falls in the level of assets accumulated when people lack the time to benefit from a market recovery. The regulatory framework should allow for innovation in designing the glide path to adapt to the needs of individuals. For example, the reduction in equity exposure may start in the last 10 years before retirement when participants are planning to take an annuity. However, if participants take regular drawdowns and remain invested during the payout phase, the reduction in equity exposure may be smoother and continue into the payout phase as the investment horizon is longer.
- The ideal level and profile of equity exposure is country-specific, and relevant stakeholders in each country should consider following a precise methodology to determine what would be the most appropriate equity exposure for default investment strategies. Default options are important for people unwilling or unable to select their own investment strategy. In some countries, policy makers may want to define a single default investment strategy for the whole population, while in others, policy makers may allow pension providers to define their own default option within a harmonised framework. Selecting an appropriate default investment strategy requires pension providers and policy makers to solve a trade-off between maximising the level of retirement income for plan members and minimising the risk that some plan members may get a retirement income that is deemed too low (OECD, 2020[10]). To solve this trade-off and select a default investment strategy, countries could follow the OECD framework, which involves five steps: i) pre-selecting the

investment strategies to be assessed; ii) assessing these strategies using a stochastic model to reflect the uncertainty of possible outcomes; iii) calculating indicators reflecting their potential riskiness and performance; iv) defining thresholds for risk indicators that reflect the importance given to the downside risk relative to the upside potential; and v) selecting the investment strategy meeting the thresholds for the risk indicators and maximising the performance indicators (OECD, 2020[10]). In implementing this framework, pension providers and policy makers should also take into account the role of defined contribution schemes in the overall pension system, the population's level of risk aversion and the characteristics of the target population for the default option, especially the length of the contribution period, the contribution level, and the payout options they tend to select.

1.5. The design of the retirement phase of defined contribution pensions should consider their role within the broader pension system, as well as the financial needs and risks they are intended to address in retirement.

The design of the retirement phase of asset-backed pensions should ensure that people are protected against longevity risk. It should also account for the overall structure of the pension system and the expected financial needs of different population groups.

Chapter 5 argues that a well-designed framework for the payout of retirement savings in defined contribution plans should consider the role of those plans in financing different needs in retirement (Figure 1.5) in the context of the pension system, as well as how individual and economic circumstances may influence the optimal solution for payout. It should also support individuals in accessing the most appropriate options for their situation at retirement.

Figure 1.5. Financial needs in retirement

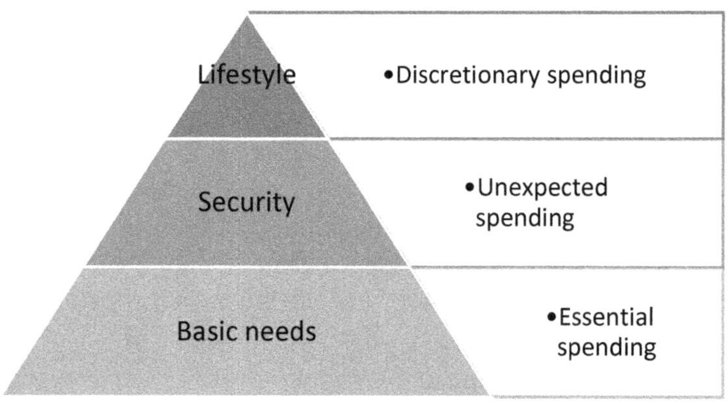

The chapter provides policy guidelines for designing the framework for the payout of retirement savings in defined contribution pension plans:

- Understand the role of defined contribution plans in financing retirement. Consumption benchmarks are useful to illustrate how much savings is needed to finance different living standards in retirement. Comparing expected retirement income from other sources with these benchmarks can provide an indication of whether savings in defined contribution plans will likely be used to finance essential, unexpected or discretionary spending needs.

- Consider the financial solutions best suited to meeting different financial needs in retirement. The role of the retirement savings plans in financing retirement will inform the payout options that should be available to individuals. Optimal solutions to finance essential, unexpected and discretionary spending will differ in the risks they should mitigate (Figure 1.6). Essential spending needs are well served with a guaranteed lifetime income that also mitigates inflation risk. Unexpected spending needs will require liquidity while allowing for returns to at least keep up with inflation. Discretionary spending will require more flexibility, but lifetime incomes can also be useful for regular discretionary spending needs to allow individuals to optimise their spending budget over their retirement.

Figure 1.6. Illustration of the risks that should be mitigated for different spending needs in retirement and the corresponding type of solutions

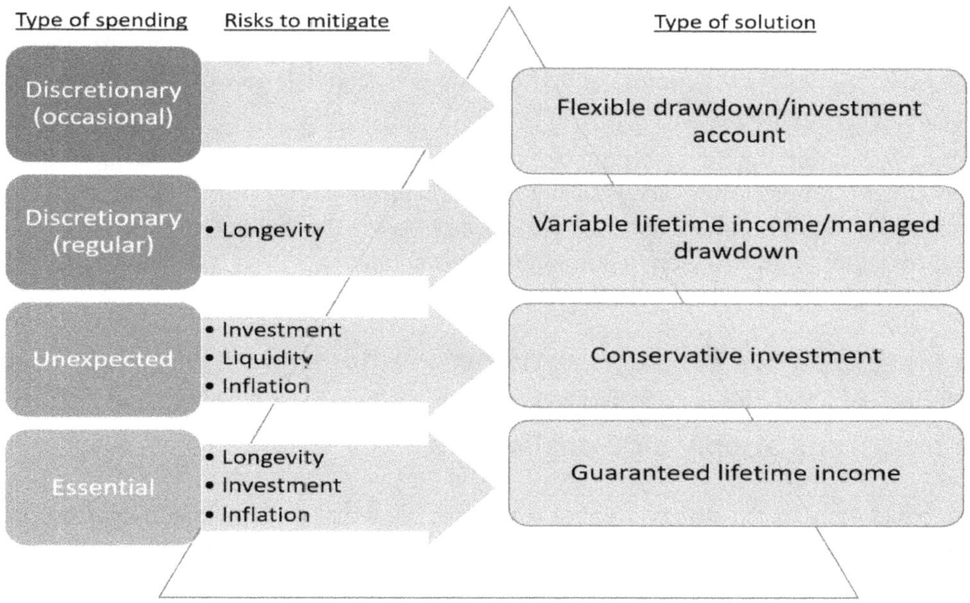

- Ensure essential spending needs are met while considering individual and market circumstances. While guaranteed lifetime incomes are well suited to meeting essential spending needs in most cases, flexibility may be needed in certain circumstances. Individual circumstances may imply that alternative options would be better suited for their retirement, and unfavourable market conditions may be detrimental to people if they have to lock in losses to obtain a guaranteed lifetime income.
- Allow retirees to set aside a portion of their retirement savings to cover unexpected expenses. Requiring that retirees convert their entire balance into an income may restrict their ability to adapt to unexpected events, particularly if that income is relatively low.
- Allow for flexibility to meet discretionary spending needs while encouraging options that provide a regular income. Discretionary spending needs are likely to be more heterogenous across the population, and thereby require more flexibility as to the options available at retirement. Nevertheless, regular discretionary spending needs are well met by options providing a regular income, and these options should be available. Individuals having higher balances or savings in voluntary pension plans are more likely to use their savings for discretionary spending needs.
- Establish any default option with care and only when the solution is not likely to cause undue harm. Most individuals defaulted into a particular payout solution are likely to simply accept the default rather than consider whether other options may be more suitable for their situation. As such, the implementation of a default option for payout needs to consider whether harm is likely for any

particular group, and ideally should allow individuals to later adapt if the solution is not appropriate for their needs.

- Promote awareness and education about the payout options that individuals have at retirement. Increased awareness and knowledge can help individuals to better engage with and understand their options and consider which may be most appropriate for their situation.
- Promote the development and use of digital tools to facilitate individuals' comprehension of and access to different options at retirement. Such tools can show personalised information, facilitating communication and promoting engagement with decisions at retirement.
- Leverage behavioural insights to nudge individuals towards appropriate payout options. Nudges, like highlighting the consequences of different choices, can be effective at guiding individuals towards appropriate outcomes but should be accompanied by tools that promote awareness and engagement with financial decisions at retirement.
- Encourage and facilitate the provision and uptake of personalised guidance. Such guidance can improve financial outcomes for individuals, but often people are not aware how to access it. Additionally, regulatory requirements do not always distinguish between guidance and advice in a sufficiently clear manner.
- Monitor and support the development of digital solutions for personalised advice. Digital advice has the potential to improve the accessibility of financial advice by reducing the cost of providing it. Nevertheless, such solutions are not yet developed for the payout of pensions, and individuals remain reluctant to fully rely on technology-based solutions.

1.6. Home equity release products can improve homeowners' financial resources during retirement, but they require adequate consumer protection and must overcome numerous supply side challenges.

Homeowners could use home equity release products to improve financial outcomes in retirement. Retirees who own their homes can use these products to increase their available financial resources in retirement. However, policymakers need to ensure that the regulatory framework surrounding these products guarantees their suitability for homeowners, while also addressing potential risks to homeowners and considering the need for providers to manage their own risk exposures. The regulatory framework for these products should consider established good practices for product design and contractual terms, as well as the potential supply side challenges.

Chapter 6 looks at the different designs and features of home equity release products available across OECD countries. It highlights that adequate consumer protection measures need to be in place given the potential complexity of these products and discusses numerous supply side challenges for the provision of these products.

Home equity release products come in several forms, and are largely based on two models, a loan-type model, and a sale-type model. The loan-type is often referred to as a reverse mortgage, which is a loan backed by the home as collateral. There are two types of products that involve a full or partial sale of the home equity. One is a home reversion, which involves selling all or part of the home equity to another party while retaining the right to reside in the home. The other is a sell and rent back scheme, whereby the home is sold to a third party and rented back to retain occupancy. They can structure payments in different ways (Table 1.3).

Table 1.3. Type of home equity release products and payouts possible, by country

Country	Reverse mortgage				Home reversion			Sell and rent back	
	Lump sum	Fixed annuity	Line of credit	Life annuity	Lump sum	Fixed annuity	Life annuity	Lump sum	Fixed annuity
Australia	x	x	x		x			x	x
Canada	x	x	x						
France					x		x		
Germany	x	x			x				
Hungary					x		x		
Ireland	x				x				
Italy	x	x			x		x		
Japan	x	x	x						
Korea	x	x		x					
Netherlands	x	x						x	
New Zealand	x	x				x			
Norway	x	x							
Poland	x	x							
Spain	x	x		x	x		x	x	
Sweden	x								
United Kingdom	x	x	x		x			x	
United States	x	x	x	x					

Home equity release products can provide a valuable additional source of financing for individuals' needs in retirement, but they are not suitable for every situation. These products should be targeted at individuals who are most likely to benefit from them.

Home equity release products are most beneficial for older individuals who would like to continue living in their current home for the rest of their life. As such, home equity release products are not likely to be suitable for those who plan to downsize at some point, as they can limit the flexibility to change homes and would reduce the value that people would get from the sale of their property. Younger retirees are more likely to have a change in circumstances that could require them to change homes, making the suitability of a home equity release product more uncertain. Additionally, reverse mortgages are relatively more costly for younger retirees because the debt accumulates over a longer period, reducing the amount of equity they are able to release with the product. Home equity release products can be particularly valuable for homeowners who need additional financial resources in retirement. Using home equity to pay off outstanding debt can reduce essential income needs in retirement. Home equity can also help retirees to absorb expenses that they may not be able to afford otherwise, such as home repairs. It can also provide individuals with a source of financing of last resort to support extraordinary expenses such as long-term care or divorce.

Home equity release products are better suited for those who do not prioritise leaving their home as a bequest to their heirs. These products reduce the home's value that can be left to heirs, either by increasing the debt heirs will need to repay or by reducing the equity owned in the home, thereby reducing the value of the bequest.

The regulatory framework should include measures to ensure that these products are suitable for the homeowners accessing them. These include requirements for advice or guidance, mandatory disclosures of relevant information, and the opportunity for homeowners to reflect on whether their decision is the right one.

Several jurisdictions require the involvement of an independent professional for an individual to acquire a home equity release product to help to ensure that the product is suitable. The role of these professionals can be to ensure that the individual understands the product and its financial implications, to assess whether the product is suitable given the individual's financial situation, or to verify the competence of the individual to make an informed decision in their own best interest. These professionals can also serve to flag any sign of potential elder abuse, where a family member or acquaintance may be pressuring the individual to take a home equity release product in order to take advantage of them.

Product disclosures should ensure that individuals are aware of the financial implications of taking a home equity release product and have the information needed to be able to assess whether the product is suitable for them. Good practice for reverse mortgage disclosures includes projections of the accumulated debt and home value, helping individuals understand how much home equity may remain in the future. Disclosures should also clearly highlight any potential tax owed on the proceeds of the home equity release product, as well as the impact it may have on other means-tested benefits that retirees receive.

Some jurisdictions require that home equity release products allow for a cooling-off period to give individuals the time to reflect on their decision and change their mind about taking the product if they decide the product is not right for them. These cooling-off periods are typically around 30 days.

While home equity release products have the potential to improve retirement outcomes for certain groups, they can also present significant risks to homeowners. The regulatory framework should aim to mitigate these risks and minimise any potential harm. Industry groups have already come up with numerous good practices in product design that regulatory frameworks can borrow from, and international experience provides additional examples of product features that can be beneficial for homeowners.

Home equity release products should provide tenancy protections that allow for individuals to remain in their homes for their remaining lifetime. Indeed, this is one of the main draws of home equity release products and prevents people from losing their home in old age. Ideally, declared spouses should also be granted the right to lifetime residency, even if they are not on the contract for the home equity release product or on the title of the home. If these protections are not granted, spouses could lose their home without having any means to relocate to a new home. Simply disclosing the consequences of not having tenancy protections for spouses is not always effective at getting people to understand them. A couple of jurisdictions take measures to allow for this protection, either through the use of trusts or through specific provisions in the regulation.

Other product features limit the debt that borrowers of reverse mortgages accumulate, including interest rate caps, limits on the debt owed, penalty-free repayments, and by allowing for multiple disbursements of funds. Where interest rates are variable, industry good practice is to introduce a cap on the interest rate to limit how much debt can accumulate over the borrower's lifetime. An important product feature to protect borrowers is the no negative equity guarantee (NNEG), which makes the loan non-recourse by preventing the lender from requiring heirs to pay back debt in excess of the home value. An equity guarantee is a similar feature that is available in some jurisdictions and guarantees that the owner retains a minimum percentage of equity in their home. This feature is useful where home equity can be an important source of financing for long-term care needs and prevents borrowers from exhausting their available home equity and losing that source of financing of last resort for significant financial shocks. Industry standards also allow for penalty-free repayments if borrowers choose to reduce their debt levels by repaying all or part of their reverse mortgage. Finally, another useful feature is to allow individuals to receive their payments over time rather than only as a lump-sum. This prevents debt from accumulating on a sizable lump-sum that individuals may not need immediately, and instead allows for a disbursement of payments over time as income or as a line of credit for borrowers to use as needed.

The contractual terms of home equity release products should ensure that homeowners will have adequate protections and will be treated fairly regarding the receipt and repayment of funds. Some jurisdictions ensure that homeowners are guaranteed to receive the amounts they are contractually entitled to even if the provider goes insolvent. This is normally insured by a government-backed guarantee, and this protection can involve an explicit premium.

Individuals should also be treated fairly if the provider enforces any payments due to a breach of contractual terms. Before enforcing payments or foreclosure on the home, providers should engage with individuals and attempt to remedy the situation, and failing this, they should provide a notice period before commencing any enforcement proceedings.

When payment to the provider becomes due, either because of death or permanent departure from the home to a long-term care facility, providers should allow for sufficient time for the sale of the home and the fulfilment of contractual obligations. Family members managing the estate normally have around 12 months to manage selling the home, and the grace period can be extended in the event of departure due to long-term care needs to allow more time to sort out the financial situation of the occupant.

While product design needs to limit risks to consumers, measures also need to be in place to allow providers to effectively mitigate their own risk exposures such as moral hazard, crossover risk, and the length of time until the home is sold.

Providers are exposed to moral hazard because individuals have less incentive to ensure the upkeep and maintenance of their home if they will not benefit financially from doing so. This could lead to a deterioration in the home value, reducing the price at which it can be sold and thereby increasing the risk that providers incur a loss. One way to mitigate this risk is to ensure that homeowners have sufficient resources to finance required maintenance, insurance payments, and property tax. Approaches taken to mitigate moral hazard include requiring adequate financial resources for an individual to qualify for the equity release product, requiring that a certain amount of the funds be set aside for maintenance and upkeep, or requiring that home occupants allow for regular home inspections to ensure the home is adequately cared for.

A key risk exposure for providers of reverse mortgages is the crossover risk that the accumulated loan balance exceeds the market value of the home. For non-recourse loans with NNEGs, this would result in providers not getting full repayment of the loan. Some jurisdictions require an explicit premium for a third party to cover this risk. Another measure to limit risk exposure is to limit the amount that individuals can borrow as a function of their home value and their age. Limits are lower for younger borrowers, say 15% of the home value of someone aged 60, increasing up to around 50% for older borrowers aged 80 and over. Such limits reduce the risk that debt will accumulate to a level exceeding the value of the home.

Imposing a minimum age to access a home equity release product reduces somewhat the uncertainty around when the provider will be repaid by reducing the expected duration of the product. A minimum age of 60 to access home equity release products targeting the elderly is common.

Nevertheless, other risks to providers remain, and supply-side challenges can go beyond the regulatory framework around home equity release products. For example, financing and capital requirements are a major barrier to entry, which can result in a concentrated and uncompetitive market.

Authorities could consider the introduction of a government-backed programme to ensure the availability of and access to good-value products to homeowners where the supply of home equity release products is lacking and where authorities feel such products could improve financial outcomes in retirement. Several jurisdictions have taken this approach. However, uptake remains low and further consideration is needed to promote retirees' awareness of and demand for home equity release products to capitalise on the assets they have available to them in retirement.

1.7. Communication to individuals can be improved using individual pension dashboards if they are carefully designed and operated.

Communication to members when designing, promoting, and reforming asset-backed pensions should be effective, personalised, regular, consistent and unbiased. Chapter 7 examines individual pension dashboards as useful tools to assist individuals in planning for their retirement. It recommends to carefully considering various design and operational aspects in the development of individual pension dashboards to ensure their success.

Chapter 7 presents good practices and lessons for jurisdictions looking to develop an individual pension dashboard to facilitate individuals' access to information about their pensions and their expected future retirement income to help planning. It looks at some of the individual pension dashboards that have been developed or are being developed to improve retirement planning and the delivery of pensions (Table 1.4).

Table 1.4. Summary of the scope and functionality of individual pension dashboards

Jurisdiction	Platform	Pillars covered	Functionality
Australia	myGov	2	Information, Limited account management
Belgium	Mypension.be	1, 2	Information, Data
Chile	Pension Simulator	2, 3	Information
Croatia	My Pension (Moja Mirovina)	1, 2 (3 planned)	Information
Denmark	PensionsInfo	1, 2, 3	Information
Estonia	Minu Pension	1, 2, 3	Information
Germany	Digitale Rentenübersicht	1, 2, 3	Information
Hong Kong, China	eMPF	2, ~3	Information, Data, Account management, Administrative functions
Ireland	PensionsVault	2, 3	Information
Israel	Pension Clearing House	2	Information
Latvia	Government Services Portal	1, 2	Information, Limited account management
Mexico	AFORE Movil	2	Information, Account management
Netherlands	Mijnpensioenoverzicht.nl	1, 2	Information
Norway	Norsk Pensjon	1, 2, 3	Information, Data
Slovak Republic	Orange Envelope	1,2,3	Information
Spain	Plataforma Digital Común	2 (partial)	Information, Data
Sweden	MinPension	1, 2, 3	Information
UK	Pensions Dashboard	1, 2, 3	Information

Pension dashboards that provide individuals with information on their accumulated pensions are expanding globally and have the potential to greatly improve communication to individuals about the retirement incomes they can expect. These platforms can offer an accessible and user-friendly format to engage individuals with their retirement planning and provide a comprehensive picture of retirement preparedness across different sources of retirement income. In addition, they can serve to make the operations and management of pensions easier and more efficient, and potentially provide relevant stakeholders with information to monitor the system's success in delivering adequate pensions.

Policy makers need to make sure that the purpose and functionality of the dashboard is clearly defined and coherent. Individual pension dashboards should provide functionalities in line with a clear purpose and objective.

They should also make sure that dashboards include content that is relevant and useful for individuals' retirement planning and present information in a way that is easily understandable and effective in engaging users.

- Dashboards should automatically include all sources of retirement income where possible and relevant.
- Dashboards should provide an estimate of future retirement income in real terms.
- Projections should convey the uncertainty around estimations.

- Retirement income calculators are a useful tool to aid decision-making.
- Retirement income should, where possible, be shown over time, not only at the point of retirement, and should reflect the different payout options available.
- Additional variables affecting retirement outcomes (e.g. investment returns, fees) are also useful to include.
- Allowing users to download a summary of the information presented can facilitate the use of the information for retirement planning.
- Information should be presented using a layered approach.
- Technical vocabulary and jargon should be avoided.
- Visuals can aid user understanding and engagement.
- Including information on what people can do to change outcomes is important to positively impact retirement planning.
- User testing is essential to identify the most effective formats for engaging different types of individuals.

There are numerous practical aspects involved in the development of individual pension dashboards, including how to organise various stakeholders to support, develop and manage the platform, how to ensure the accuracy and security of data provided to the platform, and how to promote awareness and use of the platform.

- Mandating pension providers to connect to the dashboard is effective in ensuring broad and timely coverage.
- The management of publicly owned dashboards by independent public or semi-public entities can mitigate potential conflicts of interest and ensure the appropriate expertise.
- Single access points can simplify the promotion of the dashboard but may not appeal to all potential users.
- Multiple stakeholders should be involved in the dashboard's governance.
- Dashboards should have a clear source of financing and a dedicated budget.
- Providers of data to the platform need to conform to a minimum set of common data standards.
- Unique identifiers are required to link pension accounts to individual users.
- Data protection measures are crucial to safeguard the security of individual data.
- The choice between a centralised database and a live-access model needs to consider cost, security, service objectives and data needs.
- Legislation should outline the authorised use of data stored in a centralised database by relevant stakeholders for policy developments.
- Communication plans are crucial for the success of dashboards.
- Pension providers can be useful to help promote dashboards.

Finally, policy makers should be aware that the development of individual pension dashboards is a long process that will likely require improvements over time as well as regular monitoring of usage and retirement outcomes to ensure dashboards are effective in achieving their objectives. Therefore, the development of a dashboard should establish clear objectives with a timeline of milestones to achieve them, and measurable metrics should be used to assess the impact of the dashboard given its objectives.

References

OECD (2023), *Annual survey on financial incentives for retirement savings: OECD country profiles 2023*, OECD Publishing, Paris, https://doi.org/10.1787/2154cc08-en. [8]

OECD (2023), *Pension Markets in Focus 2023*, OECD Publishing, Paris, https://doi.org/10.1787/28970baf-en. [1]

OECD (2022), "How best to involve employers in the provision of asset-backed pension arrangements", in *OECD Pensions Outlook 2022*, OECD Publishing, Paris, https://doi.org/10.1787/41f6fe2a-en. [6]

OECD (2022), "Policy guidance on developing asset-backed pension arrangements", in *OECD Pensions Outlook 2022*, OECD Publishing, Paris, https://doi.org/10.1787/f2537a8b-en. [3]

OECD (2022), *Recommendation of the Council for the Good Design of Defined Contribution Pension Plans*, https://legalinstruments.oecd.org/en/instruments/OECD-LEGAL-0467. [5]

OECD (2020), "Selecting default investment strategies", in *OECD Pensions Outlook 2020*, OECD Publishing, Paris, https://doi.org/10.1787/1c7381db-en. [10]

OECD (2018), "Improving retirement incomes considering behavioural biases and limited financial knowledge", in *OECD Pensions Outlook 2018*, OECD Publishing, Paris, https://doi.org/10.1787/pens_outlook-2018-8-en. [9]

OECD (2018), "Policy guidelines to improve the design of financial incentives to promote savings for retirement", in *Financial Incentives and Retirement Savings*, OECD Publishing, Paris, https://doi.org/10.1787/9789264306929-9-en. [7]

OECD (2016), *Recommendation of the Council on Core Principles of Private Pension Regulation*, https://legalinstruments.oecd.org/en/instruments/344. [4]

OECD (2016), "The changing pensions landscape: The growing importance of pension arrangements in which assets back pension benefits", in *OECD Pensions Outlook 2016*, OECD Publishing, Paris, https://doi.org/10.1787/pens_outlook-2016-4-en. [2]

Note

[1] The OECD annually collects updated information on financial incentives for retirement savings across OECD countries (OECD, 2023[8]).

2 Improving access to asset-backed pension plans through arrangements pooling multiple employers

Stéphanie Payet

This chapter discusses the extent to which multi-employer pension arrangements increase access to asset-backed pension plans by encouraging or facilitating employer provision of pension plans. It looks at the characteristics, advantages and disadvantages of the different models of multi-employer pension arrangements.

The involvement of employers in the provision of asset-backed pension plans presents several advantages. Employers can facilitate employee savings through payroll deductions and contribute on behalf of their employees. They can tailor the design of occupational pension plans to match the preferences of their employees and select features that can facilitate decision-making for employees, such as by introducing default options. Employers may also bear some of the investment and longevity risks, as well as some of the costs associated with operating the plan. They can also provide financial education to their employees, thereby increasing awareness among employees of the need to save for retirement (OECD, 2022[1]).

However, employers may find it difficult to sponsor and administer an occupational pension plan for their employees. Barriers preventing employers from sponsoring a plan include concerns over business profitability, the complexity of establishing and administering a plan, as well as the associated costs and administrative burden (OECD, 2022[1]). These barriers are likely to affect small employers more.

Pension arrangements pooling multiple employers have the potential to increase the number of workers having access to asset-backed pension plans by encouraging or facilitating employer provision of pension plans. These arrangements, which are called "multi-employer pension arrangements"[1], may reduce costs by achieving scale and alleviate the administrative burden on employers (OECD, 2022[1]).

This chapter discusses the extent to which these pension arrangements pooling multiple employers increase the number of workers having access to asset-backed pension plans by encouraging or facilitating employer provision of pension plans. The chapter looks at the characteristics of these arrangements and covers all types of pension plans and funds where employers have a role to play in pension provision, beyond just deducting and paying contributions. That is, they may establish the plan or fund, administer the plan, select the plan administrator or fund manager, or enrol employees into the plan. This includes occupational pension plans and workplace personal pension plans, but excludes personal pension plans that individuals join without their employer's intervention (e.g. mandatory individual account systems in Chile or Latvia).

The analysis shows that multi-employer pension arrangements have features that may encourage or facilitate employer provision of asset-backed pension plans, especially among small employers. There are two main models of multi-employer pension arrangements depending on which stakeholders establish them, either financial institutions ("financial institution model"), or employer and worker representatives ("representative model"). The different models lead to different management and governance structures, employer and worker levels of access, and onboarding processes. Multi-employer pension arrangements have advantages over single-employer arrangements. In particular, achieving scale by pooling multiple employers can reduce costs and the administrative burden on each employer, improve governance and provide more diverse investment opportunities. However, multi-employer pension arrangements also come with challenges, such as excluding certain types of employers or workers, or providing fewer options to employers to tailor the plan to their needs. Depending on the model, some of the advantages and challenges vary in importance.

Countries willing to promote employer provision of asset-backed pension plans may consider introducing a mix of different models of multi-employer pension arrangements complementing each other to provide access to all types of employers and workers. As multi-employer pension arrangements established by employer and employee representatives through collective agreements can usually only be accessed by those covered by such agreements, there is a need for multi-employer pension arrangements established by financial institutions to cater to the needs of other employers as well as the self-employed. Moreover, a public provider of last resort could be useful for small employers when existing multi-employer pension arrangements fail to appropriately serve their needs.

The chapter describes in Section 2.1 the different models of multi-employer pension arrangements and their management and governance structures. Section 2.2 analyses which employers and workers may have access to these arrangements, while Section 2.3 describes the onboarding process for employers.

Sections 2.4 and 2.5 discuss, respectively, the advantages and challenges these arrangements may bring, focusing on the policy objective of improving access to asset-backed pension plans. The final section concludes.

2.1. Different models of multi-employer pension arrangements

This section describes the two main models of multi-employer pension arrangements, as well as the management and governance structure of the arrangements. Multi-employer pension arrangements are vehicles pooling together different employers to offer occupational pension plans or workplace personal pension plans. They allow related or unrelated employers to join forces and pool resources to administer the pension plans and manage the assets. A multi-employer pension arrangement may include only one pension plan for all employers covered, with the same plan parameters for all employees covered. Employers within the same multi-employer pension arrangement may also decide to have several pension plans for different categories of employees. Alternatively, each employer within the same multi-employer pension arrangement may have its own pension plan with specific plan parameters.

The two main models of multi-employer pension arrangements are the "representative model" and the "financial institution model". In the former, worker and employer representatives, such as trade unions, associations of self-employed workers, groups of employers and business associations, establish jointly or separately multi-employer pension arrangements on behalf of workers and employers. In the later, financial institutions establish multi-employer pension arrangements, which different employers can join.[2] Multi-employer pension arrangements exist in many OECD countries and in some the two models co-exist (Table 2.1).

Table 2.1. Models of multi-employer pension arrangements in selected OECD countries

Country	Pension plan / fund	Model of multi-employer pension arrangement	Establishment
Australia	Industry superannuation funds	Representative	Through collective agreements at the industry level
	Retail superannuation funds	Financial institution	By financial institutions
Austria	Multi-employer pension funds	Financial institution	By pension companies
Belgium	Sectoral pensions	Representative	Through collective agreements at the sector level
Canada	Multi-employer registered pension plans (RPP)	Representative	By a group of employers or by trade unions and participation requires a collective agreement at the firm level
	Pooled registered pension plans (PRPP)	Financial institution	By licensed administrators
	Group Registered Retirement Savings Plans (RRSP)	Financial institution	By banks, credit unions, trusts or insurance companies
Denmark	Occupational pensions	Representative	Through collective agreements at the sector level or through profession-wide agreements for the self-employed
		Financial institution	By life insurance companies
Finland	Statutory earnings-related pensions (1)	Representative	Through collective agreements at the industry or firm level
		Financial institution	By pension insurance companies
Germany	Occupational pensions (1)	Representative	Through collective agreements at the industry level
		Financial institution	By financial institutions
Greece	Occupational Insurance Funds (TEA) (1)	Representative	By a group of employers that do not need to be in the same sector
Iceland	Occupational pensions	Representative	Through collective agreements at the industry level or profession-wide agreements for the self-employed

Country	Pension plan / fund	Model of multi-employer pension arrangement	Establishment
Ireland	Master trusts	Financial institution	By insurance companies or employee benefit consultancy firms
Italy	Contractual pension funds	Representative	Through collective agreements at the national level
	Open occupational pension funds	Financial institution	By banks, insurance companies, investment firms and asset management companies
Japan	Fund-type corporate pension plans [1]	Representative	By a group of employers and participation requires a collective agreement at the firm level
	Contract-type corporate pension plans	Financial institution	By trust banks, life insurance companies or pension management organisations
Korea	Retirement pension plans	Financial institution	By retirement pension trustees
Netherlands	Industry pension funds	Representative	Through collective agreements at the industry level
	Professional pension funds	Representative	Through profession-wide agreements for the self-employed
	General pension funds	Financial institution [2]	By financial institutions
New Zealand	KiwiSaver	Financial institution	By KiwiSaver scheme providers
Norway	Occupational pensions [1]	Representative	By a group of employers and participation requires a collective agreement at the firm level
		Financial institution	By life insurance companies, banks or mutual funds
Poland	Employee capital plans (PPK)	Financial institution	By investment funds, pension funds or insurance companies
Portugal	Closed pension funds [1]	Representative	By a group of employers
	Open pension funds	Financial institution	By pension fund management companies or life insurance companies
Slovenia	Open mutual pension funds	Financial institution	By banks, pension companies and insurance companies
Spain	Simplified occupational pension plans	Representative	Through collective agreements at the sector level, or by associations of self-employed workers, public administrations, cooperatives or labour societies
	Joint-promotion occupational pension plans	Representative	By a group of employers
		Financial institution	By pension fund management companies
Sweden	Occupational pensions	Representative	Through collective agreements at the national level
Switzerland	Common foundations	Representative	By professional associations
	Collective foundations	Financial institution	By insurance companies, banks or trustee companies
Türkiye	Automatic enrolment system	Financial institution	By pension companies
United Kingdom	Master trusts	Financial institution	By pension providers
	Group personal pensions	Financial institution	By pension providers
United States	Multiemployer pension plans	Representative	Through collective agreements at the industry level
	Multiple-employer pension plans	Representative	Through collective agreements at the industry level
		Financial institution	By banks or insurance companies
	Employer-sponsored individual retirement accounts (IRAs)	Financial institution	By IRA providers
	State-based auto-IRAs	Financial institution	By public institutions in selected states

Notes:

1. This type of pension plan / fund may also be promoted and established by single employers.
2. In theory, general pension funds can be established by any party, but all the currently existing ones have been established by financial institutions.

Under the representative model, when social partners establish a multi-employer pension arrangement, collective bargaining agreements are necessary at the level of the firm, at the level of the industry or sector, or at the national level to establish or join the arrangement. In 10 countries out of the 25 included in

Table 2.1, the social partners (i.e. employee and employer representatives) jointly establish multi-employer pension arrangements at the industry or sector level. For example, in Belgium, when the initiative to establish an occupational pension plan comes from a sector rather than one employer, the plan is established through a collective labour agreement concluded within a commission with employee and employer representatives of the sector. When one side of the social partners establishes alone a multi-employer pension arrangement, collective bargaining agreements may need to take place at the firm level to join the arrangement (e.g. Canada, Japan, Norway). For example, in Canada, trade unions representing the employees of unrelated employers in a specific industry can establish multi-union occupational pension plans. Negotiations to join such a plan are conducted at the firm level as there is no obligation for the employers of the industry to participate in it. By contrast, in Greece, an employer can establish an occupational insurance fund with other employers or join an existing one without the need to enter into a collective agreement with its employees. Finally, the social partners can establish multi-employer pension arrangements through collective bargaining at the national level, as in Italy and Sweden. In Italy, contractual pension funds are agreed in the framework of national labour contracts and applicable at the industry level. In Sweden, central employer organisations and unions conduct collective agreements. In the private sector, the Confederation of Swedish Enterprises has established a pension plan for blue-collar workers with the union LO and another pension plan for white-collar workers with the union PTK.

The representative model also includes multi-employer pension arrangements for self-employed workers. For example, in Denmark and the Netherlands, profession-wide agreements establish mandatory occupational pension funds for certain professions, such as notaries, general practitioners, or medical specialists. In Spain, associations of self-employed workers can voluntarily establish simplified occupational pension plans for their members and other self-employed workers.

Under the financial institution model, banks, insurance companies or asset managers may directly administer pension plans and manage pension assets, or may establish a subsidiary with the sole purpose of running that business.[3] Employers do not need to have any kind of relationship to join the same multi-employer pension arrangement. The financial institution splits the arrangement between different sections for the different occupational pension plans of the employers covered. Employers are usually responsible for selecting the financial institution for their occupational pension plan.

The governance structure of multi-employer occupational pension arrangements usually reflects their ownership structure. Under the representative model, employers and employees nominate representatives in the governing body. By contrast, under the financial institution model, the governing body is composed of financial professionals. Employer and employee representatives may take part in a stakeholder body with advisory and consent rights, as is the case for general pension funds in the Netherlands, for example.

There are cases where the two models of multi-employer pension arrangements intersect. Under the representative model, the social partners may delegate the management of multi-employer pension arrangements to financial institutions. In Belgium for instance, the commission establishing a sectoral pension plan must delegate the management of the plan to a pension fund or an insurance company. In Spain, the social partners establishing simplified pension plans for private-sector employees through collective agreements need to attach the plans to one or more occupational pension funds established and managed by pension fund management entities. In Sweden, the social partners in the private sector have established two pension administration companies for the occupational pension plans covering blue-collar and white-collar workers, respectively, but they procure the insurance companies that employees can choose for the management of their assets.

Under the financial institution model, the selection of a multi-employer pension arrangement may require a consultation or an agreement with employee representatives at the firm level. For example, in Austria, joining a multi-employer pension fund requires the conclusion of a collective agreement with the sector union. In Poland, employers must conclude a PPK management agreement with a financial institution in agreement with the trade union organisation in their company. If there is no trade union organisation in the company, employers need to agree with employee representatives.

The governing body of certain multi-employer pension arrangements combines employer and employee representatives with financial professionals. This is the case for example for selected commercial pension companies in Denmark (e.g. PFA Pension). In Finland, the supervisory board and the board of directors of pension insurance companies, which are financial institutions, have to include members chosen among the persons suggested by the central labour market organisations that represent employers and employees. There must be an equal number of such representatives for the employees and for the employers, and their combined number must be at least half of the total number of members in the supervisory board and board of directors, respectively. In Spain, while pension fund management entities and their board of directors are responsible for the management of occupational pension funds to which occupational pension plans are attached, employer and employee representatives are part of supervisory bodies at the plan and fund levels.[4]

In the case of multi-employer pension arrangements with defined benefit (DB) plans, employers may share biometric and financial risks, or transfer the risks to the provider of the arrangement. Under the representative model, employers usually share risks collectively. For example, in Canada, if a DB plan in an arrangement with more than one participating employer or union is underfunded and one of the participating employers goes bankrupt, regulators will not force a plan termination as long as at least one participating employer or union remains. Under the financial institution model, multi-employer pension arrangements running DB plans may allow employers to transfer risks to a third party. For example, in the United Kingdom, employers can transfer their DB plan to a DB superfund, allowing them to pass on the responsibility of guaranteeing pension payments to plan participants to the superfund, which uses a capital buffer to secure the pension commitments.

Finally, some countries provide financial incentives to employers to encourage them to contribute to multi-employer pension arrangements (OECD, 2023[2]). In Belgium, sectoral pension plans benefit from an exemption of the 4.4% premium tax on contributions. In Germany, employers contributing at least EUR 240 per year to an occupational pension plan on behalf of a low-income employee (i.e. earning less than EUR 2 575 per month) receive a tax credit of 30% of the contribution, up to a maximum contribution of EUR 960. This tax incentive applies to multi-employer and single-employer occupational pension plans. In Spain, employers can deduct from corporate income tax 10% of their contributions into an occupational pension plan in favour of employees with an annual gross remuneration of less than EUR 27 000.[5] In addition, employer contributions are not subject to social security contributions, up to a contribution limit of EUR 135.30 per worker and per month. These financial incentives are not specific to multi-employer pension arrangements, but they were introduced at the same time as a package to promote occupational pension plans.

2.2. Access to multi-employer pension arrangements

2.2.1. Employer access

Employers' access to multi-employer pension arrangements tends to be more restrictive under the representative model. Table 2.2 describes for selected OECD countries which employers can access multi-employer pension arrangements and the extent to which their participation is mandatory or voluntary. In Belgium, Korea, the Netherlands, Spain and Sweden, not all employers have access to multi-employer pension arrangements. Except for Korea, multi-employer arrangements in these countries are part of the representative model and their access is restricted to employers in certain industries or sectors, or to employers covered by a collective bargaining agreement. In Australia, Canada, Denmark, Finland, Iceland, Japan, Norway, Portugal, and the United States, multi-employer pension arrangements accessible to all employers complement other arrangements having more restricted access. For example, in Australia, retail funds and most industry funds allow any worker to join, while some industry funds are restricted to workers in specific industries. In Canada, pooled registered pension plans were introduced in 2012 to make it easier for employers not already offering an occupational pension plan to do so. The United States has been gradually allowing access to multiple-employer pension plans. The latest version of multiple-employer pension plans, called pooled employer plans, was introduced in 2021 and is accessible to any employer. Other countries, such as Austria, Ireland, Italy, New Zealand, Poland, Slovenia, Türkiye and the United Kingdom, only have multi-employer pension arrangements with unrestricted access to all employers. Except for Italy, these are part of the financial institution model.

Table 2.2. Employers' access to multi-employer pension arrangements in selected OECD countries

Country	Pension plan / fund	Employers with access	Employer participation
Australia	Industry superannuation funds	Any employer although some funds are restricted to employers in specific industries	Mandatory employer contributions to fund selected by employee or stapled fund
	Retail superannuation funds	Any employer	Mandatory employer contributions to fund selected by employee or stapled fund
Austria	Multi-employer pension funds	Any employer	Voluntary
Belgium	Sectoral pensions	Restricted to employers covered by a collective agreement at the sector level	Mandatory for employers in the sector but certain exemptions and possibility to opt out
Canada	Multi-employer registered pension plans (RPP)	Restricted to employers establishing the plan or belonging to the industry covered by the union plan	Voluntary
	Pooled registered pension plans (PRPP)	Any employer	Voluntary
	Group Registered Retirement Savings Plans (RRSP)	Any employer	Voluntary
Denmark	Occupational pensions	- Representative model: Restricted to employers covered by a collective agreement at the sector level or to certain self-employed professionals - Financial institution model: Any employer	Mandatory for employers covered by a collective agreement at the sector level and for self-employed workers covered by a profession-wide agreement
Finland	Statutory earnings-related pensions	- Representative model: Restricted to employers covered by a collective agreement at the industry level - Financial institution model: Any employer	Mandatory
Germany	Occupational pensions	Any employer	Mandatory or voluntary depending on the collective agreement
Greece	Occupational Insurance Funds (TEA)	Any employer	Voluntary
Iceland	Occupational pensions	Any employer although some funds are restricted to employees in specific unions	Mandatory
Ireland	Master trusts	Any employer	Voluntary
Italy	Contractual pension funds	Any employer based on industry, sector or geographical area	Mandatory under national labour contract
	Open occupational pension funds	Any employer	Mandatory under national labour contract
Japan	Fund-type corporate pension plans	Restricted to employers establishing the plan	Voluntary
	Contract-type corporate pension plans	Any employer	Voluntary
Korea	Retirement pension plans	Restricted to employers covered by a collective agreement	Voluntary
Netherlands	Industry pension funds	Restricted to employers covered by a collective agreement at the industry level	Mandatory for employers in the industry but certain exemptions and possibility to opt out

Country	Pension plan / fund	Employers with access	Employer participation
	Professional pension funds	Restricted to certain self-employed professionals	Mandatory for self-employed workers covered by a profession-wide agreement
	General pension funds	Restricted to employers targeted by the fund	Mandatory for targeted employers
New Zealand	KiwiSaver	Any employer	Mandatory
Norway	Occupational pensions	- Representative model: Restricted to employers establishing the plan - Financial institution model: Any employer	Mandatory
Poland	Employee capital plans (PPK)	Any employer	Mandatory
Portugal	Closed pension funds	Restricted to employers with a business, association, professional or social link between them	Voluntary
	Open pension funds	Any employer	Voluntary
Slovenia	Open mutual pension funds	Any employer	Voluntary
Spain	Simplified occupational pension plans	- Sector plans: Restricted to employers covered by a collective agreement at the sector level - Other plans: Restricted to employers targeted by the plan	- Sector plans: Mandatory or voluntary for employers in the sector depending on the collective agreement and possibility to opt out when mandatory - Other plans: Voluntary
	Joint-promotion occupational pension plans	- Representative model: Restricted to employers establishing the plan, but new employers may join it if the specifications of the plan so provide - Financial institution model: Any employer	Voluntary
Sweden	Occupational pensions	Restricted to employers covered by a collective agreement at the national level	Mandatory for employers covered by the collective agreement
Switzerland	Collective foundations	Any employer	Mandatory
	Common foundations	Restricted to members of professional associations	Voluntary for the self-employed
Türkiye	Automatic enrolment system	Any employer	Mandatory
United Kingdom	Master trusts	Any employer	Mandatory
	Group personal pensions	Any employer	Mandatory
United States	Multiemployer pension plans	Restricted to employers covered by a collective agreement at the industry level	Voluntary
	Multiple-employer pension plans	Some plans are accessible to any employer (pooled employer plans) while others are restricted to employers with some level of association (e.g. geographic location, trade or industry)	Voluntary
	Employer-sponsored IRAs	Any employer	Voluntary
	State-based auto-IRAs	Any employer	Mandatory in selected states for employers not already offering a pension plan

Participation is mandatory for employers in most countries when access to a multi-employer pension arrangement is restricted to employers covered by a collective agreement at the sector, industry or national level. For example, in Belgium, sectoral pensions are in principle mandatory for all employers of the sector (and their employees). The collective labour agreement setting up the plan may, however, exclude certain companies. In the Netherlands, although there is no obligation for employers to offer an occupational pension plan, if a representative group of employers and employees establishes an industry-wide pension plan, they can request the Minister of Social Affairs and Employment to declare that plan mandatory for all employers in the industry. In Italy, all employers hiring their employees under a national labour contract must establish a pension plan in line with their industry.[6] In Spain, participation in a simplified plan established by a statutory sectoral collective agreement is only mandatory for employers covered if the collective agreement requires it. Similarly, in Germany, participation in industry-wide occupational pension plans may be compulsory for employers depending on the collective agreement.

Employers may be allowed to opt out of the plan established through collective agreement if they offer their own, single-employer occupational pension plan of at least similar quality as the sector plan. This is the case in Belgium, the Netherlands and Spain.

In some countries, smaller industries may be allowed to join the multi-employer pension arrangement created by a larger related industry. In Italy for instance, the contractual pension fund for the steel industry also covers employers in the manufacturing, metal and machinery industries.

A multi-employer pension arrangement can play the role of default option or provider of last resort. In Italy, there is a contractual pension fund of last resort for employers in industries not attached to a specific fund by collective agreement. This fund used to be a public entity, but now one of the private providers plays that role. In the United Kingdom, Nest was set up by the government and has an obligation to accept all employers that want to use it for their automatic enrolment duties. In Switzerland, if an employer does not establish or join a pension institution, all the covered employees of this employer are affiliated by law to a pension institution known as the Substitute Occupational Benefit Institution, which was established by the employer federations and trade unions. In Sweden, the social partners procure the insurance companies members can choose, but for white-collar private sector workers, Alecta is the default option. In New Zealand, the government selects several default KiwiSaver providers by procurement for employees automatically enrolled by their employer. These employees are randomly allocated to the default fund offered by one of the selected default providers, except if they actively choose a fund or if their employer has chosen a provider.

2.2.2. Worker access

Membership in multi-employer pension arrangements may be restricted to certain workers. In Canada, multi-employer registered pension plans established by trade unions may require union membership for workers to be able to join the pension plan. If the local union agrees, non-unionised employees may be able to join the plan if the plan also counts unionised members of the same employer. In Iceland, around 60% of workers cannot choose their pension fund because they have to contribute to the pension fund corresponding their union based on their job. An employer may, therefore, have to pay pension contributions to different pension funds depending on the employee. Similarly, in Denmark and Sweden, blue and white-collar workers are covered by different collective agreements, and therefore different pension funds.[7] In Australia, some industry funds are only open to workers in specific industries. Moreover, in several countries, public sector employees have separate pension schemes. For example, Sweden has one scheme for local government employees, including municipalities, county councils, and regional and municipal companies, and another scheme for central government employees. In Norway, KLP is the pension provider for local government employees and was jointly created in 1949 by the Union of Norwegian Cities and the Norwegian Association of Rural Municipalities. In Spain, public administrations such as municipalities can establish a simplified pension plan for their employees.

Multi-employer pension arrangements do not usually cover the self-employed, and when they do, it is usually on a voluntary basis. Under the representative model, some multi-employer pension arrangements target the self-employed. Participation is mandatory for all self-employed workers in Iceland, while it is mandatory for certain professions only in Denmark and the Netherlands. In the Netherlands, this applies mainly to high-income professionals, such as doctors, notaries and dentists, but also, for instance, to self-employed painters. In Spain, self-employed workers may have the possibility to adhere voluntarily to the sectoral plan that corresponds to their activity if the collective agreement establishing the plan allows it. Besides, associations of self-employed workers can establish, on a voluntary basis, an occupational pension plan for their members in Italy, Norway, Spain and Portugal.[8] In Switzerland, the self-employed can join common foundations, the pension institution established for their employees, or the Substitute

Occupational Benefit Institution on a voluntary basis. In Australia, the self-employed can voluntarily contribute to superannuation funds open to the public. However, when the social partners establish multi-employer pension arrangements through collective agreements, the self-employed are usually excluded as agreements between employees and employers are not binding for them. Under the financial institution model, the self-employed may be able to join a multi-employer pension arrangement on a voluntary basis. In Canada and New Zealand, self-employed workers can voluntarily opt into an automatic enrolment scheme by contracting directly with a provider. Pooled employer plans in the United States can cover any employer, including self-employed workers, even if they share no common relationship or association with each other. In the United Kingdom, the self-employed can join Nest, which was established by legislation with the public service obligation to accept the self-employed.

Workers moving from dependent employment to self-employment may be able to keep contributing into the same plan. In the Netherlands, if employees are no longer covered by the same collective agreement, they may opt to defer their accrued rights until retirement age. A pension provider may accept voluntary contributions from deferred members for up to three years. When the deferred member becomes self-employed, this period is extended to 10 years. While 85% of pension funds provide the possibility of voluntary continuation in the pension scheme for the self-employed, two barriers may prevent take-up: the application and the voluntary continuation of contributions must be made shortly after termination of the employment contract (within 9 months and 15 months, respectively), and the self-employed must pay the sum of employee and employer contributions.

2.3. Onboarding process for employers

The first step for onboarding employers and employees into a multi-employer pension arrangement is usually to reach an agreement between employer and employee representatives to create an occupational pension plan. This agreement may be signed at the national, industry, sector or firm level (see Table 2.1). In Austria, Poland and Slovenia, a collective agreement is necessary even though a financial institution establishes the multi-employer arrangement (financial institution model).

Employers usually need to select a provider and sign a contract with that provider under the financial institution model. This is the case for example in Austria, Canada (PRPP), Finland (pension insurance companies), Korea, Poland, Portugal and the United Kingdom (master trusts). In Poland, employers have to conclude a PPK management agreement with a financial institution and a PPK contract in the name of and on behalf of each employee eligible for automatic enrolment. In some cases, employers only select a provider and then each employee joining the plan must directly sign a contract with that provider. This is the case for workplace personal pension plans, such as in the United Kingdom (group personal pensions) and the United States (employer-sponsored IRAs). To assist in the selection process, employers may hire a consultant to study the market and make proposals of financial institutions based on the needs of the employer. This is usually what employers do in the United Kingdom.

The onboarding process is, by contrast, smoother under the representative model. In Belgium, the social partners establishing a sectoral pension plan need to designate a plan organiser run by employer and employee representatives. This plan organiser is then responsible for the pension promise, the selection of the pension institution and the payment of the contributions to the pension institution. Each employer covered by the collective agreement only needs to pay the contributions to the plan organiser. In Denmark, if an employer is a member of the business association part of the collective agreement, then participation in the collective occupational pension plan is automatic. This is the same in Sweden, however, if an employer is not part of the Confederation of Swedish Enterprises, the employer needs to sign a collective agreement directly with the unions representing the employees of the company or, in the case of blue-collar workers, to make a direct agreement with the corresponding pension administration company. In

Spain, employers only need to adhere to the plan established at the level of the industry or sector by the social partners to offer a simplified occupational pension plan to their employees.

Some providers have fully online onboarding processes. This is the case for example of Nest in the United Kingdom. When an employer selects Nest for its enrolment duties, signing up with it is straightforward.[9] The employer first needs to create an online Nest account and then complete five tasks:

1. Read and accept Nest's terms and conditions.
2. Provide business information.
3. Give details about any delegates or third-party administrator (e.g. payroll administrator) that will help run the account.
4. Inform about how contributions will be paid (bank or credit card details).
5. Enter pay information and contribution rates.

2.4. Advantages of multi-employer pension arrangements

One of the key advantages of multi-employer pension arrangements is their potential to reduce costs through economies of scale. Although large employers can establish their own occupational pension plan and achieve scale, this may be more difficult for medium and small employers. Multi-employer pension arrangements allow businesses to pool resources and increase their negotiation power with service providers. Small employers are the ones who can benefit the most from economies of scale. Multi-employer pension arrangements should lead to lower costs for employers related to the establishment and administration of occupational pension plans, and lower fees for plan members. Sweden takes advantage of scale in two ways. First, plan administration is carried out by only two pension administration companies for all private sector employees. Second, insurance companies are put in competition to reduce fees for plan members. The advantage of pooling many employers becomes stronger when the expected number of plan members is large, either because plan membership is compulsory for employees (e.g. Australia, Belgium, Denmark, Finland, Iceland, the Netherlands, Norway, Sweden and Switzerland) or automatic with an opt-out option (e.g. Canada, New Zealand, Poland and the United Kingdom).

Another advantage of multi-employer pension arrangements is to reduce the administrative burden for employers by transferring part of it to a third party. For example, in Belgium, plan organisers, not individual employers, are responsible for sectoral plans and for ensuring that pension commitments are fulfilled. These plan organisers are set up at the level of the sector with employee and employer representatives. In the United States, pooled employer plans allow unrelated employers to outsource a large part of their fiduciary duties to the financial institution sponsoring the arrangement. This reduces the compliance burden on employers, as well as the risk of litigation in case of mistakes, although employers retain some responsibilities for selecting and monitoring the plan provider, submitting payroll files, and funding contributions timely.

Multi-employer pension arrangements are well suited to cover small employers. Indeed, the administrative and financial burdens involved in running a pension plan can be better distributed. Belgium introduced sectoral pensions with the primary objective of expanding coverage for employees in small and medium-sized enterprises. Sectoral pensions exist for example in the construction sector, the food industry, the chemical industry and the non-market sector. In Denmark, PensionDanmark is the pension provider for all blue-collar workers covered by a collective agreement and around 80% of its active members work in companies with less than 10 employees.

Multi-employer pension arrangements can also improve plan governance. Under the financial institution model, the governing body is usually composed of financial professionals who are subject to tight "fit and proper" criteria. Under the representative model, the pool of potentially suitable candidates for the governing body is usually larger than in the case of a single-employer arrangement.

Size also provides more diverse investment opportunities. By pooling resources, multi-employer pension arrangements may allow pension entities to invest in more complex asset classes through higher-skilled investment teams and increased ability to negotiate lower fees with asset managers. For example, only large investors can access direct unlisted equity investment in infrastructure projects as these investments require scale, good governance to oversee the programme and a long-term investment horizon (OECD, 2022[3]).

Multi-employer pension arrangements may also improve portability. This is particularly the case for multi-employer pension arrangements established through collective agreements and covering an entire industry or sector. Employees changing jobs within the same collective agreement automatically remain in the same plan. Under the financial institution model, frictionless portability may not be guaranteed, however. For example, in the United Kingdom, Nest merges the accounts of members enrolled through different employers, but some master trusts cannot consolidate the accounts of members covered under different sections of their arrangement.[10]

Multi-employer pension arrangements under the representative model may bring additional advantages. Plans established by the social partners may have more stable rules as they should represent a long-term commitment from employees and employers in a particular industry, and thereby may be less subject to changes in governments. Additionally, the institutions managing the plans may run on a non-for-profit basis, as it is the case for example in Australia, Denmark and Italy. Finally, plans agreed at the level of an industry may better fit the needs of workers in that industry. For example, in Australia and Denmark, pension funds also offer insurance products and adjust their product coverage to the characteristics of their members.

2.5. Challenges associated with multi-employer pension arrangements

Multi-employer pension arrangements may provide fewer options to employers and reduce the possibilities of tailoring the plan to their needs when compared to single-employer occupational pension arrangements. Under the representative model, the same plan rules apply to all employers and employees covered by the same collective agreement ("one-size-fits-all"). In Belgium, the Netherlands and Spain, employers can opt out of the sectoral plan if they offer an occupational plan of at least similar quality. In Belgium, the employer may also offer an occupational pension plan in addition to the sectoral plan. This is called "opting up". Under the financial institution model, employers can usually select some of the design parameters, such as the contribution rate and the investment options. For the latter, however, the financial institution may limit the number of available options to reduce costs.

Financial institutions may not pass on economies of scale to employers and plan members under the financial institution model.[11] For example, the Australian Productivity Commission found that fees charged by industry funds (representative model) are well below those charged by retail funds (financial institution model) (Productivity Commission, 2018[4]). Similarly, the Italian pension supervisor shows that the average synthetic cost indicator for a representative member with a holding period of 10 years is lower for contractual pension funds (representative model) than for open pension funds (financial institution model), at 0.47% versus 1.35% in 2022 (COVIP, 2023[5]).

Additionally, multi-employer pension arrangements may not avoid unequal participation rates across different types of workers when participation is voluntary. For example, in Italy, multi-employer pension arrangements are mandatory for employers but voluntary for employees. Employees are enrolled automatically when they join the labour market, but they can opt out. Employee participation rates are much higher in industrial sectors, such as energy, chemicals and pharmaceuticals (between 70% and

90%) than in the retail, tourism and services sectors (around 10%) (Jessoula, 2018[6]). The fact that firms tend to be larger and to have greater union representation in the industrial sectors may lead to more efforts to foster employee participation. Additionally, the retail, tourism and services sectors tend to have smaller firms and more vulnerable workers, such as women, younger workers and low-income earners. Moreover, employer contributions into occupational pension plans come from their mandatory severance pay contributions (called *Trattamento di Fine Rapporto*, TFR). Smaller employers may encourage employees to opt out of occupational pension plans to keep these contributions in the company, as they may provide readily accessible financing. Meanwhile, vulnerable workers may be more likely to opt out of occupational pension plans as they may prefer to keep the TFR as a severance allowance, which provides a guaranteed rate of return and is accessible when leaving the company.

Small employers may be at a disadvantage under the financial institution model. For example, in the United Kingdom, some master trusts refuse to serve small employers because they are less economically beneficial. By contrast, Nest is a master trust with a legal requirement to accept all employers. Moreover, some master trusts establish their price based on the number of members, the membership age structure and the expected contribution flows. Smaller employers, therefore, are charged relatively higher given the lower number of covered employees. Finally, some master trusts also offer fewer options to smaller employers as they are reluctant to set up specific products for a small number of potential members. By contrast, they tend to offer more bespoke options to larger employers to attract them.[12]

Another challenge with multi-employer pension arrangements relates to the composition of the governing body and the suitability of its members. Under the financial institution model, the governing body usually lacks employee and employer representatives, and this may reduce its accountability towards these stakeholders. Under the representative model, the governing body is not likely to represent the interests of the whole range of employers and employees covered given that they may have very diverse characteristics. In addition, employer and employee representatives may lack sufficient skills and knowledge to properly administer and manage the scheme.

Under the representative model, the behaviour of a subgroup of employers participating in a multi-employer pension arrangement may negatively affect the other participating employers. For example, when an arrangement runs a DB pension plan, the funding position of the plan may be weakened by employers leaving the arrangement. For instance, in the United States, employers can exit a multiemployer plan at any time, and when they do, they have to pay a withdrawal liability corresponding to their share of the underfunding, if any. However, the withdrawal liability may be insufficient to cover the full cost of the vested benefits of their workers who remain in the plan, creating a financial burden for remaining employers (Munnell, Aubry and Crawford, 2017[7]). Another example is when one employer failing to comply with certain legal requirements of a multi-employer pension arrangement can penalise all the other participating employers. This is the case for instance in the United States for multiple employer plans, which may lose their tax-qualified status if only one employer is not compliant.[13]

Multi-employer pension arrangements established through collective agreements between social partners may raise fairness issues. Indeed, they may exclude workers outside collective agreements. This concerns self-employed workers but also employees in companies not interested in entering collective bargaining agreements. For example, in Sweden, IT companies with young employees may not be covered by collective agreements. In Denmark, around 10% of employees do not have an occupational pension plan. Moreover, when occupational pension plans also offer disability insurance, pension funds covering blue-collar workers may not be able to provide as large retirement pensions as those covering white-collar workers because the former may face higher costs related to disability pensions (e.g. Iceland).

Contributions may be lower in multi-employer pension arrangements established through collective agreements compared to single-employer plans. In sectors with small employers and low wages, employers and employees may have few resources to pay pension contributions. In Belgium, employees participating in a sectoral pension plan had an average contribution rate of 1.5% and a median contribution rate of 0.9% in 2019. In the case of employer-sponsored occupational pension plans, the average and median contribution rates stood at 5.2% and 3.6%, respectively (Sigedis, 2021[8]). This may reflect the fact that sectoral plans mostly concern less productive sectors paying low wages (e.g. construction and hospitality sectors).[14] Indeed, sectoral plans were introduced by the Act on Supplementary Pensions in 2004 to boost access to occupational pension plans, which at the time were mostly offered by large companies in productive sectors (e.g. the chemical industry and the banking sector). In Spain, employers can decide to pay higher contributions to a simplified pension plan than those specified in the collective agreement.

Finally, there may be challenges related to the transition from single-employer to multi-employer pension arrangements, in particular under the financial institution model. Although single-employer pension funds may be cost-efficient and well governed, in particular with large employers, some countries with many small single-employer occupational pension funds may want some of them to consolidate and transition to multi-employer pension arrangements. For example, in Ireland, the transposition of the IORP II Directive of the European Union led to increased governance requirements and a consolidation of occupational pension plans within master trusts, which have governance structures in line with the new requirements. Even though the transition to a master trust is smooth for most pension plans, those with complex assets or benefit structures may be difficult to replicate in a master trust.[15] Moreover, employer inertia may limit the development of master trusts as employers may lack good understanding of the new governance requirements and may not realise that a master trust could be more cost-effective for their plan. In addition, data challenges related to members' contact details may prevent a smooth transition to a master trust.

2.6. Conclusion

This chapter shows that pension arrangements pooling multiple employers have features that may encourage or facilitate employer provision of asset-backed pension plans, especially among small employers. It discusses the extent to which these multi-employer pension arrangements improve access to asset-backed pension plans by encouraging or facilitating employer provision of pension plans. It also analyses the characteristics of these multi-employer pension arrangements.

There are two main models of multi-employer pension arrangements depending on which stakeholders establish them, either worker and employer representatives (representative model), or financial institutions (financial institution model).

Under the representative model, a multi-employer pension arrangement for employees requires a collective bargaining agreement at the level of the firm, at the level of the industry or sector, or at the national level. The governing body comprises employer and employee representatives, but the management of the arrangement may be delegated to a financial institution. Only employers in certain industries or sectors covered by a collective bargaining agreement have access to the arrangement and participation is usually mandatory for employers. Membership is also usually restricted to certain employees depending on their union membership, industry or sector. Onboarding into the arrangement is automatic for employers covered by a collective agreement, or requires simple adherence to the plan in case of voluntary participation. The self-employed tend to be excluded as agreements between employees and employers are not binding for them. However, some arrangements specifically target these workers.

Under the financial institution model, a multi-employer pension arrangement can cover employers without any kind of relationship between one another. The governing body comprises financial professionals, although a mixed governance structure with employer and employee representatives exists in some countries. The employer is usually responsible for selecting the financial institution for its pension plan. Nevertheless, a consultation or an agreement with employee representatives may be required at the firm level. The arrangement provides unrestricted access to all employers, but some providers may refuse to cover selected employers (e.g. small employers). Onboarding into the arrangement requires the employer to select and sign a contract with the provider of the arrangement. The self-employed may be able to join the arrangement on a voluntary basis.

Multi-employer pension arrangements have advantages over single-employer arrangements that may encourage a broader range of employers to offer a pension plan to their employees, in particular small employers. They also bring challenges. Table 1.1 shows that these advantages and challenges vary slightly depending on the model.

Table 2.3. Main advantages and challenges of multi-employer pension arrangements

<table>
<tr><th></th><th>Representative model</th><th>Financial institution model</th></tr>
<tr><td rowspan="7">Advantages</td><td colspan="2">Reduce costs through economies of scale</td></tr>
<tr><td colspan="2">Reduce the administrative burden on employers</td></tr>
<tr><td colspan="2">Improve plan governance</td></tr>
<tr><td colspan="2">Provide more diverse investment opportunities</td></tr>
<tr><td>Improve portability</td><td></td></tr>
<tr><td>Can be run by non-for-profit institutions</td><td></td></tr>
<tr><td>Can fit the needs of workers in the industry</td><td></td></tr>
<tr><td rowspan="10">Challenges</td><td colspan="2">Provide fewer options to employers to tailor the plan to their needs</td></tr>
<tr><td colspan="2">May not prevent unequal participation rates across different types of workers when participation is voluntary</td></tr>
<tr><td colspan="2">Governing body less representative of specific employers and employees</td></tr>
<tr><td>Employers can be negatively affected by the behaviour of other participating employers</td><td></td></tr>
<tr><td>Exclude employees outside collective agreements</td><td></td></tr>
<tr><td>Contribution rates may be low</td><td></td></tr>
<tr><td>Members of the governing body may lack sufficient skills and knowledge</td><td></td></tr>
<tr><td></td><td>Economies of scale may not be passed on to employers and plan members</td></tr>
<tr><td></td><td>Small employers may be excluded, charged higher prices or provided with fewer options</td></tr>
<tr><td></td><td>Transition may be complex</td></tr>
</table>

Countries contemplating multi-employer provision of asset-backed pension plans may consider introducing a mix of different models so that they complement each other to provide access to all types of employers and workers. On the one hand, while multi-employer pension arrangements established by employer and employee representatives through collective agreements can cover a wide range of employers and employees across sectors and industries, they tend to exclude employers not covered by collective agreements as well as the self-employed. Multi-employer pension arrangements established by financial institutions and by associations of self-employed workers may fill that gap. On the other hand, multi-employer pension arrangements established by financial institutions can cover a wide range of unrelated employers but may not serve well small employers. Multi-employer pension arrangements established through collective agreements in industries with many small employers or public providers of last resort could better serve the needs of small employers.

References

COVIP (2023), *Supplementary pension funds in Italy at end-2022: Main data*, https://www.covip.it/sites/default/files/relazioneannuale/supplementary_pension_funds_in_italy_at_end_2022_-_main_data.pdf. [5]

Jessoula, M. (2018), "Pension multi-pillarisation in Italy: actors, 'institutional gates' and the 'new politics' of funded pensions", *Transfer: European Review of Labour and Research*, Vol. 24/1, pp. 73-89, https://doi.org/10.1177/1024258917748275. [6]

Munnell, A., J. Aubry and C. Crawford (2017), *Multiemployer pension plans: Current status and future trends*, Center for Retirement Research at Boston College, https://crr.bc.edu/wp-content/uploads/2017/12/multiemployer_specialreport_1_4_2018.pdf. [7]

OECD (2023), *Annual survey on financial incentives for retirement savings*, https://www.oecd.org/content/dam/oecd/en/topics/policy-sub-issues/asset-backed-pensions/Financial-incentives-retirement-savings-2023.pdf. [2]

OECD (2022), "How best to involve employers in the provision of asset-backed pension arrangements", in *OECD Pensions Outlook 2022*, OECD Publishing, Paris, https://doi.org/10.1787/41f6fe2a-en. [1]

OECD (2022), *Strengthening Asset-backed Pension Systems in a Post-COVID World*, OECD Publishing, Paris, https://doi.org/10.1787/288cb3cf-en. [3]

Productivity Commission (2018), *Superannuation: Assessing Efficiency and Competitiveness, Inquiry Report*, https://www.pc.gov.au/inquiries/completed/superannuation/assessment/report/superannuation-assessment-overview.pdf. [4]

Sigedis (2021), *La constitution d'une pension complémentaire chez les salariés en Belgique: Participation et montant des cotisations en 2019*, https://pensionstat.be/file/cc73d96153bbd5448a56f19d925d05b1379c7f21/e32f207825d09109e17dcd1037e39cd8c11c0315/Rapport%20th%C3%A9matique,%20La%20constitution%20d%E2%80%99une%20pension%20compl%C3%A9mentaire%20chez%20les%20salari%C3%A9s%20en%20Belgique.pdf. [8]

Notes

[1] Pension arrangements pooling multiple employers may have different names in different countries, such as industry funds, multi-employer plans, multiple-employer plans, pooled employer plans, group personal pensions, or master trusts. This chapter uses the term "multi-employer pension arrangements" to encompass all.

[2] The term "financial institution" does not imply that all financial institutions establishing multi-employer pension arrangements are for-profit.

[3] In some cases, pension administration and asset management may be carried out by different pension services providers, such as in Korea.

[4] In the case of publicly promoted occupational pension funds, the Special Control Commission is in charge of supervising all pension funds and comprises members appointed by a public body on the proposal of

the most representative trade union organisations, the most representative employers' organisations and the Ministry of Inclusion, Social Security and Migration.

[5] When the worker earns more than EUR 27 000, the deduction applies to the proportional part of the employer contribution that corresponds to a remuneration at that threshold.

[6] In Italy, employers may decide not to use a national labour contract, but this is rare.

[7] In Sweden, collective agreements usually apply to non-unionised employees, except when the agreement states otherwise.

[8] In Spain, a simplified plan sponsored by an association of self-employed workers may not restrict membership to workers who are members of the association.

[9] See https://www.nestpensions.org.uk/schemeweb/nest/employers/set-up-your-workplace-scheme/how-to-sign-up/what-you-need.html.

[10] Each employer has its own, separate section in the master trust.

[11] By contrast, competition between financial institutions may lead some of them to offer features below market price to attract employers. However, they may have issues to deliver.

[12] In Australia, some industry superannuation funds also tend to offer more bespoke options to larger employers.

[13] The SECURE Act created a statutory exception to that rule for certain types of multiple employer plans from 2021.

[14] Another potential explanation is that employers participating in sector or industry-wide plans may agree on the smallest common denominator for the contribution rate. It may be difficult for employers of different sizes and with different interests to agree on a common contribution rate.

[15] For example, some plans may include with-profit annuities that are no longer sold in the market.

3 Assessing the design of financial incentives for retirement savings in OECD countries

Stéphanie Payet

This chapter describes and compares the design of financial incentives for retirement savings across OECD countries. It also analyses recent trends in the design of financial incentives and assesses the extent to which countries follow the OECD policy guidelines developed in this area in 2018.

The OECD Recommendation for the Good Design of Defined Contribution Pension Plans (OECD, 2022[1]) states that policy makers should "design financial incentives to maximise the impact on enrolment and contributions", and thus encourage retirement savings, especially in voluntary plans. Indeed, most OECD countries provide financial incentives to encourage savings for retirement in asset-backed pension plans, with the aim of making complementary retirement savings more attractive (OECD, 2018[2]).

Financial incentives for retirement savings can target different stakeholders and take different forms. Most countries provide financial incentives to individuals indirectly, via the personal income tax system, or directly. Tax incentives are indirect subsidies through the tax code and arise when the tax treatment of retirement savings deviates from the tax treatment of traditional forms of savings. By contrast, non-tax incentives are direct payments into the pension account of eligible individuals. Employers may also receive tax incentives through the corporate income tax system to encourage them to offer or sponsor occupational pension plans and contribute on behalf of their employees. Finally, countries may also offer financial incentives for retirement savings to employers and individuals by providing relief on the payment of social contributions.

This chapter assesses the design of financial incentives for retirement savings in OECD countries. It describes and compares the design of financial incentives for retirement savings across countries using information from the 2023 edition of the OECD Annual Survey on Financial Incentives for Retirement Savings (OECD, 2023[3]). The chapter also analyses recent trends in the design of financial incentives and assesses the extent to which countries follow the OECD policy guidelines in this area (OECD, 2018[4]).

Most OECD countries apply a variant of the "Exempt-Exempt-Taxed" ("EET") tax regime, where the taxation of retirement savings is deferred until the individual receives pension benefits. Yet, a wide range of tax regimes exist across countries as well as within countries depending on the type of pension plan, the voluntary or mandatory nature of the plan, and who pays the contributions. Some countries provide non-tax financial incentives in the form of matching contributions and fixed nominal subsidies, either as a complement to or a substitute for tax incentives. While employer contributions are deductible from corporate income tax like any other business expenses and rarely benefit from additional tax incentives, the exemption of social security contributions can make it cheaper for the employer to contribute to the employee's pension plan than to pay the same amount in salary to the employee. Since 2015, many countries have increased financial incentives for retirement savings as asset-backed pension plans are expected to play an increasing role in financing retirement income.

The design of financial incentives for retirement savings in OECD countries is broadly aligned with the OECD policy guidelines. However, tax rules remain complex in many countries and the parameters linked to financial incentives are not always updated on a yearly basis.

The chapter describes in Section 3.1 the tax treatment of retirement savings from the point of view of individuals, looking in detail at how contributions, investment income and pension benefits are taxed in the different countries. Section 3.2 looks at the different forms of non-tax financial incentives. Section 3.3 analyses the extent to which social contributions are levied on pension contributions and pension benefits. Section 3.4 focuses on the tax treatment of employer contributions through the corporate income tax system. Section 3.5 describes recent trends in the design of financial incentives for retirement savings. Finally, section 3.6 concludes by assessing the extent to which OECD countries design their financial incentives in line with the OECD policy guidelines.

3.1. Tax treatment of retirement savings from the perspective of individuals

Tax incentives for individuals come from a differential tax treatment applied to savings in asset-backed pension plans as compared to savings in other savings vehicles. In most countries, traditional forms of savings are taxed similarly to other income and earnings, with contributions and investment income included in taxable income, and withdrawals are exempt from taxation. This is generally referred to as the "Taxed-Taxed-Exempt" or "TTE" tax regime. When the tax regime applied to asset-backed pension plans deviates from the "TTE" tax regime, individuals may pay less taxes over their lifetime.[1] Tax incentives are, therefore, indirect subsidies provided through the tax code; they are not paid in the pension account of the individuals.

Many countries apply a variant of the "Exempt-Exempt-Taxed" ("EET") tax regime to retirement savings, where both contributions and investment income are exempt from taxation while benefits are treated as taxable income upon withdrawal. Out of 38 OECD countries, 17 follow this tax regime for the main asset-backed pension plan (Figure 3.1). Yet a wide range of tax regimes can be found as well, from the "EEE" tax regime, where contributions, investment income and pension benefits are tax exempt, to regimes where two of three flows are taxed.

Figure 3.1. Overview of the tax treatment of retirement savings in OECD countries, 2023

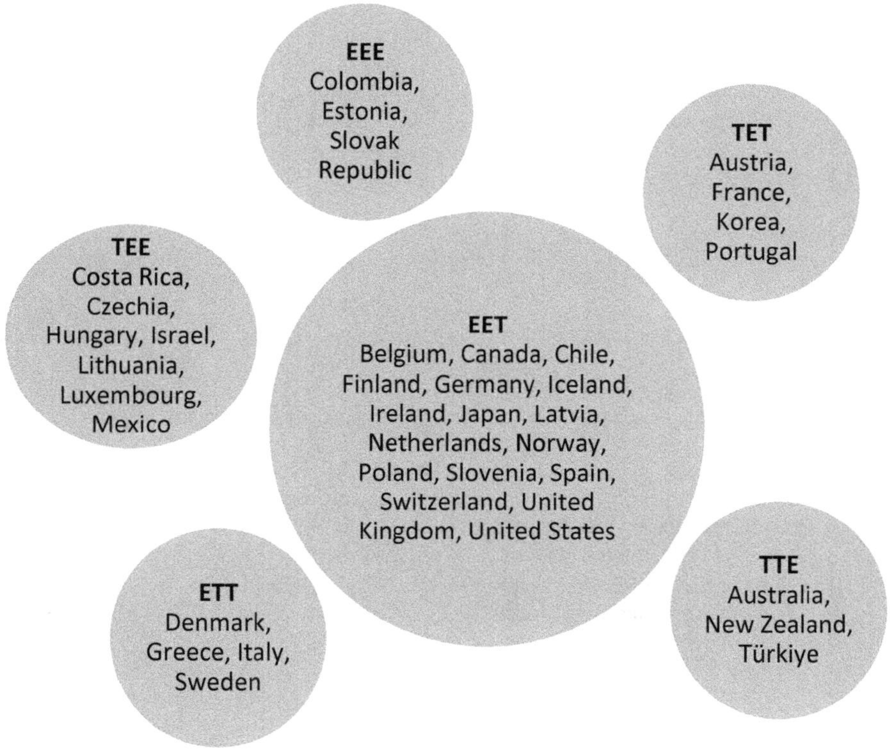

Note: Main asset-backed pension plan in each country. "E" stands for exempt and "T" for taxed for contributions, investment income and pension benefits, respectively. Countries offering tax credits on contributions are considered as taxing contributions when the tax credit does not cover the full amount of tax paid on those contributions for some individuals. The tax treatment of an annuity is assumed when different tax treatments apply to different types of retirement income payments.
Source: OECD (2023[3]), Annual survey on financial incentives for retirement savings, https://www.oecd.org/content/dam/oecd/en/topics/policy-sub-issues/asset-backed-pensions/Financial-incentives-retirement-savings-2023.pdf.

There are disparities within countries, however. Table 3.1 shows that the tax treatment of retirement savings may vary according to the type of plan, the type of contribution (i.e. mandatory or voluntary) and the source of contribution within the same plan (i.e. the employer or the individual). A unique tax treatment applies in 16 out of 38 OECD countries.[2] In the other countries, several tax treatments apply. The following subsections provide further details on the tax treatment of contributions, investment income and pension benefits.

Table 3.1. Tax treatment of retirement savings by type of plan, type of contribution and source of contribution, 2023

Country	Type of plan / contribution	Source of contribution	Tax treatment		
			Contributions	Returns	Withdrawals
Australia	Concessional contributions	All	0%/15%/30%	15%	E
	Non-concessional contributions	Individual	T	15%	E
Austria	Occupational plans	Employer	E	E	T
	Occupational and personal plans	Individual	T	E	T/PE
	State-sponsored retirement provision plans	Individual	T	E	E
Belgium	Occupational plans for employees	Employer	E	E/9.25%	10%/16.5%
		Individual	30% credit	E/9.25%	10%
	Occupational plans for self-employed	Individual	E	E/9.25%	10%/16.5%
	VAPZ plans (self-employed)	Individual	E	E/9.25%	T/PE
	VAPW plans (employees)	Individual	30% credit	E/9.25%	10%/33%
	POZ plans (self-employed)	Individual	30% credit	E/9.25%	10%/33%
	Third pillar personal plans	Individual	30%/25% credit	E/9.25%	8%/10%
Canada	All	All	E	E	15% credit
Chile	Mandatory contributions	Individual	E	E	T
	Voluntary contributions, regime A	Individual	T	E	E
	Other voluntary contributions	Individual	E	E	T
Colombia	All	All	E	E	E
Costa Rica	Mandatory contributions	Individual	T	E	E
		Employer	E	E	E
	Voluntary contributions	All	E	E	E
Czechia	Supplementary plans	Individual	T/PE	E	E
		Employer	E	E	E
Denmark	Age savings plans	All	T	15.3%	E
	Other plans	All	E	15.3%	T
Estonia	Mandatory contributions	All	E	E	E
	Voluntary contributions	Individual	20% credit	E	E
Finland	All	All	E	E	T
France	All	All	T/PE	E	T/PE
Germany	Occupational plans and *Riester* plans	All	E	E	T
	Private pension insurance	Individual	T	E	T/PE
Greece	Occupational insurance funds	All	E	5%	T
	Group pension insurance contracts	All	E	5%	15%
	Personal pension plans	All	T	5%	E
Hungary	All	All	T	E	E
Iceland	All	All	E	E	T
Ireland	All	All	E	E	T/PE
Israel	All	Individual	35% credit	E	E
	All	Employer	E	E	E
Italy	All	All	E	12.5%/20%	9% - 15%
Japan	All	All	E	E	T/PE
Korea	Occupational plans	Employer	E	E	T/PE
	All	Individual	13.2%/16.5% credit	E	T/PE
Latvia	Mandatory contributions	Individual	E	E	T
	Voluntary contributions	Individual	E	20%	E
		Employer	E	20%	T
Lithuania	Pillar 2 plans	Individual	T/PE	E	E
	Pillar 3 plans	All	E	E	E
Luxembourg	Occupational plans	Employer	20%	E	E
	All	Individual	E	E	T/PE

Country	Type of plan / contribution	Source of contribution	Tax treatment		
			Contributions	Returns	Withdrawals
Mexico	All	Employer	E	E	E
	Mandatory contributions	Individual	T	E	E
	Long-term voluntary contributions	Individual	E	E	E
	Short-term voluntary contributions	Individual	T	T	E
Netherlands	All	All	E	E	T
New Zealand	All	All	T	10.5% - 28%	E
Norway	Occupational defined contribution plans	Employer	E	E	T
		Individual	T/PE	E	T
	Individual pension saving	Individual	T/PE	E	T/PE
	Occupational plans for the self-employed	Individual	E	E	T
Poland	OFE plans	Individual	E	E	T
	IKZE plans	Individual	E	E	10%
	PPK, PPE and IKE plans	All	T	E	E
Portugal	Occupational plans	Employer	E	E	T
	All	Individual	T/PE	E	T/PE
Slovak Republic	Pillar 2 plans	Employer	E	E	E
		Individual	T	E	E
	Pillar 3 and PEPP plans	All	T/PE	19%	E
Slovenia	All	All	E	E	T/PE
Spain	All	All	E	E	T
Sweden	Premium Pension	Individual	E	E	T
	Other plans	All	E	15%	T
Switzerland	All	All	E	E	T
Türkiye	Personal plans	All	T	5%/10%/15%	E
United Kingdom	All	All	E	E	T/PE
United States	Roth contributions	Individual	T + credit (0% - 50%)	E	E
	Other contributions	All	E + credit (0% - 50%)	E	T

Note: T = Taxed; E = Exempt (usually up to a limit); T/PE = Taxed but partially exempt; credit = Tax credit. The tax treatment of an annuity is assumed when different tax treatments apply to different types of retirement income payments.
Source: OECD (2023[3]), Annual survey on financial incentives for retirement savings, https://www.oecd.org/content/dam/oecd/en/topics/policy-sub-issues/asset-backed-pensions/Financial-incentives-retirement-savings-2023.pdf.

3.1.1. Tax treatment of contributions

Countries generally provide tax relief on pension contributions (Table 3.2). Tax relief on contributions can take different forms:

- **Tax exemption**: Tax exempt contributions are not subject to personal income tax and provide tax relief at the individual's marginal tax rate. In most countries, employer contributions are not considered as taxable income for the employee and, therefore, are fully tax exempt from the perspective of the individual.
- **Tax deduction**: The most common approach to provide tax relief on contributions paid by individuals is to make them deductible from taxable income, up to a limit. Similar to a tax exemption, tax relief is provided at the individual's marginal tax rate as contributions are deducted before calculating personal income tax. Tax deduction may only be partial. In Portugal, for example, only 20% of employee contributions to all their pension plans is tax deductible. In Denmark, France and Norway, pension contributions are deductible for the calculation of some taxes but not others.[3]
- **Tax credit**: Tax relief on individual contributions may also be provided in the form of a non-refundable tax credit. Contributions are not tax deductible, but the individual receives a tax credit

that reduces the amount of personal income tax due. The tax credit is expressed as a percentage of the contributions paid, up to a limit. It reduces the individual's tax liability potentially down to zero but not beyond (the excess tax credit is lost to the individual). Tax credits can be found in Belgium (with a credit rate of 30%), Estonia (20%), Israel (35%), Korea (13.2% or 16.5% for lower earners) and the United States (0% to 50% depending on income). Depending on the individual's marginal tax rate, the tax credit may be as generous, more generous or less generous than a tax deduction.[4]

- **Reduced taxation**: Tax relief may also occur when contributions are taxed but at a lower rate than other income. For example, in Australia, employer contributions to superannuation accounts are taxed at the fixed rate of 15% for most employees.[5] As this rate is usually lower than their marginal tax rate, most individuals benefit from a tax rate relief on their contributions.

Table 3.2. Tax relief on contributions in OECD countries by type of relief and source of contribution, 2023

Source of contribution	Tax exemption	Tax deduction	Tax credit	Reduced taxation	No tax relief
Individual / Employee		Canada; Chile; Colombia; Costa Rica (v); Denmark; Estonia (m); Finland; France; Germany; Greece; Iceland; Ireland; Italy; Japan; Latvia; Lithuania (p3); Luxembourg; Mexico (v); Netherlands; Norway; Poland (OFE, IKZE, PPE, PPK); Portugal; Slovak Republic (p3); Slovenia; Spain; Sweden (IPS); Switzerland; United Kingdom; United States	Belgium; Estonia (v); Israel; Korea; United States		Australia; Austria; Costa Rica (ROP); Czechia; Denmark (age savings); Germany (private pension insurance); Greece (personal plans); Hungary; Lithuania (p2); Mexico (m); New Zealand; Poland (IKE); Slovak Republic (p2); Türkiye; United States (Roth)
Employer	Austria; Belgium; Canada; Colombia; Costa Rica; Czechia; Denmark; Estonia; Finland; France; Germany; Greece; Iceland; Ireland; Israel; Italy; Japan; Korea; Latvia; Lithuania; Mexico; Netherlands; Norway; Portugal; Slovak Republic (p2); Slovenia; Spain; Sweden; Switzerland; United Kingdom; United States			Australia; Luxembourg	Hungary; New Zealand; Poland (PPE; PPK); Portugal (PPR); Slovak Republic (p3); Türkiye
Self-employed		Belgium (IPT, VAPZ); Israel; Norway	Belgium (POZ)	Luxembourg	

Note: m=mandatory; v=voluntary; p2=pillar 2; p3=pillar 3.
Source: OECD (2023[3]), Annual survey on financial incentives for retirement savings, https://www.oecd.org/content/dam/oecd/en/topics/policy-sub-issues/asset-backed-pensions/Financial-incentives-retirement-savings-2023.pdf.

Pension contributions do not get tax relief when they are included in the taxable income of the individual. In that case, contributions are considered to be taxed at the individual's marginal tax rate. In Austria,

Hungary, New Zealand and the Republic of Türkiye (hereafter Türkiye), individual contributions never attract tax relief (Table 3.2).

Employer contributions are fully taxable for individuals in a few countries only. Table 3.2 shows that in Hungary, Poland (PPE and PPK plans), Portugal (PPR plans), the Slovak Republic (third pillar) and Türkiye, employer contributions are considered taxable income for the employee and added to the employee's income before calculating personal income tax.[6] Such employer contributions are therefore taxed at the individual's marginal tax rate. In New Zealand, the employer superannuation contribution tax is calculated based on the employee's salary in the previous tax year and the tax rate applicable to employer contributions for the employee varies from 10.5% to 39%.[7] By contrast, in some cases, employer contributions are treated as taxable income for the employee but are deemed to be made by the employee for tax relief purposes, meaning that they are deductible within the individual's tax deductibility limit. This is the case for example in Ireland for employer contributions into retirement annuity contracts.

There is usually a limit on the contributions attracting tax relief. This contribution limit may be defined as a percentage of the individual's income. Figure 3.2 shows the maximum limit on contributions attracting tax relief expressed as a percentage of income that exists in each country. The contribution limit does not exceed 10% of income in eight countries. At the other extreme, contributions attracting tax relief are capped at 100% of income in the United Kingdom and the United States. In several countries, the limit covers both employee and employer contributions.[8] Figure 3.2, however, hides disparities within countries across different types of plans. For example, in Belgium, contributions up to 3% of gross salary are eligible for the tax credit in VAPW plans, while contributions up to 9.4% of professional income are deductible from professional income for the self-employed in social VAPZ plans.

Figure 3.2. Maximum limit on contributions attracting tax relief expressed as a percentage of income, 2023

As a percentage of the individual's income

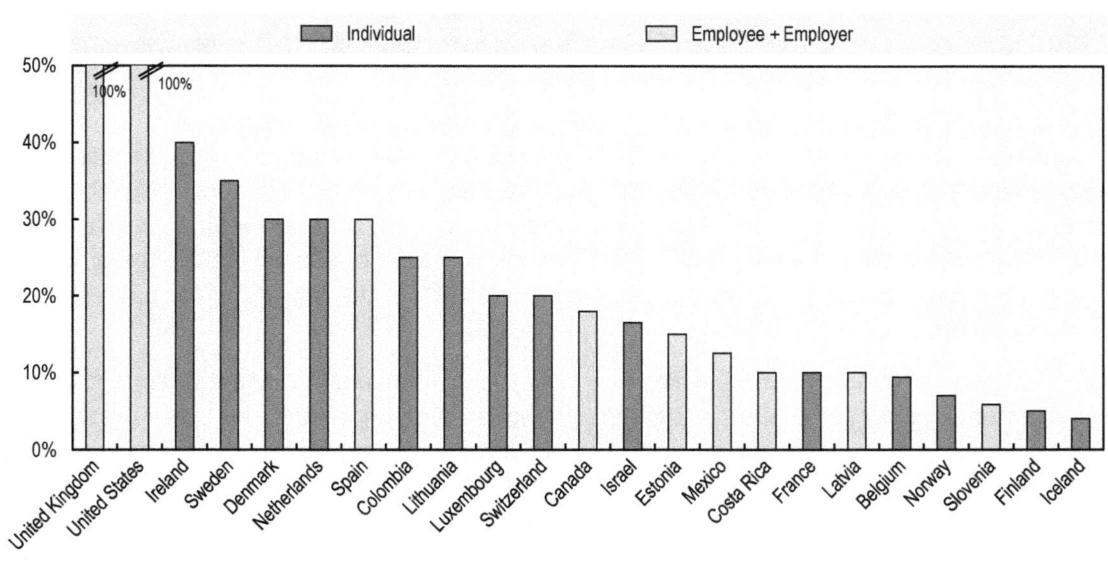

Source: OECD (2023[3]), Annual survey on financial incentives for retirement savings, https://www.oecd.org/content/dam/oecd/en/topics/policy-sub-issues/asset-backed-pensions/Financial-incentives-retirement-savings-2023.pdf.

The limit on contributions attracting tax relief may also be a fixed amount. In most countries expressing the contribution limit as a percentage of income, there is also a cap in absolute amount to put a ceiling on the tax relief granted to high-income earners. Additionally, in many countries, the limit on contributions attracting tax relief is the same for all individuals and is directly expressed as a fixed amount. This fixed limit is sometimes a multiple of a reference value in the country. For example, in Germany, the joint limit for employer and employee contributions to occupational pension plans attracting tax relief is equal to 8% of the social security contribution ceiling, i.e. 8% of EUR 87 600 in 2023.[9] Figure 3.3 shows the maximum fixed limit on contributions attracting tax relief expressed as a percentage of the average wage in each country. In Australia, Chile, Colombia, Poland, Sweden and the United Kingdom, this limit exceeds 100% of the average wage for certain types of plans (left panel of Figure 3.3). For example, in Australia, the limit for voluntary contributions (AUD 110 000) represents 119% of the average wage.[10] In most countries, the fixed contribution limit represents less than 40% of the average wage (right panel of Figure 3.3) and can be as low as 1% in the Slovak Republic for contributions to third pillar pension plans (EUR 180).

Figure 3.3. Maximum limit on contributions attracting tax relief expressed as a fixed amount, 2023

As a percentage of the average wage in the economy in 2022

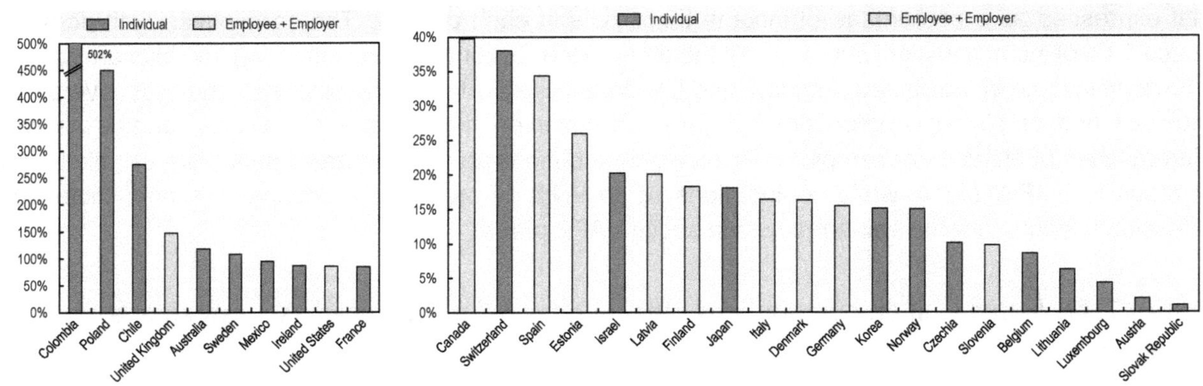

Notes: Countries in the left panel have limits above 80% of the average wage. Countries in the right panel have limits up to 40% of the average wage.
Source: OECD (2023[3]), Annual survey on financial incentives for retirement savings, https://www.oecd.org/content/dam/oecd/en/topics/policy-sub-issues/asset-backed-pensions/Financial-incentives-retirement-savings-2023.pdf.

Some countries allow individuals to carry forward the limits on contributions attracting tax relief unused in the previous years. This is possible in Australia, Canada, Italy and the United Kingdom. Individuals can carry forward up to five years of unused limits on contributions attracting tax relief in Australia and three years in the United Kingdom. In Italy, employees can recoup the unused annual tax relief of their first 5 years of participation during the following 20 years, up to 50% of the maximum annual relief per year. There is no time constraint in Canada.

Limits on contributions attracting tax relief may vary with age. In Ireland and the Netherlands, older workers can deduct a higher proportion of their income than younger ones. In Ireland, the contribution limit varies from 15% of earnings for individuals younger than 30 years old to 40% for individuals aged 60. In the Netherlands, it varies from 3.9% for individuals aged 15-19 to 27.5% for individuals aged 65-67. Additionally, some countries have higher fixed contribution limits for older workers. In Denmark, the annual contribution limit to age savings plans increases from DKK 8 800 to DKK 56 900 for individuals within seven years from the retirement age. In Korea, an extra KRW 2 million of contributions can be taken into account for the calculation of the tax credit for people older than 50 years old with a gross income of up to KRW 100 million. In the United States, certain plans allow participants aged 50 years old and over to make pre-tax catch-up contributions beyond the basic limit on employee contributions. Catch-up contributions vary from USD 1 000 for IRA plans to USD 7 500 for 401(k) plans. In Portugal, only 20% of the contributions can be deducted from taxable income, and in contrast with the other countries, the deduction limit declines with age, from EUR 400 for individuals under 35, to EUR 350 for individuals aged 35-50, and EUR 300 for individuals above 50.

Some countries link the limit on employee contributions attracting tax relief to the amount contributed by the employer. Several countries have joint contribution limits for employee and employer contributions in occupational or personal pension plans. This is the case in Canada, Colombia, Costa Rica, Denmark, Estonia, Finland, Germany, Italy, Japan, Latvia, Mexico, the Netherlands, Slovenia, Spain, the United Kingdom and the United States (Figure 3.2 and Figure 3.3). In Austria, Japan (corporate defined contribution plans) and Norway, employee contributions cannot exceed employer contributions. However, in Austria, the employee may still contribute up to EUR 1 000 if the employer contributes less than this amount. In Spain, employees can contribute more than the employer in an occupational pension plan only if the employer contributes less than EUR 1 500 annually. In Finland, if the employee contributes more than the employer in a voluntary occupational group plan, the excess amount is not tax deductible. Additionally, some countries adjust the contribution limit to personal pension plans to whether the individual is already covered by an occupational pension plan. In Japan, individual contribution limits to personal pension plans depend on whether their employer sponsors an occupational plan and the type of occupational plan. The limit is the lowest when the employer already sponsors a defined benefit plan (JPY 12 000 monthly) and the highest when the employer does not sponsor any occupational plan (JPY 23 000). Similarly, in Switzerland, the contribution limit to personal plans is higher when the individual is not covered by an occupational pension plan (CHF 35 280 as opposed to CHF 7 056).

Some countries distinguish limits on contributions attracting tax relief between employees and self-employed workers. Contribution limits tend to be lower for employees than for the self-employed because the former can receive employer contributions, which are usually tax exempt for the employee. For example, in Belgium, contributions by the self-employed to free supplementary pension plans (VAPZ) cannot exceed 8.17% of professional income up to EUR 3 859.40, while contributions by employees in the equivalent plans (VAPW) cannot exceed EUR 1 830 or 3% of gross salary received two years before, whichever is higher. In France, employees can deduct 10% of their earnings net of professional costs of the previous year up to EUR 35 194, while self-employed workers and heads of agricultural holdings can deduct 10% of taxable profit capped at 8 times the annual social security ceiling, plus 15% of taxable profit between 1 and 8 times the annual social security ceiling. In Norway, employee contributions into occupational pension plans up to 4% of salary are deductible from ordinary income but not from personal income, while contributions by self-employed workers into voluntary occupational plans are deductible from both ordinary income and personal income, up to 7% of imputed personal income from self-employment up to 12 G.[11] By contrast, in Spain, the contribution limit is lower for the self-employed. An initial EUR 1 500 contribution limit applies to all workers. This limit can be increased by EUR 8 500 if the contribution is done by the employer or by the employee into the same occupational plan, or by EUR 4 250 if the contribution is done by a self-employed worker into a simplified occupational pension plan.

Finally, tax relief may be provided for contributions made on behalf of a spouse with low earnings. For example, in Australia, a tax credit may apply to after-tax contributions made on behalf of non-working or low-income-earning spouses. It is payable to the contributor, not to the spouse. The tax credit is calculated as 18% of the lesser of AUD 3 000[12] and the total amount of contributions paid. However, few people make use of this option (OECD, 2021[5]). In Spain, an individual can deduct up to EUR 1 000 per year for contributions paid to his/her spouse's pension plan when the spouse's net income is less than EUR 8 000. This deduction can be carried forward for five years. If the spouse is disabled, the individual can make an additional deductible annual contribution of up to EUR 10 000 to the spouse's pension plan. Individuals can also contribute to their spouse's pension plan in Canada, Chile, the Czech Republic (hereafter Czechia), Latvia, New Zealand, Hungary, Lithuania, the United Kingdom and the United States. In these countries, contributions to the spouses' account are included in the contributor's own contribution limit.

3.1.2. Tax treatment of investment income

Countries generally exempt from taxation investment income resulting from assets earmarked for retirement. Only 12 OECD countries tax investment income at least for selected pension plans.[13] In Belgium, investment income is only taxed when the yearly investment return exceeds the guaranteed return, and the individual is granted a share of the excess return. In Latvia, investment income is only taxed in voluntary pension schemes. In the Slovak Republic, it is only taxed in voluntary personal pension schemes (third pillar). In France, Mexico, the Slovak Republic and Türkiye, investment income is taxed when the individual retires and not during the accumulation phase. The part of pension income originating from investment income is taxed separately.

Some countries tax investment income in asset-backed pension arrangements at a fixed rate that is usually lower than the one applying to other forms of saving vehicles. A fixed tax rate applies to investment income in Australia (15%), Denmark (15.3%), Greece (5%), Latvia (10%), the Slovak Republic (19%) and Sweden (15%). In the case of Sweden, the 15% tax rate applies on an imputed return on investment rather than on the actual return on investment generated by the assets of the pension plan. The imputed return corresponds to the previous year's average government borrowing rate, but it cannot be negative.

Different tax rates may apply to investment income depending on various parameters. In Australia, investment income becomes tax free when the assets accumulated at retirement are transferred, up to a cap, to an account supporting a retirement income stream. In Italy, the taxation of investment income depends on the type of asset class. Investment income is taxed at a 20% standard rate, but income from government bonds held by the pension fund is taxed at a more favourable rate of 12.5%. In New Zealand, the taxation of investment income depends on the type of scheme and on the taxable income of the plan member. If the scheme is an occupational pension plan, a single tax rate of 28% applies. If the scheme is a Portfolio Investment Entity (e.g. all *KiwiSaver* default schemes), the tax rate varies from 10.5% to 28% depending on taxable income. In Türkiye, the tax rate on investment income depends on when the individual receives benefits. The tax rate varies from 5% if the individual is aged at least 56 and has been a member of the scheme for at least 10 years, to 10% if the individual is younger than 56 and has been a member of the scheme for at least 10 years, and to 15% if the individual has been a member of the scheme for less than 10 years.

3.1.3. Tax treatment of pension benefits

Countries generally tax pension benefits. Some countries that tax pension benefits provide some tax relief when compared to other types of income. For example, in Canada, a 15% tax credit is provided on the first CAD 2 000 of eligible pension income. In France, annuities are taxed at the individual's marginal tax rate after a 10% deduction. In Italy, pension benefits are taxed at a fixed rate of 15%, with a reduction of 0.3% for every year of participation beyond 15 years. The maximum reduction is 6%, leading to a 9% tax rate after 35 years of participation. In Japan, a pension-related deduction jointly applies to public pensions and private pension annuities. In Slovenia, only half of the amount of the calculated annuity is taxed at the individual's marginal tax rate.

The tax treatment of pension benefits is usually identical across all types of retirement income payments (e.g. annuities, drawdowns, lump sums). However, lump sums and pensions paid over a minimum period may attract different tax treatments. In particular, lump sums may be tax free up to a certain amount or only partially taxed. The rationale is to reach a more neutral tax treatment across the different types of retirement income payments as lump sums can be quite large and significantly increase the individual's marginal tax rate the year of withdrawal. For example, in Ireland, individuals can withdraw up to 25% of their savings (capped at EUR 200 000) as a lump sum tax free. In Switzerland, the federal government taxes lump sums as capital income. This tax is progressive and is equal to 1/5 of the income tax that would be generated if lump sums were separately taxed as income. In the United Kingdom, an individual can have a tax-free lump sum up to 25% of the total value of the pension account (capped at GBP 268 275).

Only four OECD countries use tax incentives to encourage people to take a lifetime annuity or to withdraw their assets over a minimum length of time. In Czechia, lifetime annuities and drawdowns over more than 10 years are tax free, while drawdowns over shorter periods and lump sums are taxed. In Estonia, lifetime annuities and pensions paid over the average remaining life expectancy are tax exempt. The tax rate for shorter periods and for full lump sums is 10%. In Korea, individuals taking an annuity for the part of benefits originating from employer contributions only pay 70% of the amount due in the case of a lump sum. In Türkiye, the government pays a subsidy equal to 5% of participants' savings at retirement for those who choose a minimum 10-year annuity.

A minority of countries use the tax system to discourage early withdrawals. The age limit defining early withdrawals differs in each country and there may be more than one limit to define different tax treatments. For example, in Australia, pensions are taxed at the individual's marginal tax rate before the preservation age, there is a 15% tax offset between the preservation age and 59 years old, and pensions are tax free from age 60.[14] Other countries discouraging early withdrawals with the tax system include Belgium, Denmark, Estonia, France, Italy, Lithuania, Türkiye, the United Kingdom and the United States.

Finally, only Ireland taxes the total amount of funds accumulated at the point of retirement once it exceeds a certain limit.[15] The limit has been set at EUR 2 million since 1 January 2014. Upon withdrawal, the amount of assets exceeding this limit is subject to an upfront income tax charge at the higher rate of income tax (currently 40%).

3.2. Non-tax financial incentives

Several countries have introduced more direct financial incentives to encourage participation in, and contributions to, asset-backed pension plans, especially for low-income earners. Non-tax incentives considered herein include matching contributions from the government or from the employer, and government fixed nominal subsidies. These payments are provided to eligible individuals who participate in or make voluntary contributions to an asset-backed pension plan. Both matching contributions and subsidies are paid into the pension account, thus increasing the assets accumulated to finance retirement income. They are never considered taxable income for individuals. Table 3.3 shows that 17 OECD countries have such incentives.

Table 3.3. Non-tax financial incentives, 2023

Country	Type of plan / contribution	Employer matching contribution	Government matching contribution	Government fixed nominal subsidy	Tax treatment
Australia	Non-concessional contributions		50% up to AUD 500 / year		TtE
Austria	State-sponsored retirement provision plans		4.25% up to EUR 136.94 / year		TEE
Chile	Mandatory contributions		50% up to 50% of 10% of monthly minimum wage for 24 months	18 × 10% of monthly minimum wage	EET
	Voluntary contributions, regime A		15% up to 6 UTM (1)		TEE
Colombia	All		20%		EEE
Czechia	Supplementary plans		20% up to CZK 230 / month		TEE
Estonia	Mandatory plans			4% of national average wage up to	EEE

Country	Type of plan / contribution	Employer matching contribution	Government matching contribution	Government fixed nominal subsidy	Tax treatment
				3 years / child	
Germany	Occupational plans	15% match			EET
	Riester plans			EUR 200 when joining < age25 EUR 175 / year EUR 300 / year / child born after 2008	EET
Hungary	Personal plans		20% up to HUF 100 00, HUF 130 000 or HUF 150 000 / year depending on plan		TEE
Iceland	Personal plans	Minimum 2% of salary			EET
Italy	Occupational plans	Depend on collective agreement			Ett
Lithuania	Pillar 2 plans			1.5% of national average gross salary / year	TEE
Mexico	Solidarity savings plans		325% up to 6.5 times the worker's basic salary		TEE
	Mandatory contributions			Depend on number of days worked and salary level	TEE
New Zealand	*KiwiSaver* plans	3% of salary	50% up to NZD 521.43 / year		TTE
Poland	PPK plans	Minimum 1.5% of salary		PLN 250 when joining PLN 240 / year	TEE
Türkiye	Personal plans		30% up to 30% of annual gross minimum wage	TRY 1 000 when joining	TtE
United Kingdom	Automatic enrolment	Minimum 3% of salary			EET
United States	Qualified Automatic Contribution Arrangement	100% on the first 1% worker contribution + 50% on the next 5% contributions			EET
	Thrift Savings Plan		100% on the first 3% worker contribution + 50% on the next 2% contributions		EET

Note: The UTM is a monthly unit for taxation purposes. It was set at CLP 63 326 in July 2023. The letter "t" in lowercase represents cases where the income flow is only partially taxed or taxed at a lower rate than the marginal tax rate.
Source: OECD (2023[3]), Annual survey on financial incentives for retirement savings, https://www.oecd.org/content/dam/oecd/en/topics/policy-sub-issues/asset-backed-pensions/Financial-incentives-retirement-savings-2023.pdf.

Matching contributions are the most common type of non-tax financial incentive used to promote retirement savings. Governments or employers may pay matching contributions. Matching contributions encourage contributions from the individual as their payment is conditional on the individual contributing. Government matching contributions are expressed as a proportion of the individual's own contribution, up to a maximum amount. The generosity of the match rate varies greatly across countries, from 4.25% in Austria to 325% in Mexico (solidarity savings programme for civil servants).[16] The most common match rates are 20% (Colombia, Czechia, Hungary) and 50% (Australia, Chile, New Zealand). The maximum entitlement varies across countries and represents between 0.3% of the average wage in Austria and 3.3% of the average wage in Chile. Employer matching contributions are usually expressed as a minimum contribution rate (i.e. as a percentage of salary).

Governments can use matching contributions to target specific groups of workers, in particular low earners. For example, in Australia, the government super co-contribution is for individuals with a total income below AUD 58 445 making voluntary non-deducted contributions.[17] The match rate provided is 50% with a maximum entitlement of AUD 500 (0.5% of the average wage). For every dollar that the individual earns above AUD 43 445, the maximum entitlement is reduced by 3.333 cents. In Chile, workers aged between 18 and 35 with an income lower than 1.5 times the minimum wage are entitled to a government matching contribution for their first 24 monthly continuous or discontinuous contributions to the pension system. The matching contribution is equivalent to 50% of the mandatory contribution of the worker if his/her wage is lower than or equal to the minimum wage, or 50% of the mandatory contribution over the minimum wage if his/her wage is greater than the minimum wage and lower than 1.5 times the minimum wage. In Colombia, the BEPS programme encourages voluntary contributions by low-income earners. At retirement, individuals receive a 20% matching contribution from the government.

Seven OECD countries provide government subsidies to promote retirement savings. Government subsidies are fixed nominal amounts and are therefore more valuable to low-income earners, as the fixed amount represents a higher share of their income. In Chile, Estonia, Germany and Lithuania, at least some of the subsidies are targeted at women:

- In Chile, women aged 65 or older are entitled to a government subsidy for each child alive at birth. The subsidy is equivalent to 18 months of mandatory contributions (10%) over the minimum wage in place at the birth of the child, and earning the returns of fund type C since 2009 or since the birth of the child, whichever is later.
- In Estonia, one of the parents is entitled to monthly contributions equal to 4% of the national average wage into their mandatory asset-backed pension plan for a maximum duration of three years per child (whether or not the parent has returned to work), for children born after 1 January 2013.
- In Germany, the child subsidy is paid into the *Riester* account of the parent receiving child allowances, which is the mother by default. The maximum subsidy amounts to EUR 185 per year and per child born before 1 January 2008, or EUR 300 per year and per child born on or after 1 January 2008.
- In Lithuania, the government contributes 1.5% of the average gross salary of the year before the last in the account of people who have children up to three years old and who receive maternity benefits. For persons with more than one child under the age of three, the government pays contributions for all children to one of the parents.

Governments usually pay subsidies and matching contributions directly in the pension account of entitled individuals. In some countries, matching contributions are technically tax credits paid directly in the pension account instead of coming as a deduction of the tax liability. This is the case for example in New Zealand. Pension providers may also claim the financial incentive from the government on behalf of members. For example, in the United Kingdom, the employer may deduct pension contributions to an occupational pension plan from the employee's salary either before or after deducting personal income tax, depending on the pension scheme. In the second case, the pension provider claims tax back from the government at the basic rate of 20% and the tax refund is paid in the pension account.[18]

In most countries, non-tax incentives complement tax incentives coming from the preferential tax treatment of retirement savings. This could be because it is difficult to remove incentives already in the tax code. The three exceptions are Australia, New Zealand and Türkiye, where government matching contributions essentially substitute tax incentives.

3.3. Treatment of contributions and benefits with respect to social contributions

Besides the personal income tax system, contributions to asset-backed pension plans and benefits paid from these plans can be subject to social contributions. Social contributions are usually levied on gross salaries and wages to finance, among other things, health insurance, unemployment insurance, public pensions and disability pensions. Table 3.4 classifies OECD countries according to whether social contributions are fully levied, partially levied or not levied on pension contributions and pension benefits.

Table 3.4. Social contributions levy on pension contributions and benefits, 2023

	Not levied	Partially levied	Fully levied
Individual contributions	Costa Rica (voluntary), Finland, Greece, Iceland, Israel, Japan, Korea, Netherlands, New Zealand	Czechia, Germany	Australia, Austria, Belgium, Canada, Chile, Colombia, Costa Rica (mandatory), Estonia, France, Hungary, Ireland, Italy, Lithuania, Luxembourg, Mexico, Poland, Slovak Republic, Slovenia, Spain, Switzerland, Türkiye, United Kingdom, United States
Employer contributions	Australia, Austria, Canada, Costa Rica (voluntary), Czechia, Finland, Greece, Iceland, Ireland, Israel, Japan, Korea, Netherlands, New Zealand, Poland, Portugal, Slovenia, Spain, Türkiye, United Kingdom, United States	Belgium, France, Germany, Hungary, Italy, Norway, Sweden	Estonia, Luxembourg, Mexico, Slovak Republic, Switzerland
Pension benefits	Australia, Canada, Costa Rica, Czechia, Estonia, France, Hungary, Iceland, Italy, Korea, Latvia, Lithuania, Mexico, New Zealand, Portugal, Slovak Republic, Slovenia, Spain, Sweden, Switzerland, Türkiye, United Kingdom, United States	Austria, Belgium, Chile, Colombia, Finland, Germany, Greece, Ireland, Japan, Netherlands, Norway, Poland	Israel, Luxembourg

Note: Denmark does not collect social contributions.
Source: OECD (2023[3]), Annual survey on financial incentives for retirement savings, https://www.oecd.org/content/dam/oecd/en/topics/policy-sub-issues/asset-backed-pensions/Financial-incentives-retirement-savings-2023.pdf..

Several countries use the social security system to encourage employer contributions. Employer contributions in many countries are not subject to social contributions or benefit from a reduced rate. This preferential treatment of employer contribution makes it cheaper for an employer to contribute to an employee's pension plan than to pay the same amount in salary to that employee. For example, in Australia, Austria, Belgium, Ireland, Italy, Poland, Slovenia and the United Kingdom, employer contributions are not included in the income base to calculate social contributions, or they benefit from a reduced rate. In Italy for instance, employer contributions are subject to a rate of 10% instead of the standard 24% rate, on earnings up to a ceiling.

While pension benefits are usually not subject to social contributions, some countries levy part of the social contributions usually applicable to wages and salaries on pension benefits. In particular, several countries only levy social contributions related to health and long-term care insurance on pension benefits.

3.4. Perspective of the employer

Employer contributions to asset-backed pension plans are always considered as tax-deductible business expenses for the purpose of corporate income tax. However, certain limits may apply for these contributions to qualify as tax deductible. For example, employer contributions cannot exceed 6% of salary in the Slovak Republic and Slovenia, 7% in Norway[19] and Poland (PPE plans), 10% in Austria and Latvia, 20% in Luxembourg, and 35% in Sweden (up to a ceiling). In Belgium, employer contributions to an occupational pension plan are deductible as business expenses to the extent that total retirement benefits, including the statutory pension, do not exceed 80% of the last gross annual salary. In Portugal, annual contributions made by the employer cannot exceed 15% of the annual total costs with wages and salaries. In Türkiye, the sum of contributions paid by employers to the individual pension system and personal insurance premiums paid by employees cannot exceed 15% of the employee's monthly wage and the annual minimum wage per annum.[20]

In addition to the possibility of exempting employer contributions from social contributions discussed in section 3.3, only four countries provide additional financial incentives to employers to encourage contributions to pension plans:

- In Chile, workers aged between 18 and 35 with an income lower than 1.5 times the minimum wage are entitled to a government matching contribution for the first 24 monthly contributions to the pension system. This contribution consists of two payments: a subsidy to employers for hiring this type of worker and a direct contribution to the worker's pension account of the same amount. The matching contribution is equivalent to 50% of the mandatory contribution of the worker if their wage is lower than or equal to the minimum wage, or 50% of the mandatory contribution over the minimum wage if their wage is greater than the minimum wage and lower than 1.5 times the minimum wage.
- In Germany, if employers contribute at least EUR 240 per year to an occupational pension plan on behalf of a low-income earner (earning less than EUR 2 575 monthly), they get a tax allowance of 30% of the contribution, up to a maximum contribution of EUR 960 (i.e. the tax allowance varies between EUR 72 and EUR 288 per year). The allowance is administered through the wage tax and reduces the employer's wage tax liability.
- In Korea, charges for the Wage Claim Guarantee Fund are reduced by up to 50% if employers set up occupational pension plans rather than severance payment schemes.
- In Spain, employers can deduct from corporate income tax 10% of their contributions into an occupational pension plan in favour of employees with an annual gross remuneration of less than EUR 27 000. When the worker earns more than EUR 27 000, the deduction applies to the proportional part of the employer contribution that corresponds to a remuneration at that threshold.

3.5. Recent trends in the design of financial incentives for retirement savings

Beyond the changes to income thresholds and limits on contributions attracting tax relief that some countries update on a yearly basis, most countries have made changes to the design of their financial incentives since 2015 when the OECD started monitoring this information.[21] The main trend has been to increase financial incentives to encourage people to save more for retirement. However, some countries reduced financial incentives to lower the fiscal cost and limit the share of the fiscal cost benefitting high-income earners. Countries followed different approaches to change the value of financial incentives.

3.5.1. Increase in the value of financial incentives for retirement savings

Some countries eliminated certain taxes that penalised high-income earners contributing too much to asset-backed pension plans. For example, Australia eliminated the excess concessional contributions charge on 1 July 2021. This charge was penalising high-income earners receiving mandatory employer contributions above the concessional contributions cap.[22] In Slovenia, since 1 January 2020, individuals taking a lump sum from their pension plan may request that the portion corresponding to contributions made in excess of the annual tax-deductible contribution cap is excluded from the annual taxable base upon withdrawal. This eliminated the double taxation of excess contributions. The United Kingdom eliminated the tax charge that applied when an individual had built up pension savings worth more than the lifetime allowance as of the tax year 2023/24.[23] It also increased in 2021 the income limit from which the annual allowance is reduced, from GBP 150 000 to GBP 240 000. This reduced the proportion of individuals exceeding their annual contribution limit and paying the annual allowance charge.

Some countries also reduced or eliminated certain taxes to encourage specific behaviours. For example, Estonia and Korea increased the attractiveness of retirement income options paying benefits over a minimum period. Lifetime annuities and pensions paid over the average remaining life expectancy are no longer taxable since 2021 in Estonia. Korea reduced the taxation of pension benefits taken over periods exceeding 10 years in 2020. To encourage employer contributions on behalf of employees, Ireland since 2023 no longer considers employer contributions paid into a PRSA as taxable income for employees. Finally, in Italy, returns on new investment in stocks of Italian and European companies made since 2017 are tax free (instead of a standard tax rate of 20%) if the securities are held for at least five years.

Several countries increased the limits on contributions attracting tax relief beyond the normal indexation rules to encourage individuals to contribute more to their pension plans. For example, in 2017, Czechia doubled the level of tax-deductible contributions that members can pay annually from CZK 12 000 to CZK 24 000. They also increased the level of employer contributions not considered as taxable income from CZK 30 000 to CZK 50 000. In 2020, Korea increased the amount of contributions that can be taken into account for the calculation of the tax credit by KRW 2 million for people aged 50 or older with a gross income of up to KRW 100 million. Norway increased in 2019 the tax-deductibility limit for contributions by self-employed workers into voluntary defined contribution occupational plans from 6% to 7% of imputed personal income from self-employment between 1 and 12 G.[24] They removed the lower income threshold of 1 G in 2023. In 2023, the Netherlands increased the tax-deductibility limit for contributions to voluntary personal plans from 13.3% to 30% of annual income. The goal was to create a level playing field when it comes to the taxability of pension accrual between occupational and personal plans. Spain increased the tax deductibility limit for the combined employer and employee contributions in 2021, from EUR 8 000 to EUR 10 000. However, contributions from individuals could not exceed EUR 2 000 and the extra EUR 8 000 could only be paid by employers into occupational pension plans. In 2022, the limit for contributions to occupational plans increased to EUR 8 500, while the limit for individual contributions decreased to EUR 1 500 (keeping the overall limit at EUR 10 000), and employees were allowed to pay part of the contributions to occupational plans. Finally, the United Kingdom increased the annual contribution limit (annual allowance) from GBP 40 000 to GBP 60 000 in 2023.

Some countries introduced new tax incentives. In Germany and Spain, the new tax incentives targeted employers and were meant to encourage employer contributions into their employees' pension plan. In Germany, since 2018, employers contributing at least EUR 240 per year to an occupational pension plan on behalf of a low-income earner (earning less than EUR 2 575 monthly) get a tax allowance of 30% of the contribution, up to a maximum contribution of EUR 960. In Spain, starting from 2023, employers can deduct from corporate income tax 10% of their contributions into an occupational pension plan, up to an employee's annual gross remuneration of EUR 27 000. Moreover, Denmark introduced an extra tax exemption in 2018 to keep up the pension saving incentives and avoid the interaction problem with income-related government pensions and housing support. In 2018, for pension savings up to a limit, an extra exemption of 22% was obtained the last 15 years before retirement, while for pension savers with more than 15 years to retirement, the extra exemption was 8%. The extra exemptions were further increased in 2020 to 32% and 12% respectively, meaning that 132% or 112% of contributions are tax exempted instead of 100%. Finally, Korea introduced in 2022 a tax credit of 10% for individuals transferring their deposits in an individual savings account reaching maturity into a pension account.

Alternatively, several countries introduced new non-tax financial incentives. In Lithuania, Poland and Türkiye, these non-tax incentives were introduced at the same time as automatic enrolment. In Lithuania, individuals contributing at least 3% of gross income in voluntary personal pension plans (second pillar) receive a government subsidy equivalent to 1.5% of the pre-last year's average gross national salary. In Poland, PPK members benefits from an employer matching contribution and from government subsidies equal to PLN 250 when the member joins the plan and PLN 240 annually when the employee contributes at least 1.5% of salary. In Türkiye, the government initially matched 25% of individual pension contributions up to 25% of the annual minimum wage at the time of the introduction of the automatic enrolment mechanism in 2017. Both rates were increased to 30% in 2022. The government also pays a one-time TRY 1 000 contribution for individuals who do not opt out within the first two months, and a subsidy equal to 5% of participants' savings at retirement for those who choose a minimum 10-year annuity. Germany also introduced employer matching contributions in 2018. Employers must pay a 15% matching contribution if employees ask to convert part of their salary into a contribution to an occupational pension plan and if the employer pays less in social insurance contributions due to the salary conversion.

Finally, some countries reduced the taxation of early withdrawals of retirement savings, in particular during the COVID-19 pandemic. Australia, Chile, France, Iceland, Spain, Portugal, and the United States allowed special early access to retirement savings in 2020 and beyond in order to provide short-term relief for members affected by the COVID-19 crisis. Their approach regarding the taxation of these early withdrawals varied, however. In Spain, Portugal and the United States, special COVID-19 withdrawals remained taxed as any other withdrawals or benefits but did not incur the penalties that early withdrawals usually trigger. In addition, in the United States, individuals could report the taxable portion of the withdrawal proportionally over 2020, 2021 and 2022 to smooth tax payment, and could repay all or part of the withdrawal within three years to avoid paying the tax on it. In France, the self-employed could withdraw up to EUR 8 000, but only EUR 2 000 was tax exempt. In Australia and Chile, the special COVID-19 withdrawals were generally tax free, while early withdrawals would normally be taxed.[25] Iceland is the only country where withdrawals linked to the pandemic remained taxed the same way as any other early withdrawals, i.e. subject to the individual's marginal income tax rate.

Beyond the pandemic, Canada, Iceland and Portugal used the tax system to favour the withdrawal of retirement savings to buy a residence. In these three countries, the rules concern only voluntary personal pension plans. In Canada, since 1 April 2023, RRSP funds can be transferred to a Tax-Free First Home Savings Account, subject to a lifetime limit of CAD 40 000, and then be withdrawn tax-free for the purpose of buying a first home. Iceland passed a law in June 2014 allowing active members in voluntary personal pension plans to withdraw assets tax free to pay down residential housing debt, up to ISK 750 000 per year for couples taxed together and ISK 500 000 per year for single persons. Individuals who do not own their residential housing can withdraw up to ISK 500 000 per year and per person to invest in residential housing. This kind of tax-free withdrawal was initially supposed to end in 2019 but has been extended several times, currently until 31 December 2024. Portugal approved a law in October 2022 allowing the redemption of PPRs until 31 December 2023 without penalties and for any motive, up to the monthly limit, per taxpayer, of the social support index (EUR 480.43 in 2023). Moreover, the partial or total redemption of PPRs without penalties was allowed in 2023 for (i) the payment of instalments of mortgage-backed credit on the saver's own permanent residence; (ii) the payment of credit instalments for the construction or benefit of households for permanent and own residence; (iii) the payment of social housing corporations for permanent and own residence; and (iv) the early repayment of the credits referred above.

3.5.2. Decrease in the value of financial incentives for retirement savings

Some countries increased tax rates or introduced new taxes in relation to retirement savings. For example, Greece started to tax returns on investment in 2019 at the rate of 10%, later reduced to 5% in 2020. In Hungary, since 2019, employer contributions to voluntary pension funds and to institutions for occupational retirement provisions are considered taxable income for the employee. Before, these contributions were subject to personal income tax, but the tax was paid directly by the employer. Latvia increased the tax rate on investment returns from voluntary pension plans from 10% to 20% in 2019. New Zealand introduced in 2021 a new tax rate of 39% for employer contributions when the total amount of salary or wages earned by the employee exceeds NZD 216 000. Slovenia introduced in 2021 an insurance premium tax of 8.5% for voluntary supplementary pension contributions withdrawn during the first 10 years of a pension contract.

Other countries eliminated or reduced tax-deduction possibilities. In Austria, individual pension contributions are no longer tax deductible for new pension contracts since 2016. Japan reduced in 2020 the level of the tax deduction for annuities applicable to both public and private pensions for pensioners with income other than public pensions above certain thresholds. Since 2016, Sweden restricts the possibility to deduct contributions to voluntary personal pension plans to the self-employed and employees who completely lack pension rights in employment.

Finally, some countries reduced the limits on contributions attracting tax relief. For example, Australia introduced a range of measures in July 2017 to reduce incentives for high-income earners. The limit on contributions attracting a 15% tax rate was reduced; the income limit above which contributions are taxed at 30% was lowered; and a cap of AUD 1.6 million was introduced to the amount that can be transferred to a retirement phase account (i.e. an account supporting retirement income streams) with tax-free investment earnings. Denmark reduced the annual contribution limit to the age pension scheme in 2018 from DNK 29 600 to DNK 5 100 for individuals with more than five years to the retirement age. However, the limit was increased to DNK 46 000 for individuals with five or fewer years to the retirement age. The higher limit was extended to individuals with up to seven years to the retirement age in 2023. Lithuania reduced the limit for tax-deductible voluntary personal pension contributions and life insurance premiums from EUR 2 000 to EUR 1 500 in 2019. Norway reduced the contribution limit for individual pension savings schemes from NOK 40 000 to NOK 15 000 in 2022.

3.6. Alignment with OECD policy guidelines

The design of financial incentives for retirement savings in OECD countries and their recent changes generally align with the OECD policy guidelines in this area, but more work still needs to be done in particular on reducing complexity. In 2018, the OECD (2018[6]) developed policy guidelines to improve the design of financial incentives for retirement savings for countries wanting to use them to support their policy goals (Box 3.1). The previous sections of this chapter examined the tax treatment of retirement savings across OECD countries and recent trends in the design of financial incentives, highlighting how some countries have increased those incentives, while others have decreased them. The next step is to look at how these financial incentives align with OECD policy guidelines.

Box 3.1. OECD policy guidelines to improve the design of financial incentives for retirement savings

1. **Financial incentives are useful tools to promote savings for retirement**. They encourage people to participate in and contribute to retirement savings plans, while keeping individual choice and responsibility for retirement planning.
2. **Tax rules should be straightforward, stable and common to all retirement savings plans in the country**. Different tax rules for different types of plan and frequent changes to those rules may create confusion and reduce people's trust in the system.
3. **The design of tax and non-tax incentives for retirement savings should at least make all income groups neutral between consuming and saving**. This tax neutrality is achieved when the way present and future consumption is taxed makes the individual indifferent between consuming and saving. The tax treatment of retirement savings should at least not discourage savings.
4. **Countries with an "EET" tax regime already in place should maintain the structure of deferred taxation**. The upfront cost incurred at the introduction of the pension system with deferred taxation is already behind in most countries and the rewards in the form of large tax collections on pension income are in the horizon.
5. **Countries should consider the fiscal space and demographic trends before introducing a new retirement savings system with financial incentives**. The maturity of the pension system and demographics influence the fiscal cost related to financial incentives.
6. **Identifying the retirement savings needs and capabilities of different population groups could help countries to improve the design of financial incentives**.
    a. **Tax credits, fixed-rate tax deductions or matching contributions may be used when the aim is to provide an equivalent tax advantage across income groups**. Financial incentives that equalise the tax relief provided on contributions for all individuals, independently of their income level and marginal income tax rate, achieve a smoother distribution of the overall tax advantage across the income scale.
    b. **Non-tax incentives, in particular fixed nominal subsidies, may be used when low-income earners save too little compared to their savings needs**. Non-tax incentives are better tools to encourage retirement savings among low-income earners, who are less sensitive to tax incentives.
7. **Countries using tax credits may consider making them refundable and converting them into non-tax incentives**. Individuals with a low tax liability can still benefit from tax credits when they are refundable. The value of the credit is strengthened when it is paid directly into the pension account, in order to help individuals to build larger pots to finance retirement.
8. **Countries where pension benefits and withdrawals are tax exempt may consider restricting the choice of the post-retirement product when granting financial incentives**. When withdrawals are tax exempt, financial incentives may lose their purpose if individuals withdraw early or take a lump sum. To counter this, policy makers could restrict the choice of when and how to withdraw the money; take back part or all of the financial incentives when individuals take a lump sum or withdraw early; or encourage people to selected post-retirement products that are more in line with the objective of people having a retirement income.
9. **Countries need to regularly update tax-deductibility ceilings and the value of non-tax incentives to maintain the attractiveness of saving for retirement**. Keeping tax-deductibility ceilings for contributions and the value of non-tax incentives (maximum matching contribution,

subsidy) constant over time may reduce the attractiveness of saving for retirement and lower the positive impact on participation and contribution levels.

Source: OECD (2018[4]), "Policy guidelines to improve the design of financial incentives to promote savings for retirement", in *Financial Incentives and Retirement Savings*, OECD Publishing, Paris, https://doi.org/10.1787/9789264306929-9-en.

OECD countries seem to acknowledge the usefulness of financial incentives to promote savings for retirement as they all provide them to individuals saving for retirement. Figure 3.1 shows that, in most countries, the tax treatment of retirement savings deviates from the "TTE" tax regime applicable to other forms of savings. Moreover, even in the three countries applying the "TTE" tax regime to retirement savings, some tax relief actually applies or non-tax incentives substitute tax incentives. Indeed, in Australia, pension contributions and investment income are taxed, but for most individuals a tax rate of 15% applies that is lower than their marginal income tax rate (Table 3.1). In New Zealand, financial incentives take the form of employer and government matching contributions. In Türkiye, individuals receive government matching contributions and fixed nominal subsidies, and the tax rate on investment income may be as low as 5% if the individual withdraws benefits from age 56 after at least 10 years of participation in the pension plan.

Tax rules are still complex in many OECD countries. Table 3.1 shows that tax rules tend to vary by type of plan, by type of contribution (mandatory or voluntary) and by source of contribution (employer or individual). Even in countries where only one tax treatment applies to all retirement savings generally, differences may exist in tax-deductibility limits, tax rates, or tax credit levels depending on the situation. For example, in Canada, contribution limits are different between defined benefit occupational plans, defined contribution occupational plans, deferred profit-sharing plans, and personal pension plans. In the Netherlands, a "TEE" tax treatment applies to contributions made on income exceeding a certain threshold, rather than "EET". Moreover, frequent changes to tax rules have been made in some countries, not necessarily towards a simplification. For example, Spain has made significant changes to the tax rules in the past 20 years, eliminating the tax reduction for lump sum payments in 2007, removing the larger contribution limit for older individuals in 2015, and constraining employee contributions into an occupational pension plan to what employers contribute into that plan in 2022. Frequent changes could deter individuals from saving in asset-backed pension plans as changes make people uncertain about the tax treatment that may apply to them in the future given the long-term nature of saving for retirement.

In general, the tax treatment of retirement savings in OECD countries is likely to provide most individuals with an incentive to save, but it may not be the case for all pension plans. The incentive to save is measured by comparing the after-tax and before-tax rates of return of a savings vehicle. A tax system is neutral when individuals are indifferent between consuming and saving and this is achieved when the after-tax rate of return is equal to the before-tax rate of return (OECD, 2018[4]). The "EET" tax regime achieves tax neutrality when the individual has the same marginal tax rate during working life and retirement. The "TEE" tax regime also achieves tax neutrality when the rate of return does not exceed the "normal return to saving" or the risk-free return (Adam et al., 2011[7]). There is a disincentive to save (or an incentive to consume rather than to save) when the after-tax rate of return is lower than the before-tax rate of return, and vice-versa. The tax treatment of selected personal pension plans in some countries provides a disincentive to save. This is the case for example in Austria and Germany, where contributions are paid from taxed income and pension benefits are partially taxed ("TEt"), and in Denmark, Greece, Mexico and the Slovak Republic, where contributions are paid from taxed income and investment income is taxed ("TtE" or "TTE").[26] Moreover, in Denmark, Greece and Sweden, some individuals may have a disincentive to save in occupational pension plans. Contributions are tax exempt, investment income is taxed, and pension benefits are taxed ("EtT"). For individuals having the same marginal tax rate throughout their life, this tax treatment provides a disincentive to save. However, many people are likely to have a lower marginal tax rate in retirement because their pension income is lower than their past work income. In that case, there may still be an incentive to save despite the taxation of investment income.

Over the past 10 years, all the OECD countries using deferred taxation, such as the "EET" tax regime, have kept this regime. In Poland, however, the fiscal cost related to financial incentives may increase in the future. Indeed, the OFE plans, to which the "EET" tax treatment applies, are losing importance as participation is no longer mandatory since 2014. Meanwhile, employees have been enrolled automatically into PPK plans since 2019, and the applicable tax regime is "TEE". If membership trends continue between the two types of plans, the fiscal cost for the Polish treasury may fall in the short term and increase in the long term as the collection of taxes on OFE pension benefits will fade away (OECD, 2018[4]).

Several OECD countries have introduced new types of asset-backed pension schemes with financial incentives over the past 10 years despite pressures on the general budget. Some of them applied the same incentives as those that were already applicable to pre-existing schemes. For example, Belgium introduced in 2019 VAPW plans for employees not already covered by an occupational pension plan and applied the same tax treatment as for other types of personal pension plans. France introduced PER plans in 2018 and the tax treatment is the same as for the pre-existing plans that they replaced. Spain introduced simplified occupational pension plans in 2022 and their tax treatment is the same as for other occupational pension plans. Several countries also introduced new schemes with automatic enrolment and provided non-tax financial incentives in addition, or as a substitute to tax incentives. For example, Poland introduced PPK plans in 2019 with a "TEE" tax treatment. In addition, the government pays fixed nominal subsidies when people join a plan and annually conditional on the employee paying a minimum contribution, and employers pay matching contributions too. Similarly, Lithuania introduced automatic enrolment in its second pillar pension scheme in 2019. The "TEE" tax treatment applies, and the government pays subsidies as a match to workers' contributions. By contrast, non-tax incentives mostly substitute tax incentives in Türkiye. The government pays matching contributions and one-off subsidies to employees enrolled automatically into personal plans since 2017, and the tax treatment is "TTE".[27]

Most OECD countries tend to provide higher overall tax advantages to middle and high-income earners. Indeed, most countries provide tax relief on contributions in the form of tax exemptions or tax deductions (Table 3.2). Moreover, personal income tax systems are progressive in most countries, meaning that tax rates increase with taxable income. This implies that the higher the earnings, the larger the tax relief provided by tax exemptions and tax deductions on each unit of contribution. By contrast, in Estonia and Hungary, a single personal income tax rate applies irrespective of the level of taxable earnings (20% and 15%, respectively), so all individuals receive the same tax incentive in proportion to their earnings. Additionally, Belgium, Estonia, Israel, Korea and the United States use tax credits. This form of tax incentive provides the same tax relief on contributions to all individuals, except in Korea and the United States where higher credit rates are provided to lower earners. Matching contributions also achieve a smoother distribution of incentives by income level and can be found in Australia, Chile, Colombia, Czechia, Hungary, New Zealand, Türkiye and the United States, for example. In addition, the cap associated with state matching contributions reduces the value of the incentive for higher earners. Finally, fixed nominal subsidies favour lower-income earners and can be found in Chile, Estonia, Germany, Lithuania, Mexico, Poland and Türkiye.

Tax credits are non-refundable in all the countries using this form of tax relief on contributions, meaning that individuals with a tax liability lower than the tax credit only partially benefit from the tax credit. In Hungary and New Zealand, tax credits are paid into the pension account of entitled individuals instead of coming as a deduction of the income tax liability, making them state matching contributions. However, in Hungary, the tax credit is non-refundable.

Among the countries exempting pension benefits from taxation, at least for selected types of plans, most restrict how and when individuals can take money out. Some countries tax withdrawals taken before reaching a certain age or a minimum length of the pension contract (e.g. Australia, Chile, Hungary,

Lithuania, Mexico, Poland, United States). For example, in Lithuania, pension benefits from third pillar pension funds are taxed at 15% if the pension contract lasted less than five years or if the individual is more than five years before the statutory age of retirement. Other countries condition the tax-free status of pension benefits to selected types of retirement income payments (e.g. Austria, Czechia, Estonia). For example, in Czechia, annuities and programmed withdrawals paid over at least 10 years are tax free, while lump sums and programmed withdrawals over shorter periods are taxable. Another approach is to take back financial incentives if certain conditions are not met regarding the withdrawal of pension benefits (e.g. Austria, Chile, Poland). For example, in Poland, early, unconditional withdrawals from PPK plans are possible but, in that case, returns on investments are taxed at 19% (instead of being tax free), 30% of the employer matching contributions are transferred to the social security institute, and government subsidies are transferred back to the general budget. Still, some countries do not restrict tax-free withdrawals, such as Colombia, Costa Rica, Denmark (age savings), Greece (personal pensions), Latvia (voluntary pensions), New Zealand, the Slovak Republic and Türkiye.

Finally, many countries do not update the parameters linked to financial incentives on a yearly basis. While some countries update income thresholds and contribution limits for tax relief purposes in line with inflation or wages (e.g. average wage, minimum wage) on an annual basis, this was not the case between 2022 and 2023 for all thresholds and limits in countries such as Australia, Austria, Czechia, Estonia, Finland, Greece, Ireland, Italy, Japan, Korea, Latvia, Lithuania, Luxembourg, New Zealand, Portugal, the Slovak Republic, Slovenia and Spain. Moreover, countries offering government matching contributions or subsidies tend to update the maximum entitlements discretionally only, at best. For example, Germany has increased the maximum subsidy in *Riester* plans only once since 2008, from EUR 154 to EUR 175 in 2018. The maximum entitlements for government matching contributions in Australia (AUD 500) and New Zealand (NZL 521.41) have not been updated at least since 2015, when the OECD started to monitor this information. This reduces the attractiveness of financial incentives over time.

References

Adam, S. et al. (2011), *Tax by design*, Oxford University Press, https://ifs.org.uk/books/tax-design. [7]

OECD (2024), *Asset-backed pensions*, https://www.oecd.org/en/topics/asset-backed-pensions.html. [8]

OECD (2023), *Annual survey on financial incentives for retirement savings*, https://www.oecd.org/content/dam/oecd/en/topics/policy-sub-issues/asset-backed-pensions/Financial-incentives-retirement-savings-2023.pdf. [3]

OECD (2022), *OECD Recommendation for the Good Design of Defined Contribution Pension Plans*, https://legalinstruments.oecd.org/en/instruments/OECD-LEGAL-0467. [1]

OECD (2021), "Gender implications of the design of retirement savings plans", in *Towards Improved Retirement Savings Outcomes for Women*, OECD Publishing, Paris, https://doi.org/10.1787/8be79bb8-en. [5]

OECD (2018), "Does the design of financial incentives provide a tax advantage when people save for retirement?", in *Financial Incentives and Retirement Savings*, OECD Publishing, Paris, https://doi.org/10.1787/9789264306929-5-en. [2]

OECD (2018), *Policy guidelines for improving the design of financial incentives to promote savings for retirement*, https://web-archive.oecd.org/2018-12-03/501157-Policy-guidelines-for-improving-the-design-of-financial-incentives-to-promote-savings-for-retirement-Policy-Brief-4.pdf. [6]

OECD (2018), "Policy guidelines to improve the design of financial incentives to promote savings for retirement", in *Financial Incentives and Retirement Savings*, OECD Publishing, Paris, https://doi.org/10.1787/9789264306929-9-en. [4]

Notes

[1] OECD (2018[2]) calculates the overall tax advantage that individuals saving in asset-backed pension plans may enjoy over their lifetime in OECD countries based on 2018 tax rules.

[2] Canada, Colombia, Finland, France, Hungary, Iceland, Ireland, Italy, Japan, the Netherlands, New Zealand, Slovenia, Spain, Switzerland, Türkiye and the United Kingdom.

[3] In Denmark, employee contributions are deductible for personal income tax but not for labour market tax. In France, contributions are deductible for personal income tax but not for social taxes (CSG and CRDS). In Norway, employee contributions to occupational plans are deductible from ordinary income but not from personal income.

[4] For example, in Belgium, individuals earning up to EUR 15 200 in 2023 paid personal income tax at a marginal rate of 25%, while those earning up to EUR 26 830 paid personal income tax at a marginal rate of 40%. The 30% tax credit was, therefore, more advantageous than a tax deduction for the lower earners, but less advantageous for the higher earners.

[5] Individuals on adjusted taxable income of up to AUD 37 000 receive a tax offset of up to AUD 500 annually from the government that is effectively a refund of the 15% tax paid on employer contributions. For individuals for whom the sum of adjusted taxable income and employer contributions exceeds AUD 250 000, a tax rate of 30% instead of 15% is applied on the portion of employer contributions that are above the AUD 250 000 threshold.

[6] In Luxembourg, employer contributions are taxed at the rate of 20% and this tax is paid directly by the employer.

[7] The tax rates are the same as for personal income tax, but the thresholds are higher. This implies that, for some individuals, the tax rate applied to employer contributions is lower than their marginal tax rate.

[8] In Belgium, Canada (defined benefit plans) and the Netherlands (defined benefit plans), there is a limit on the accrual rate or on the total pension entitlement rather than a limit on contributions.

[9] This limit only applies to occupational pension plans implemented via direct insurance and pension funds (*Pensionskassen* and *Pensionsfonds*). There are no corresponding limits for pension plans implemented via direct commitments and support funds.

[10] However, the limit for mandatory employer contributions into a superannuation account (AUD 27 500) only represents 30% of the average wage.

[11] G is the basic amount and is set to NOK 116 239 as of 1 May 2023.

[12] This amount is reduced by one dollar for every dollar that the sum of the spouse's income, total reportable fringe benefits and reportable employer superannuation contributions exceeds AUD 37 000.

[13] Australia, Belgium, Denmark, France, Greece, Italy, Latvia, Mexico, New Zealand, the Slovak Republic, Sweden and Türkiye.

[14] The preservation age is the age at which individuals can access their superannuation assets if they are retired. It depends on the date of birth (55 years old for people born before 1 July 1960, increasing gradually to 60 for people born from 1 July 1964).

[15] From the tax year 2023/24, there is no longer a tax charge in the United Kingdom when an individual builds up pension savings worth more than the lifetime allowance.

[16] For each peso that the worker contributes voluntarily for retirement purposes, the federal government in its capacity as employer contributes 3.25 pesos, with a contribution capped at 6.5 times the worker's basic salary. Workers can contribute either 1% or 2% of their basic salary.

[17] In addition, individuals must be younger than 71, at least 10% of their total income must be from employment or business, and their total superannuation balance must be less than the general transfer balance cap on 30 June of the previous financial year.

[18] Individuals paying personal income tax at a higher rate (40% or 45%) can claim the difference through their tax return or by calling or writing to His Majesty's Revenue and Customs. The extra tax refund is not paid in the pension account.

[19] In Norway, employer contributions to defined contribution schemes are capped at 7% of wages up to 12 G and 18.1% of wages between 7.1 and 12 G.

[20] If the sum of the two exceeds the limit, the employer and the employee decide upon the priority of the deduction, i.e. deducting first the insurance premiums for the employee or the employer contributions for the employer.

[21] Readers can find previous editions of the OECD Annual Survey on Financial Incentives for Retirement Savings on the OECD website (2024[8]).

[22] Contributions over the cap are taxed at the individual's marginal income tax rate, rather than at 15%.

[23] The lifetime allowance was completely abolished in April 2024.

[24] G is the basic amount in the National Insurance scheme of Norway. The tax regulations contain a number of amounts and amount limits which are directly linked to G.

[25] In Chile, there were three opportunities to withdraw between 2020 and 2021. For the second withdrawal, individuals who had an annual taxable income exceeding 30 UTA in the year of the withdrawal were required to pay taxes. The UTA is an Annual Tax Unit. It was set at CLP 759 912 in July 2023.

[26] The letter "t" in lowercase represents cases where the income flow is only partially taxed or taxed at a lower rate than the marginal tax rate.

[27] However, the tax rate on investment income can be lower than the marginal tax rate.

4 Does investing in equity markets bring better retirement income outcomes to members of defined contribution pension plans?

Stéphanie Payet

This chapter assesses whether investing in equity markets leads to better retirement income outcomes for members of defined contribution pension plans. It first looks at the current practice and trends in equity investments in defined contribution pension schemes across a wide range of countries. It then assesses the impact of investing in equities on investment performance, on the level of assets accumulated at retirement and on replacement rates.

Defined contribution (DC) pension plans rely on investing the contributions of plan members in capital markets to generate investment income and provide income in retirement.[1] However, selecting the most appropriate investment strategy is not straightforward, especially when plan members bear the investment risk individually. Contributions may be invested according to various investment strategies with different risk-return characteristics. In addition, investing these contributions involves solving a trade-off between maximising future retirement income and providing protection from extremely low retirement income (OECD, 2020[1]). Typically, equities produce higher expected returns than bonds over the long term, but they also carry more risk as equity returns are more volatile, especially in the short term (Siegel, 2023[2]). By contrast, conservative investment strategies reduce volatility, but they can result in lower retirement incomes as they generate lower expected returns. Plan members and policy makers, therefore, must find a balance when selecting the most appropriate investment strategy for themselves or for the default option.

This chapter assesses whether investing in equity markets leads to better retirement income outcomes for members of DC pension plans. It starts by looking at the current practices and recent trends in terms of equity investment of DC pension schemes across a wide range of jurisdictions to understand the relevance of that policy question. The chapter then presents three complementary analyses that provide a comprehensive assessment of the impact of equity investment on retirement income outcomes by looking at different indicators. The first analysis looks at case studies of existing DC pension schemes to analyse the link between equity investment and average performance. However, publicly available data only go back 20 years, which is insufficient to assess the impact of investing in equities over an entire career. The second analysis addresses this limitation by using historical returns on selected asset classes since 1900 in 19 OECD countries to calculate the level of assets that successive cohorts of individuals would have accumulated at retirement had a DC pension plan existed in those countries.[2] It compares various illustrative investment strategies with different levels and profiles of exposure to equities. The third analysis is forward looking and brings in, on top of investment risk, risks related to discount rates, labour markets and life expectancy. It uses a stochastic model to generate the distribution of replacement rates that the same illustrative investment strategies would provide under different payout options.

The analyses conclude that investing in equity markets would, in general, lead to better retirement income outcomes for members of DC pension plans. Investing in equities is likely to provide a higher average performance, more assets accumulated at retirement and higher replacement rates than investing only in fixed income. Even during the payout phase, people taking regular drawdowns are likely to receive higher pension benefits when investing a significant part of their savings in equities. However, investing in equities comes with caveats, as it requires individuals to invest for long periods to get the full potential from the compounded return effect, it leads to volatile outcomes for individuals and societies, and it makes pension benefits sensitive to equity market downturns happening when people are close to retirement. This trade-off makes it difficult to determine an exact or approximate optimal equity exposure. While conservative investment strategies reduce volatility, they provide only moderate protection to members of DC pension plans and lead to sub-optimal outcomes during the payout phase when taking regular drawdowns. Finally, when considering bequests, combining equity investment with regular drawdowns may bring higher total pension payments (benefits while alive plus bequests) than taking a lifelong annuity, but without full longevity protection. The main policy implication of the analysis is that countries should avoid investment regulations that favour investment strategies that are too conservative, in particular for the default option.

The findings in this chapter are consistent with the existing literature comparing investment strategies in the context of DC pension schemes. For example, two studies find that conservative investment strategies underperform life-cycle investment strategies and strategies with constant equity exposure. Anarkulova, Cederburg and O'Doherty (2023[3]) find that investing in government bills produces lower average balances at retirement and leads to a higher risk of outliving one's resources during retirement. Khemka, Steffensen and Warren (2021[4]) show that the risk-free strategy produces the lowest balance at retirement at the median and the 10th percentile. Similarly, Berardi and Tebaldi (2023[5]) compare an investment strategy providing a minimum return guarantee and investing 95% in long-term bonds and 5% in equities to three life-cyle investment strategies, and find that the minimum guarantee strategy produces the lowest internal rate of return at the median and the fifth percentile, and the lowest performance adjusted for risk.[3] In addition, several studies show that portfolios with a high allocation to equities present a trade-off between risk and return (Dunn and Berg, 2019[6]; Khemka, Steffensen and Warren, 2021[4]; Šebo, Danková and Králik, 2020[7]). By contrast, Anarkulova, Cederburg and O'Doherty (2023[3]) find that, in the United States, the internationally diversified equity portfolio outperforms all the other strategies, producing higher wealth at retirement, higher income replacement rates and higher bequests on average, without reducing outcomes in unfavourable scenarios and with a lower risk of outliving one's resources during retirement. Finally, Šebo, Danková and Králik (2020[7]) find that life-cycle investment strategies reducing linearly the exposure to equities with age are outperformed by fixed portfolio strategies with the same average equity exposure over 40 years, both in terms of balance at retirement and maximum fall in assets during the accumulation phase. They suggest that life-cycle strategies with a glide path based on age and price movements of equities perform better. For Khemka, Steffensen and Warren (2021[4]), the glide path of life-cycle investment strategies should take into account the level of risk aversion of the individual.

This chapter complements the existing literature. While most studies compare investment strategies using stochastic modelling, Monte Carlo simulations or bootstrapping, this chapter combines stochastic modelling with historical analyses that look at the actual performance of selected pension funds and use past investment returns for selected asset classes to build asset accumulations for successive cohorts of individuals. Additionally, the analysis in this chapter compares investment strategies under two different payout options, lifelong annuities and regular drawdowns. Another interesting feature of this analysis is that it covers more than one country and shows that the main results apply to a range of countries.

This chapter looks in Section 4.1 at the current practices and recent trends regarding equity investments of DC pension schemes using aggregate national data. Section 4.2 presents the case studies of existing DC pension schemes in selected OECD countries. Section 4.3 presents the results of the analysis using historical returns, while Section 4.4 presents the results of the stochastic analysis. Section 4.5 concludes and presents policy implications.[4]

4.1. Current practices regarding equity investments and recent trends

This section finds that, in many jurisdictions, equity exposure of DC pension schemes has increased over the past 20 years, although the ways they invest in equities and the trends vary across jurisdictions. The section looks at the current practices and recent trends regarding the equity investments of DC pension schemes across a wide range of jurisdictions to understand the relevance of assessing whether investing in equities leads to better outcomes for plan members. It compares the equity investments of DC pension schemes across 23 OECD countries and 15 non-OECD jurisdictions using the OECD Global Pension Statistics database.[5] It presents data on asset allocation at end-2022 and uses a sub-sample of jurisdictions to analyse the evolution of equity exposure between end-2001 and end-2022.

The allocation of DC pension schemes into equities varies greatly across jurisdictions. Figure 4.1 presents the aggregate allocation of DC pension schemes into equities (public and private), bills and bonds, cash and deposits, and other investments at the end of 2022. Investment through collective investment schemes (CIS) is only shown when the look-through into the previous asset classes is not available. In some jurisdictions, CIS investment is used to invest indirectly in equities (e.g. Bulgaria). At the end of 2022, total equity exposure represented less than 10% of total investment in Albania, the Czech Republic (hereafter, Czechia), Finland, the Maldives and Nigeria. At the other extreme, total equity exposure represented 60% or more of total investment in Estonia, Hong Kong (China), Lithuania and Poland. On average across all jurisdictions, total equity investment represented 30% of total investment at the end of 2022. Bills and bonds made up the largest share on average, at 47%.

Figure 4.1. Allocation of DC pension schemes into selected asset classes, end-2022

As a percentage of total investment

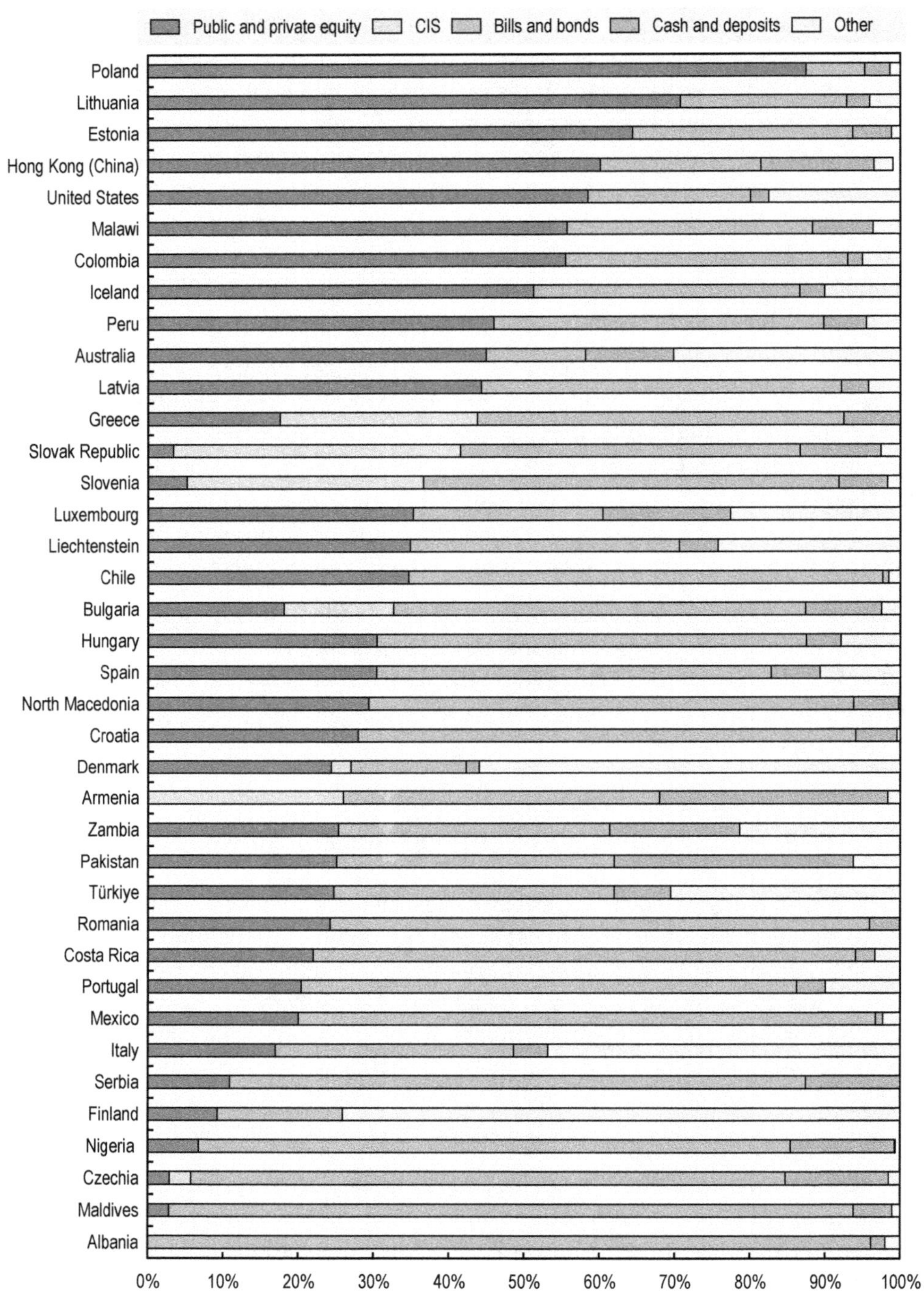

Note: The category "Collective Investment Schemes (CIS)" is shown only when the look-through into different asset classes is not available. Jurisdictions are ranked in descending order according to the aggregate allocation to equities and CIS.
Source: OECD Global Pension Statistics and Board of Governors of the Federal Reserve for the United States.

Private equity, i.e. unlisted equities and private equity funds, usually represents a small portion of total equity investment. In most jurisdictions with available data, equity investment only comprises listed equities

(Figure 4.2). This is due to the fact that many jurisdictions only authorise equites traded on regulated markets (e.g. Armenia, Bulgaria, Costa Rica, Czechia, Greece, Hong Kong (China), Pakistan and Serbia) (OECD, 2024[8]). Figure 4.2 shows that among jurisdictions reporting private equity investment, unlisted equities and private equity funds jointly represented between 2% (in Australia) and 36% (in Finland) of total equity holding at the end of 2022.

Figure 4.2. Split of equity investments of DC pension schemes, end-2022

As a percentage of the total equity holding

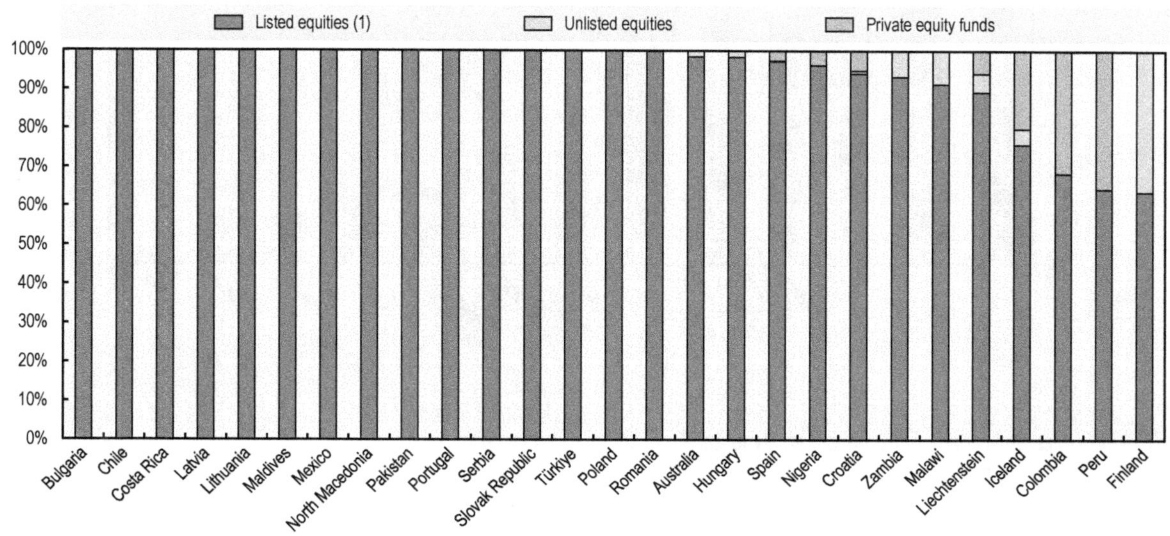

Note: (1) The category "listed equities" includes direct investment in listed equities and equity investments through collective investment schemes.
Source: OECD Global Pensions Statistics.

The extent to which DC pension schemes invest in equities through foreign or domestic companies varies widely across jurisdictions. Figure 4.3 shows that foreign equities represented more than 50% of total equity exposure at end-2022 in Chile, Croatia, Lithuania, Mexico and North Macedonia. By contrast, DC pension schemes in some countries invest in equities mostly through domestic companies. At the end of 2022, foreign equities represented 10% or less of total equity exposure in Latvia, Poland and Portugal.

Figure 4.3. Share of foreign equity investments in total equity exposure, end-2022

As a percentage of total equity investments

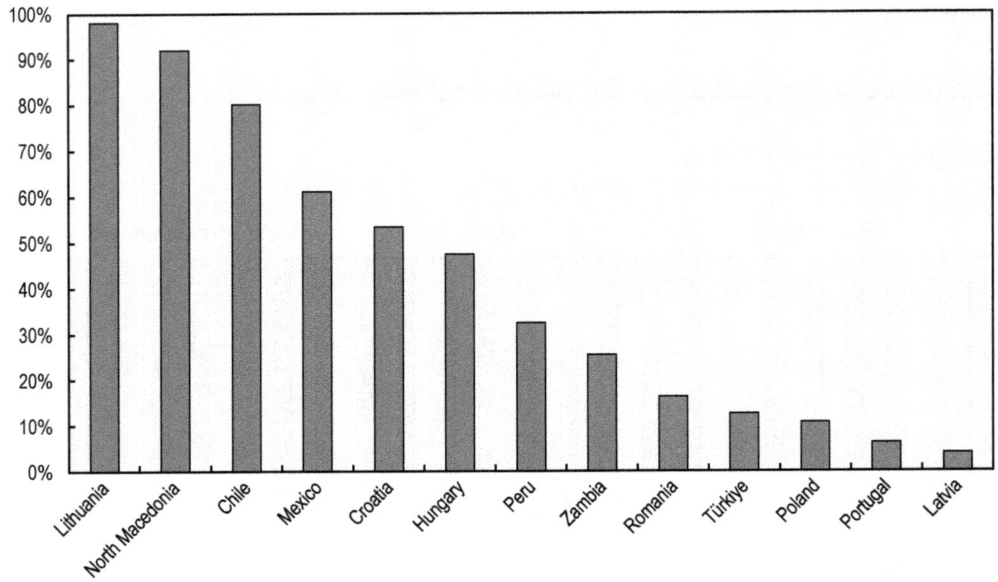

Note: The data exclude investments in private equity funds.
Source: OECD Global Pension Statistics.

Quantitative investment limits may constrain investment in equities. Several jurisdictions do not apply quantitative investment limits but request pension entities to invest according to the prudent person principle. This is the case, for example, in Australia, Denmark, Luxembourg, Malawi and the United States. Other jurisdictions have quantitative investment limits, but not for all asset classes. For example, there is no regulatory limit for equity investments in Hong Kong (China), Hungary, Italy, Latvia, the Maldives, Portugal, Slovenia, Spain and Türkiye. Among the jurisdictions with regulatory limits for equity investment, limits vary from 0%, where equity investment is not allowed, to 80% (OECD, 2024[8]).[6] At the end of 2022, equity investment, excluding private equity funds, represented 27% of the portfolio on average among the jurisdictions with quantitative limits for equities, while it was 32% on average among the jurisdictions without quantitative limits. Quantitative investment limits for equity investment may therefore be binding in some jurisdictions, although other factors may be at play.

Over the past 20 years, equity exposure has evolved differently across jurisdictions but it has in general increased in many jurisdictions. Figure 4.4, Figure 4.5, Figure 4.6 and Figure 4.7 show the evolution of equity exposure between end-2001 and end-2022, splitting selected jurisdictions into four groups according to the evolution of equity exposure in the portfolio of DC pension schemes. Figure 4.4 includes jurisdictions where equity exposure has remained relatively stable between end-2001 and end-2022, although fluctuations may have happened in-between. Figure 4.5 includes jurisdictions where equity exposure increased significantly in the first part of the period and then stabilised. Figure 4.6 includes jurisdictions where equity exposure has increased sharply in recent years to reach more than 60% of total investment at the end of 2022. Figure 4.7 includes jurisdictions where equity exposure increased gradually over 2001-22.

Figure 4.4. Evolution of equity exposure in DC pension schemes – Countries with stable exposure between end-2001 and end-2022 (as a % of total investments)

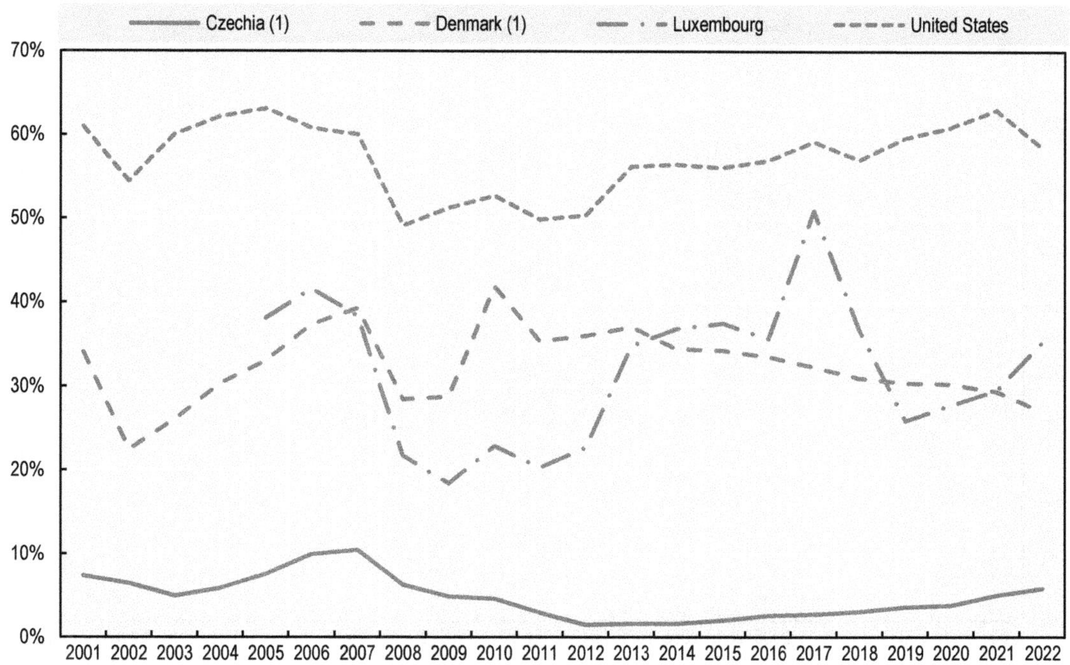

Note: 1. Equity exposure also includes investment in CIS as the look-through into different asset classes is not available.
Source: OECD Global Pension Statistics and US Federal Reserve.

Figure 4.5. Evolution of equity exposure in DC pension schemes – Countries with increased exposure and then stable exposure between end-2001 and end-2022 (as a % of total investments)

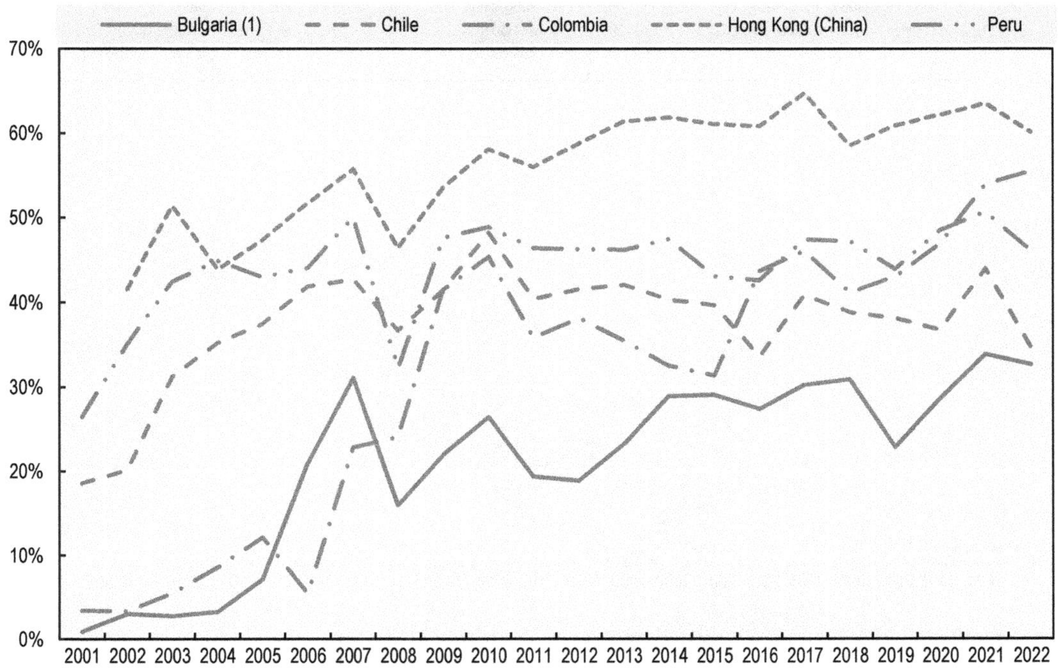

Note: 1. Equity exposure also includes investment in CIS as the look-through into different asset classes is not available.
Source: OECD Global Pension Statistics.

Figure 4.6. Evolution of equity exposure in DC pension schemes – Countries with stable exposure and then increased exposure between end-2001 and end-2022 (as a % of total investments)

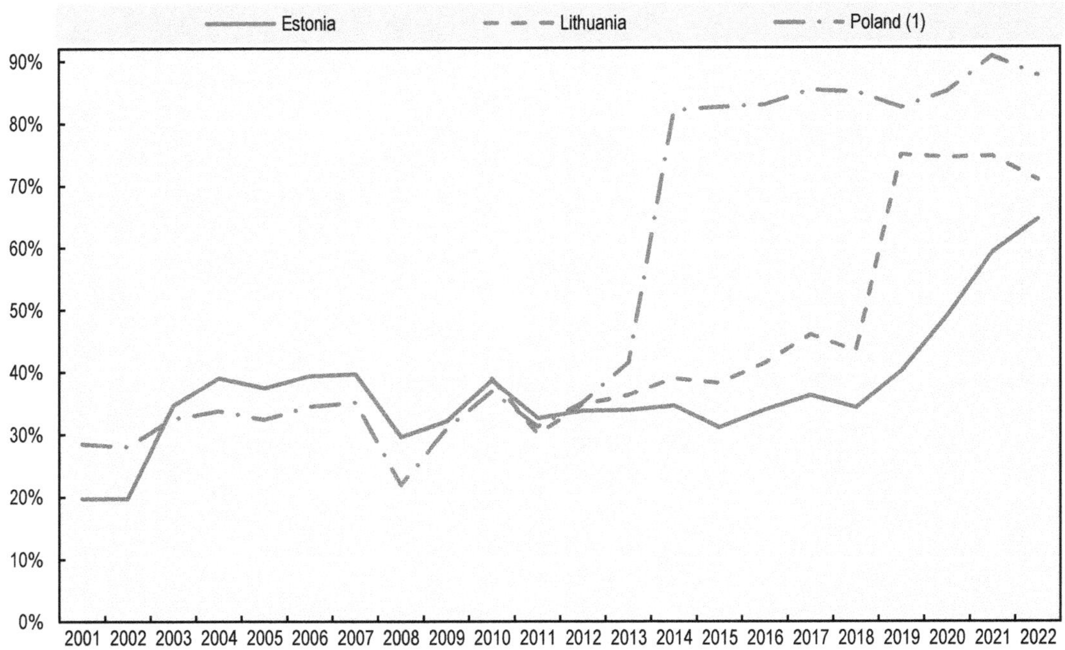

Note: 1. Equity exposure also includes investment in CIS as the look-through into different asset classes is not available.
Source: OECD Global Pension Statistics.

Figure 4.7. Evolution of equity exposure in DC pension schemes – Countries with gradual increased exposure between end-2001 and end-2022 (as a % of total investments)

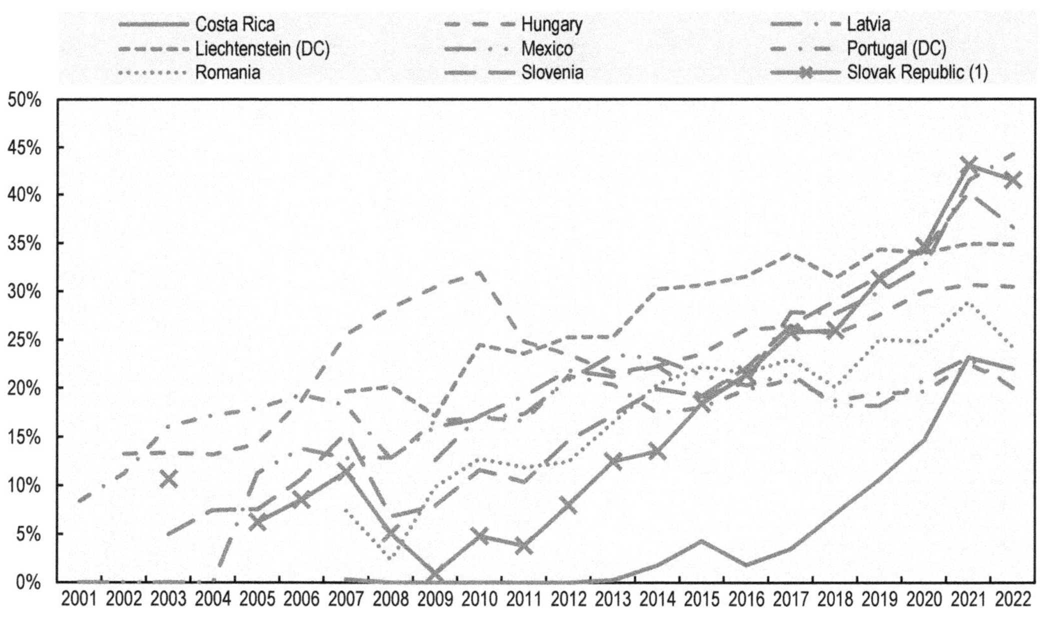

Note: 1. Equity exposure also includes investment in CIS as the look-through into different asset classes is not available.
Source: OECD Global Pension Statistics.

Several factors may explain the evolution of equity exposure. Market fluctuations change the value of assets and can affect portfolio composition when the impact varies across asset classes. For example, the 2008 global financial crisis reduced the equity exposure in most jurisdictions as equity values dropped significantly while bond values remained broadly constant. For instance, in Peru, the share of equities in total investment fell from 50% at end-2007 to 32% at end-2008. The equity share was back at 48% at end-2009 thanks to the market recovery. Additionally, in the context of DC schemes with investment choice, the reduction in equity allocations in times of market downturns may also reflect investment switches by plan members to more conservative investment strategies.[7]

Regulatory changes may also influence the evolution of equity exposure. For example, in Poland, the equity exposure doubled from 41% to 82% between end-2013 and end-2014 as a pension reform banned open pension funds from investing in domestic government bonds, which led to the transfer of all domestic government bonds held by these funds to the social security system. Lithuania introduced life-cycle funds in 2019 leading to a substantial re-allocation of assets from bonds to equities. Between end-2018 and end-2019, equity exposure increased from 43% to 75% of total investment. Estonia relaxed some investment restrictions in 2019 for the second pension pillar. Under the Investment Fund Act 2019, the equity investment limit was raised from 0% to 10% for conservative funds and from 75% to 100% for the other funds. Following this change, pension funds gradually began to increase their equity investments and new funds with full equity exposure were created. Chile introduced the multi-funds system in 2002, leading to an increase in equity exposure in the following years. Before 2002, assets could only be invested in Fund C (with 15% to 40% in equities) and Fund E (with up to 5% in equities). With the introduction of additional funds, a growing proportion of assets has been invested in riskier funds, especially in Fund B (with 25% to 60% in equities) that became the default option for new entrants up to age 35.

The level of maturity of the DC pension system can also explain the evolution of the equity exposure. When jurisdictions introduce a new DC system, equity exposure tends to be small initially and to increase as the system matures, i.e. when DC plan sponsors and members gain comfort in equity investing, often as the domestic capital market deepens and grows. For example, Bulgaria introduced a mandatory DC scheme in 2000. Equity exposure increased gradually from 1% at end-2001 to 31% at end-2007 and then fluctuated around that level up to 2022.

4.2. Equity exposure and investment performance: case studies

This section studies the link between equity exposure and average investment performance. It provides anecdotal evidence that average performance of DC pension schemes tends to increase with equity exposure, although other aspects of portfolio composition also affect performance, regardless of the equity exposure.[8] Equity exposure also increases the volatility of annual investment returns. The section studies existing DC pension funds at the country level for Chile, Czechia and France, and at the pension entity level in Australia (AustralianSuper and QSuper), Denmark (PFA), Sweden (AP7 and Alecta), the United Kingdom (Nest) and the United States (Thrift Savings Plan). Annex 4.A provides a brief description of the pension funds studied. Publicly available data cover the past 7 to 21 years, depending on the fund.[9]

Members of DC pension plans have access to a wide range of exposures to equities within countries and within pension entities. Table 4.1 presents the average equity exposure, the average performance and the volatility of returns of the studied DC pension funds over the longest available period up to the end of 2022. It shows that equity exposure varies significantly across pension funds.[10] In several countries or entities there are pension funds with extreme equity exposures (0% or 100%) used as building blocks for diversified or life-cycle investment strategies.

Table 4.1. Average equity exposure, geometric average annual real return and standard deviation of real returns of selected DC pension funds over the longest period available

Country / Entity	Pension fund	Average equity exposure	Geometric average annual real return	Standard deviation of real returns	Period analysed
Chile [1]	Funds E	3.5%	3.3%	4.7%	2002-22
	Funds D	18.2%	3.7%	6.2%	
	Funds C	38.0%	4.1%	8.8%	
	Funds B	58.6%	4.4%	12.8%	
	Funds A	78.2%	5.1%	17.1%	
Czechia	Transformed funds	0%	-2.7%	3.9%	2014-22
	Participating funds	7.7%	-2.6%	5.7%	
France	Cash funds	0%	0.1%	1.7%	2000-21
	Bond funds	0%	1.1%	2.4%	
	Diversified funds	>0%	1.2%	7.7%	
	Equity funds	100%	1.4%	15.9%	
Australia / AustralianSuper [2]	Stable	21.5%	3.0%	4.0%	2009-22
	Conservative Balanced	41.0%	3.7%	6.2%	
	Balanced	58.0%	4.6%	8.0%	
	Socially Aware	58.0%	4.7%	7.4%	
	Indexed Diversified [3]	70.0%	4.3%	6.5%	
	High Growth	73.8%	4.8%	9.7%	
Australia / QSuper [4]	Moderate	23.0%	0.7%	..	2016-22
	Sustain 2	29.6%	-0.3%	..	
	Sustain 1	35.7%	1.0%	..	
	Focus 3	39.0%	1.6%	..	
	Focus 2	45.0%	2.2%	..	
	Balanced	48.4%	3.0%	..	
	Focus 1	50.9%	2.8%	..	
	Aspire 2	51.0%	2.7%	..	
	Socially Responsible	54.8%	1.4%	..	
	Aggressive	59.3%	3.8%	..	
	Outlook	59.5%	3.5%	..	
	Aspire 1	59.5%	3.7%	..	
Denmark / PFA [5]	Profile A	24.3%	2.6%	6.6%	2011-22
	Profile B	48.6%	3.8%	8.1%	
	Profile C	72.8%	5.0%	10.0%	
	Profile D	97.1%	6.2%	12.2%	
Sweden / Alecta	40% target equity	40%	4.1%	9.2%	2012-22
	50% target equity	50%	4.7%	9.8%	
	60% target equity	60%	6.3%	12.7%	
Sweden / AP7	Fixed Income Fund	0%	-1.6%	5.0%	2011-22
	Equity Fund	100%	11.%	17.7%	
United Kingdom / Nest	Lower Growth	0%	-2.3%	..	2013-22
	2022 Retirement Fund	30.2%	2.6%	..	
	2059 Retirement Fund	52.7%	3.9%	..	
	2040 Retirement Fund	63.2%	5.2%	..	
	Higher Risk	69.8%	6.7%	..	
United States / Thrift Savings Plan	G Fund	0%	-0.5%	..	2013-22
	F Fund	0%	-1.3%	..	
	L2030 [6]	60.1%	4.5%	..	
	L2040 [6]	71.8%	5.2%	..	

Country / Entity	Pension fund	Average equity exposure	Geometric average annual real return	Standard deviation of real returns	Period analysed
	L2050 [6]	81.8%	5.9%	..	
	C Fund	100%	9.7%	..	
	S Fund	100%	6.9%	..	
	I Fund	100%	2.3%	..	

Notes: See Annex 4.A for a brief description of the different pension funds. ".." means "not available. Returns are measured in local currency. 1. Average equity exposure measured over 2008-2022.

2. Strategic equity exposure as of July 2022.

3. Performance measured over 2012-22.

4. Equity exposure at end-2022.

5. Equity exposure at end-2022 and performance measured for people 30 years before retirement age.

6. Target equity exposure as of January 2023.

Source: OECD calculations based on data collected from the websites of pension supervisors and pension entities, and on data from Europerformance.

In general, performance increases with equity exposure. Table 4.1 shows that when comparing within countries or pension entities, funds with a higher average equity exposure have usually obtained a higher average annual real return. For each country or pension entity, Table 4.1 ranks pension funds in increasing order of equity exposure from top to bottom. In most of the cases, performance increases with equity exposure. For example, in Chile, there is a nearly linear positive relationship between the average exposure to equities and the average annual real return over the past 20 years. For every 10 percentage points increase in average equity exposure, the average annual real return increases by 22 basis points on average.

Equity is not the only asset class affecting performance and some funds have achieved lower average returns than other funds with lower equity exposure. For example, the Indexed Diversified option of AustralianSuper reached a lower performance (4.3%) than the Balanced and Socially Aware options (4.6% and 4.7% respectively) over 2009-22, despite having a higher equity exposure (70% compared to 58%). Beyond differences in equity exposure, the Indexed Diversified option relies on indexing strategies, has a larger exposure to fixed income than the two other funds (25% compared to 9%) and does not diversify through investment in infrastructure, private equity and property, unlike the two other funds.

The destination of investment may also affect the performance of equities. For example, in the United States, the I Fund of the Thrift Savings Plan is fully invested in global equities and achieved a lower performance over 2013-22 than the C Fund and the S Fund, which are fully invested in US equities. Similarly, the Socially Responsible option of QSuper barely invests in Australian equities and reached a lower performance over 2016-22 than the Balanced option and several of the life-cycle funds (with a mix of Australian and international equities), despite having a higher overall equity exposure.

Funds with higher equity exposure tend to experience a greater volatility of investment returns. Table 4.1 presents the standard deviation of real returns for all funds with available information. It shows that higher equity exposure is associated with higher volatility. This is not the case, however, for the Indexed Diversified option of AustralianSuper, which experienced a lower volatility of returns than other funds with lower equity exposure. Its larger exposure to fixed income may have reduced return volatility.

4.3. Equity exposure and level of assets at retirement: historical returns

This section complements the previous analysis to assess whether investing in equities provides higher levels of assets accumulated at retirement. It expands the analysis to a full career of 40 years instead of the limited periods of time between 7 and 21 years available for the case studies. More importantly, it looks at the level of assets that individuals accumulate at the time of retirement as it matters more to them than the annual returns they get along the way.

This section calculates the level of assets that successive cohorts in 19 OECD countries would have accumulated at retirement, had a DC pension plan existed. It looks at different illustrative investment strategies and uses historical performance for different asset classes to compare outcomes across investment strategies with different levels and profiles of equity exposure. Box 4.1 describes the methodology.

Box 4.1. Brief description of the methodology

The calculations assume that each cohort is represented by a typical individual. That individual joins the labour market at age 25 and receives wages that grow in line with historical inflation and a fixed productivity rate of 1.25%.[1] Under the baseline assumptions, contributions are paid continuously over 40 years based on a constant contribution rate of 5%.[2] The individual pays an annual 1% asset-based fee and retires at age 65. The assets accumulated at retirement are expressed as a multiple of the sum of contributions paid.

The analysis uses historical data on returns and inflation between 1900 and 2021 for 19 OECD countries. Assuming a career of 40 years (from age 25 to 65), this means that the level of assets accumulated at retirement is calculated for 83 successive cohorts retiring between 1939 and 2021 for each country.

The analysis compares the level of assets accumulated at retirement that the following illustrative investment strategies would have produced:

- A fixed portfolio invested in domestic fixed income - 88% in government bonds and 12% in cash and deposits ("domestic fixed income")[3,4]
- A fixed portfolio invested 70% in domestic equities and 30% in international equities ("diversified equities")[5]
- A fixed portfolio invested 60% in equities and 40% in fixed income, with an equal mix of domestic and international securities for equities and government bonds ("diversified 60/40 portfolio")[6]
- A life-cycle investment strategy with a proportion invested in equities (70% domestic and 30% international) starting at 80% and declining linearly during the last 10 years before retirement to 20%, and with equities substituted by domestic fixed income ("life cycle 10y")
- A life-cycle investment strategy with a proportion invested in equities (70% domestic and 30% international) starting at 80% and declining linearly during the last 20 years before retirement to 20%, and with equities substituted by domestic fixed income ("life cycle 20y").

Notes:

1. The analysis does not assume productivity improvement across cohorts. Each cohort has the same starting wage at age 25.
2. The assumed contribution rate reflects the fact that, in many OECD countries, DC pension plans are voluntary and complement public pay-as-you-go pension plans. In countries where DC pension plans are mandatory and represent the main source to finance retirement, contribution rates tend to be higher, between 10% and 20%.
3. These proportions are based on the average asset allocation of pension assets at the end of 2022 across OECD countries.
4. Treasury bill returns are used as a proxy for returns of cash and deposits.
5. In the case of countries from the European Union (EU), the domestic equity portfolio becomes an EU equity portfolio from 1990 to take into account the full liberalisation of capital movements between EU countries enacted that year.
6. The fixed-income part uses the same proportions between government bonds and cash and deposits as the domestic fixed income investment strategy.

The analysis shows that most cohorts in all countries would have accumulated significantly more assets at retirement had they invested at least part of their contributions in equities instead of only in domestic fixed income. For the minority of cohorts for which investing in domestic fixed income would have turned out to produce higher levels of assets accumulated at retirement, the additional level of assets achieved compared to investing in equities would have been modest. The analysis also shows that people need to save for retirement for long periods to get the full potential of investing in equities because the compounded return accumulates over time. However, higher investment in equities also leads to more volatile outcomes across cohorts.

Portfolios with some equity exposure would have led to higher assets accumulated at retirement on average across cohorts than a portfolio with only domestic fixed income. Figure 4.8 shows the average level of assets accumulated at retirement across cohorts by investment strategy for the different countries. The portfolio with domestic fixed income would systematically have produced lower accumulated assets on average compared to the other investment strategies. For the portfolio with domestic fixed income, the average level of accumulated assets varies between 1.9 and 3.5 times the sum of contributions depending on the country. By contrast, for the portfolio with diversified equities, the average level of accumulated assets varies between 4.5 and 11.2 times the sum of contributions. The other investment strategies usually fall in-between these two extremes.[11]

Figure 4.8. Average level of assets accumulated at retirement across cohorts, by investment strategy and country

As a multiple of total contributions paid

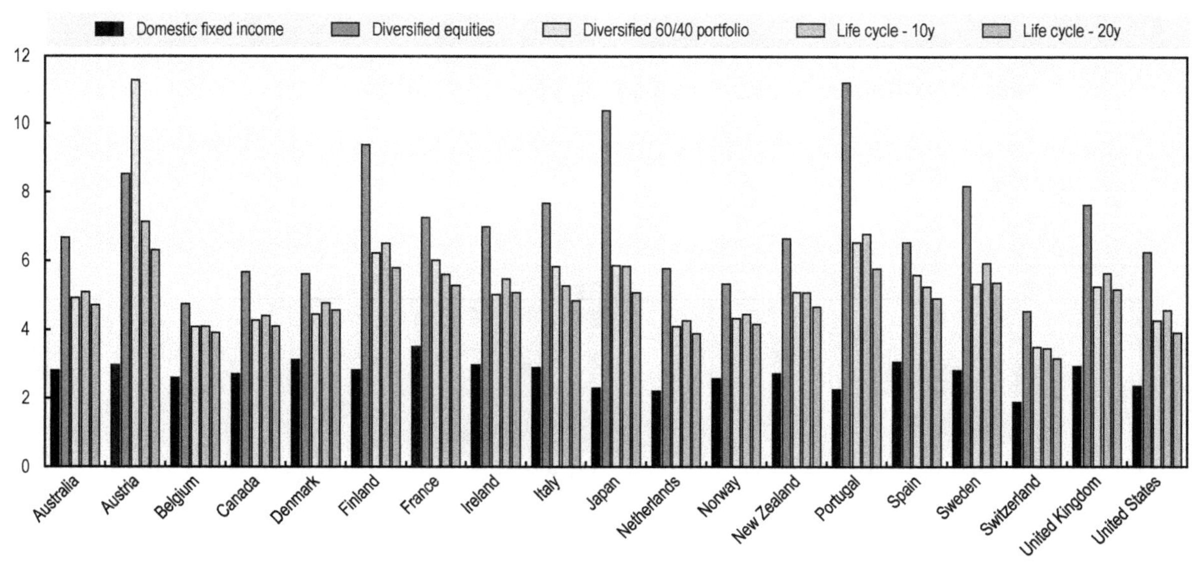

Most cohorts would have been better off investing in equity markets. Figure 4.9 shows the proportion of cohorts that would have accumulated more at retirement by investing at least part of their contributions in equities rather than investing them only in domestic fixed income. In all countries, at least 80% of the 83 cohorts analysed would have been better off investing in equity markets. This proportion reaches 100% for the four portfolios with equity exposure in Australia, Austria, Belgium, Finland, New Zealand, Portugal and the United Kingdom. Looking for example at Denmark, Figure 4.10 shows that only four cohorts among all those retiring between 1939 and 2021 would have accumulated more at retirement with the portfolio with domestic fixed income than with the portfolio with diversified equities.

Figure 4.9. Proportion of cohorts better off investing in equities rather than in domestic fixed income only, by investment strategy and country

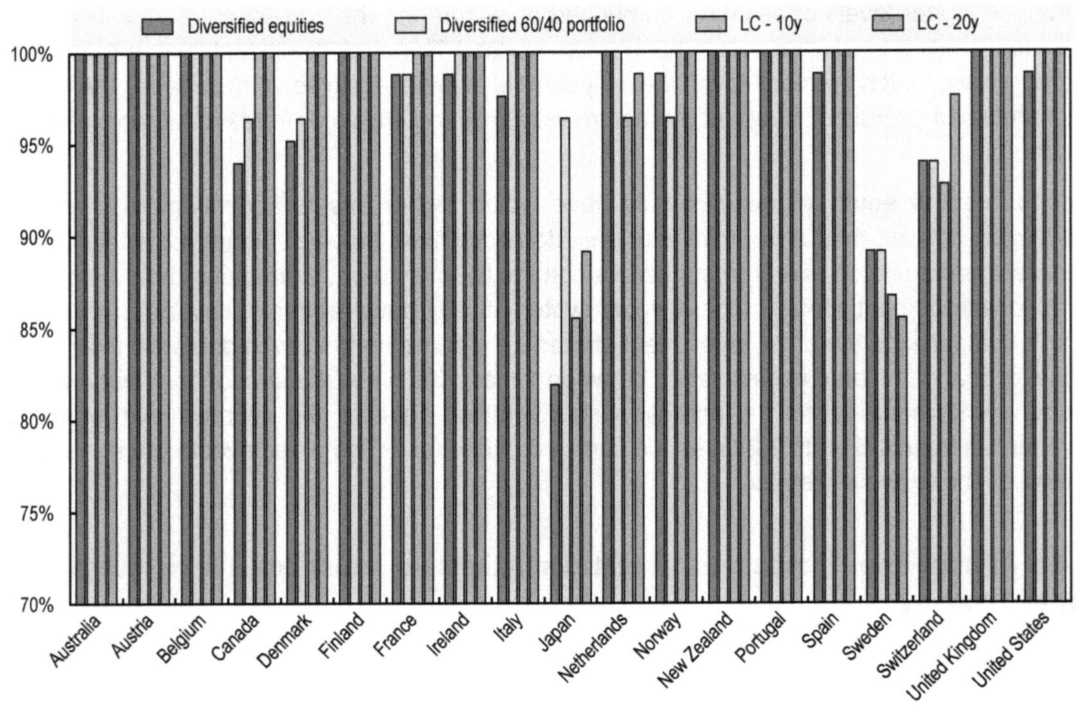

Figure 4.10. Assets accumulated at retirement by successive cohorts in Denmark, by investment strategy

As a multiple of total contributions paid

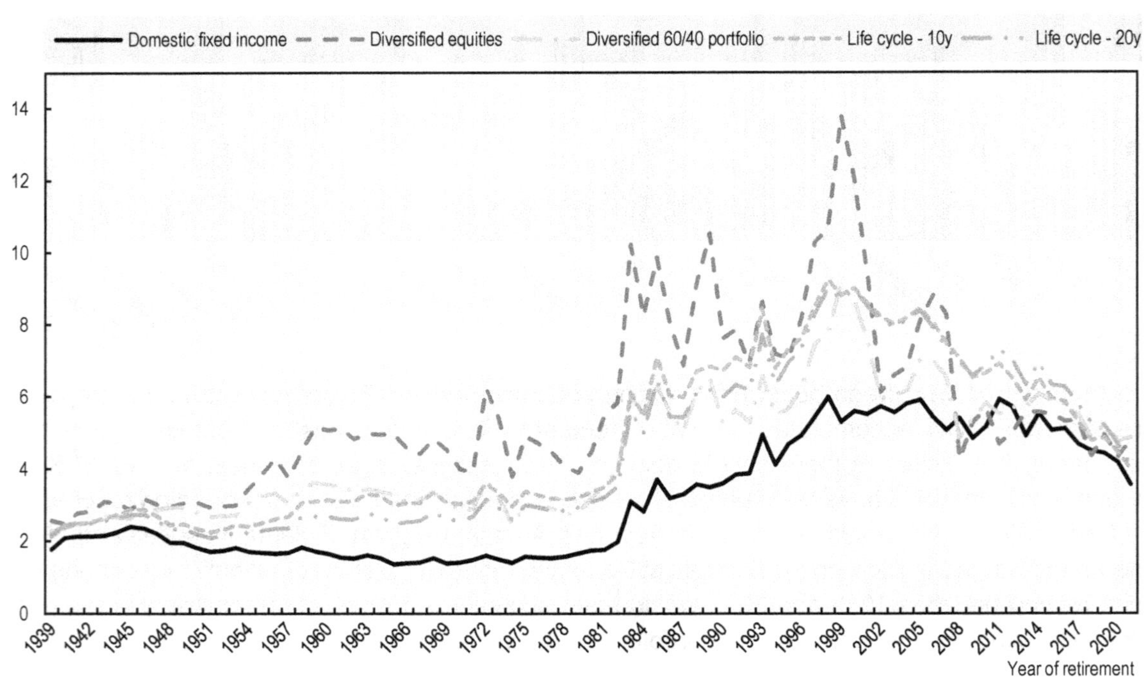

Assets accumulated at retirement would have been significantly higher when investing in equities rather than only in domestic fixed income. Figure 4.11 presents the average difference in accumulated assets between the portfolio with domestic fixed income and the other four investment strategies. Panel A compares the portfolio with domestic fixed income with the portfolio with diversified equities. The blue bars show the average difference in accumulated assets for the cohorts that would have been better off with the portfolio with diversified equities, while the black bars show the average difference in accumulated assets for the cohorts that would have been better off with the portfolio with domestic fixed income. The other panels do the same, comparing the portfolio with domestic fixed income with the diversified 60/40 portfolio (light-grey bars), the life-cycle investment strategy reducing the equity exposure 10 years before retirement (light-blue bars) and the life-cycle investment strategy reducing the equity exposure 20 years before retirement (grey bars), respectively. Among cohorts better off with investment strategies with some equity exposure, the additional level of assets they would have accumulated at retirement compared to the portfolio with domestic fixed income tends to be substantial. For example, in Sweden, for cohorts better off with the portfolio with diversified equities (74 cohorts), the additional level of assets they would have accumulated at retirement compared with the portfolio with domestic fixed income reaches 6.1 times the sum of contributions on average. The average difference in accumulated assets corresponds to 2.8 times the sum of contributions for the diversified 60/40 portfolio, 3.7 times for the life-cycle investment strategy reducing the equity exposure 10 years before retirement, and 3.0 times for the life-cycle investment strategy reducing the equity exposure 20 years before retirement.

Figure 4.11. Average difference in accumulated assets when the equity portfolios are superior to the portfolio with fixed income and vice-versa, by country

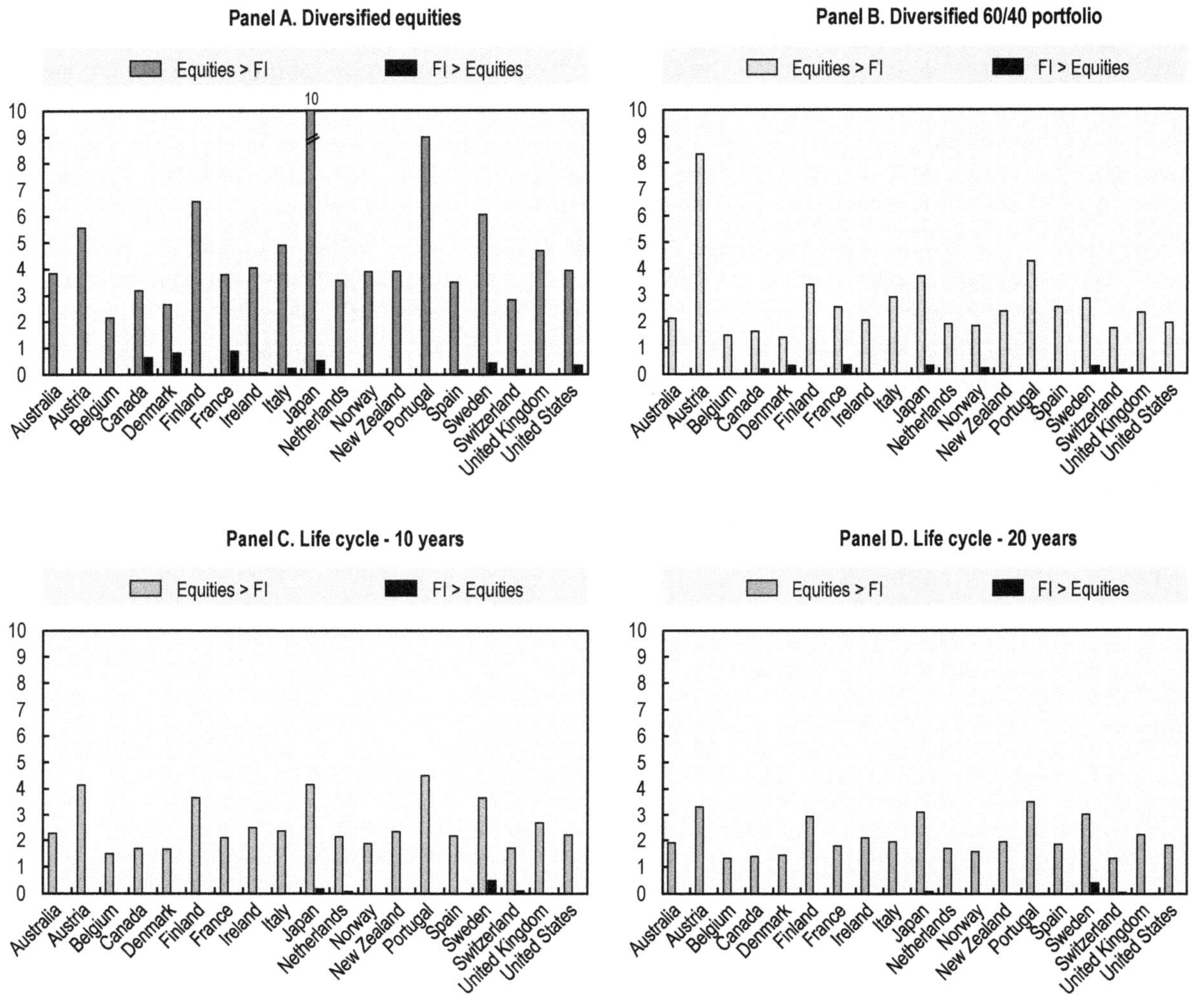

Note: FI means fixed income.

By contrast, for the few cohorts better off with the portfolio with domestic fixed income, the additional accumulated assets at retirement would have been modest compared to what would have been accumulated with the other investment strategies. Still in Sweden, the average additional level of accumulated assets achieved with the portfolio with domestic fixed income corresponds to 0.4 time the sum of contributions when comparing with the portfolio with diversified equities, 0.3 time when comparing with the diversified 60/40 portfolio, 0.5 time when comparing with the life-cycle investment strategy reducing the equity exposure 10 years before retirement, and 0.4 time when comparing with the life-cycle investment strategy reducing the equity exposure 20 years before retirement. Therefore, cohorts that would have invested in equities would have been neutral or only moderately worse off in the minority of cases when the portfolio with domestic fixed income would have produced higher assets accumulated at retirement. In the other cases, they would have been significantly better off.

However, given that portfolios with equity exposure produce more volatile outcomes, the likelihood for a cohort to accumulate a level of assets at retirement different than the other cohorts is greater when investing in equities than when investing in fixed income only. Figure 4.12 shows that the standard deviation of accumulated assets is higher for the portfolios with equity exposure in all countries. The longer and the higher the exposure to equities is, the higher the variability of accumulated assets tends to be. Hence, in most countries, the portfolio with diversified equities is the one producing the most volatile outcomes, leading to greater differences in accumulated assets across cohorts. By contrast, accumulated assets are much more comparable across cohorts with a portfolio with domestic fixed income only. However, this comes at the cost of lower levels of assets accumulated for most cohorts.

Figure 4.12. Standard deviation of accumulated assets, by investment strategy and country

As a multiple of total contributions paid

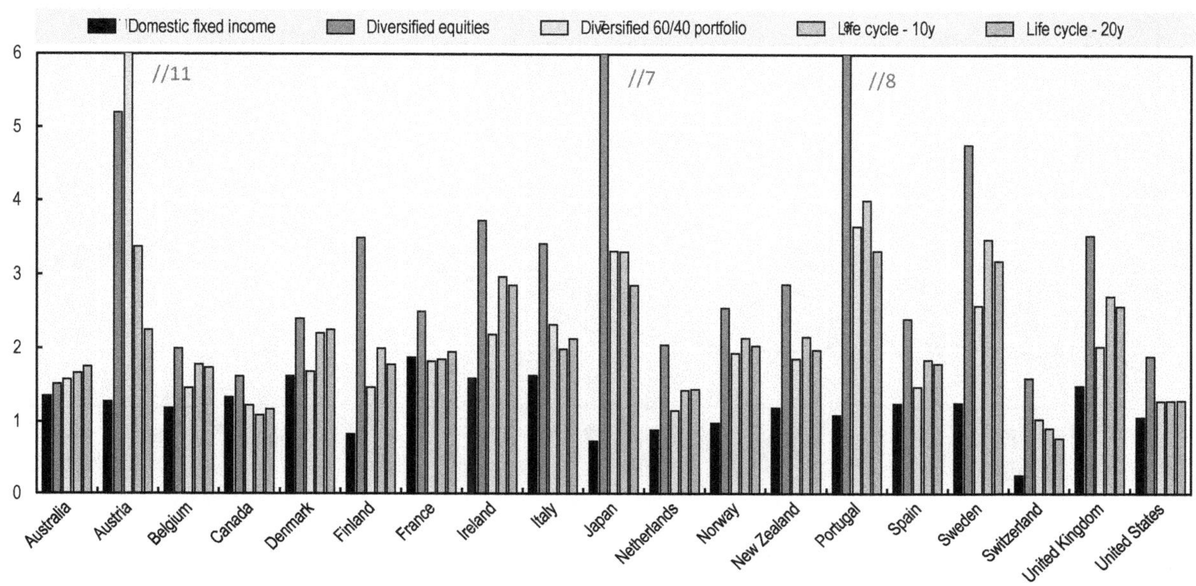

Life-cycle investment strategies can partially address the issue of volatility across cohorts when equity market downturns happen at the end of the accumulation phase. On average across cohorts, the level of assets accumulated at retirement with the life-cycle investment strategies would have been lower in all countries than with the portfolio with diversified equities (Figure 4.8). This is because reducing the equity exposure prior to retirement lowers the overall rate of return. However, accumulated assets would have fallen less from one cohort to the next with the life-cycle investment strategies had equity markets dropped towards the end of the accumulation phase. For example, Figure 4.13 shows that in Belgium, accumulated assets with the portfolio with diversified equities would have fallen from 12.3 times the sum of contributions for the cohort retiring in 1999 to 5.6 times for the cohort retiring just 3 years later in 2002. With the life-cycle investment strategy reducing the equity exposure 10 years before retirement, the accumulated assets would have been stable at around 7 times the sum of contributions across cohorts retiring between 1999 and 2002.

Figure 4.13. Assets accumulated at retirement by different cohorts in Belgium, by investment strategy

As a multiple of total contributions paid

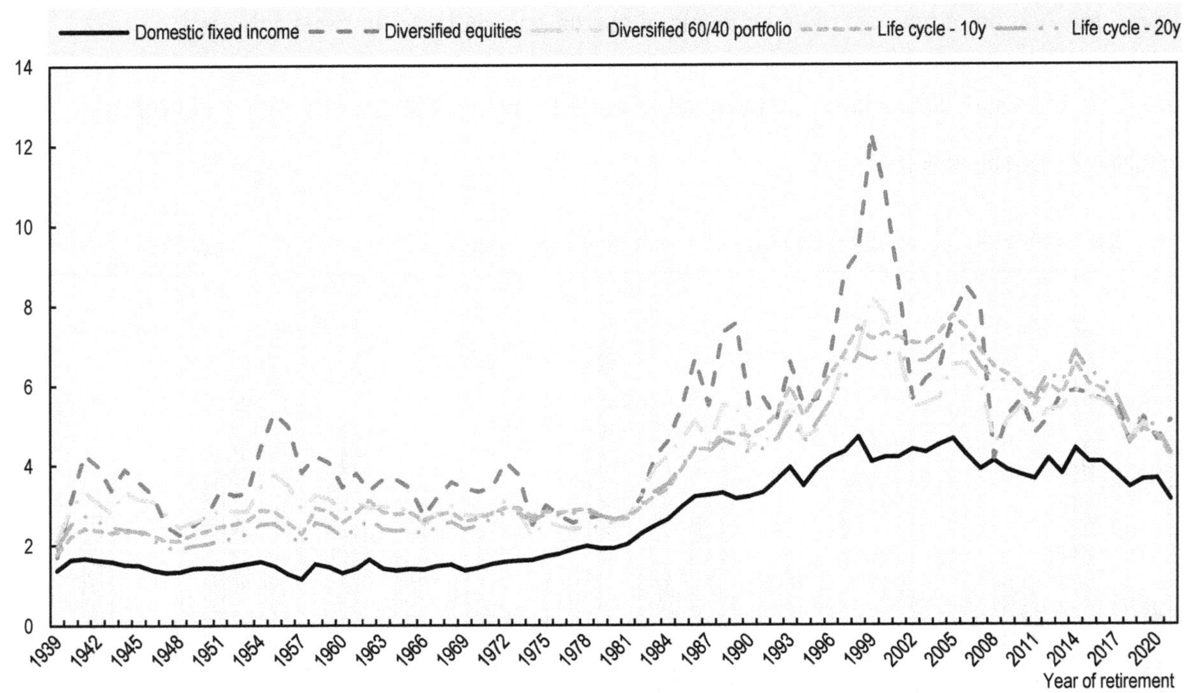

Investing in equity markets produces better results when people save for retirement for long periods as the compounded return accumulates over time. Many individuals may not be able to save for retirement during a full career. When participation in a pension plan is voluntary some individuals may delay saving into their 40s or 50s. Changing the length of the contribution period has different implications for the different investment strategies. In all the countries, average levels of accumulated assets across cohorts increase with the length of the contribution period for all investment strategies, but in greater proportions for portfolios with equity exposure. For example, Figure 4.14 shows that in the case of the United Kingdom, after only 20 years of contributions (starting to save from age 45 instead of 25), the different investment strategies would have produced relatively comparable outcomes, with average accumulated assets across cohorts ranging from 1.4 time the sum of contributions with the portfolio with domestic fixed income to 2.3 times with the portfolio with diversified equities. Differences are much larger after 40 years of contributions, with average levels of accumulated assets across cohorts ranging from 2.9 times the sum of contributions with the portfolio with domestic fixed income to 7.6 times with the portfolio with diversified equities. As the length of the contribution period increases, the effect of compounded return becomes stronger, in particular for portfolios with higher average returns.

Figure 4.14. Average level of assets accumulated at retirement across cohorts in the United Kingdom, by length of the contribution period and investment strategy

As a multiple of total contributions paid

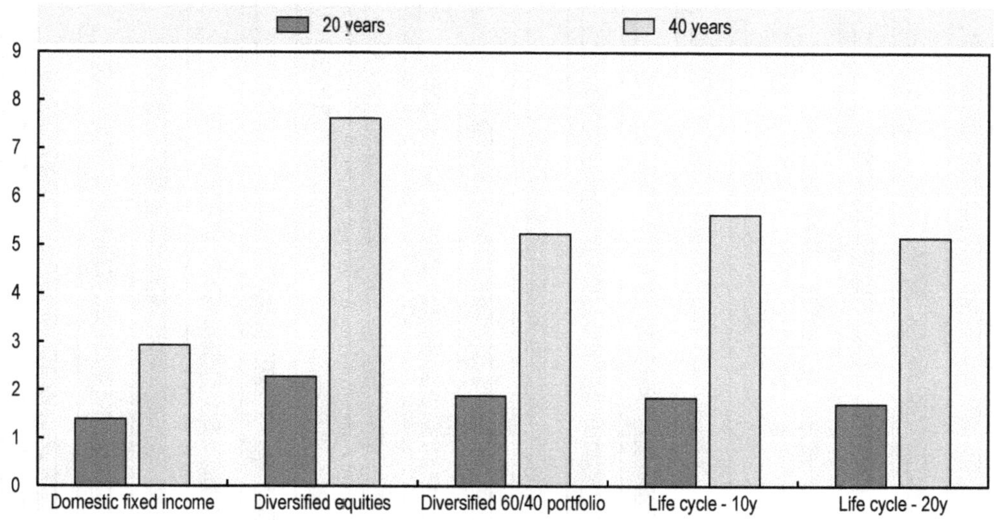

Shorter contribution periods reduce the proportion of cohorts that would have been better off investing in equity markets. However, most cohorts would have remained better off even with 20 years of contributions. Figure 4.15 compares the proportion of cohorts that would have accumulated more assets at retirement with the portfolio with diversified equities than with the portfolio with domestic fixed income after 20 or 40 years of contributions. For all the countries, the proportion of cohorts better off investing in equities increases with the length of the contribution period. With 20 years of contributions, the proportion of cohorts better off with diversified equities is still higher than 69% across countries, showing that investing in equities would still have been worthwhile for most people. Results are similar when comparing the diversified 60/40 portfolio and the life-cycle strategies with the portfolio with domestic fixed income.

Figure 4.15. Proportion of cohorts better off investing in diversified equities rather than in domestic fixed income only, by length of the contribution period and country

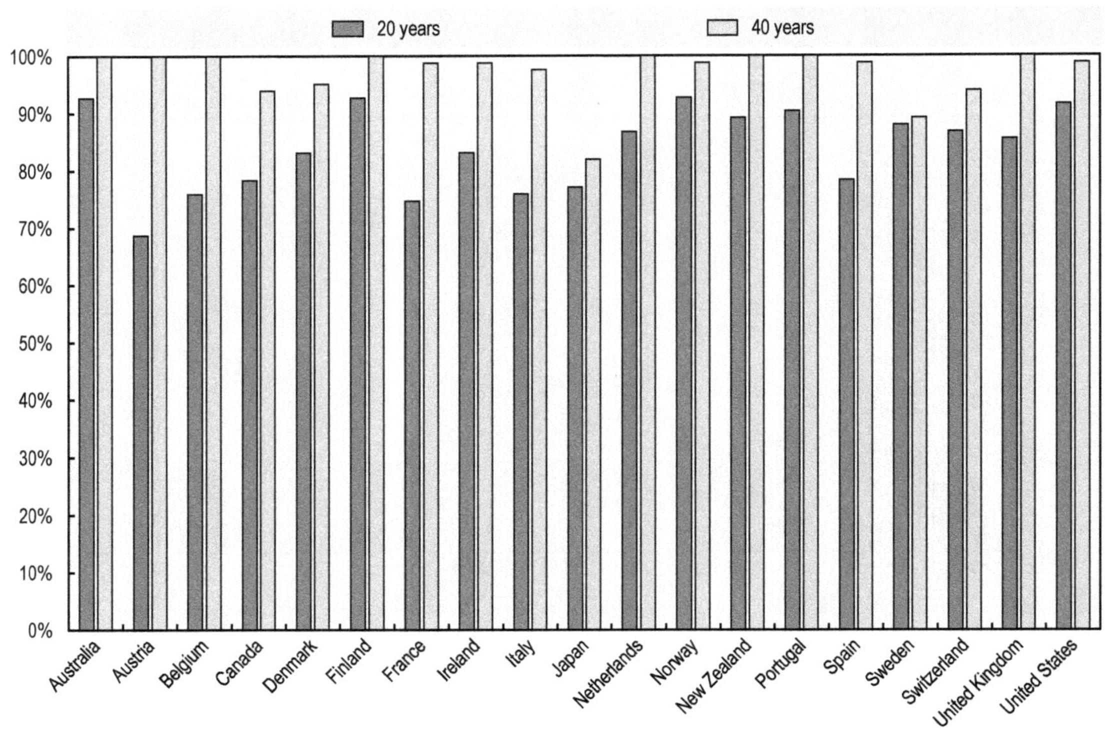

4.4. Equity exposure and replacement rates: stochastic modelling

The analysis now brings a forward-looking perspective and considers risks related to capital markets, labour markets and life expectancy to complement the historical analyses. It uses a stochastic model to simulate different realisations of the world and for each of them generate the replacement rates from a generic DC pension plan under different investment strategies and payout options. This allows to compare the distribution of replacement rates across investment strategies.[12] Additionally, the analysis compares replacement rates and total pension payments (including bequests) when individuals take a lifelong annuity or take regular drawdowns in order to assess the impact of continuing investing in capital markets during the payout phase. Annex 4.B describes the stochastic model.

The analysis shows that, when assuming that individuals take a lifelong annuity, there is a probability of around 90% that investing in equities during the accumulation phase would result in a higher replacement rate than investing only in fixed income. However, high equity exposure up to the end of the accumulation phase makes the assets accumulated sensitive to equity market downturns close to retirement. When assuming that individuals take regular drawdowns, investing in equities also leads to higher replacement rates. However, higher equity exposure leads to more volatile replacement rates during retirement. When comparing the two payout options, the analysis shows that combining regular drawdowns with equity investment is likely to lead to higher total pension payments (i.e. adding up benefits while alive and bequests) than taking a lifelong annuity.

4.4.1. Replacement rates with a lifelong annuity

This sub-section compares the replacement rates that individuals taking a lifelong annuity would obtain at retirement under different investment strategies. The lifelong annuity pays fixed nominal benefits during the entire remaining lifespan of the individual in retirement. Under this payout option, individuals only invest their retirement savings during the accumulation phase.

Investment strategies with some equity exposure outperform the fixed-income portfolio when looking at the distributions of replacement rates. Figure 4.16 presents the five illustrative investment strategies in a risk-return diagram, using the median replacement rate as the return measure and the replacement rate at the fifth percentile as the risk measure.[13] The higher the median replacement rate, the better. By contrast, the lower the replacement rate at the fifth percentile, the higher the risk because it indicates that individuals would receive a lower replacement rate in case of extreme unfavourable scenarios.[14] The median replacement rate varies from 17% for the fixed-income portfolio to 39% for the equity portfolio when individuals take a lifelong annuity at retirement. Moreover, the fixed-income portfolio also produces the lowest replacement rate at the fifth percentile, meaning that in extreme negative circumstances that may only have a 5% probability of happening, the investment strategies with some equity exposure would still produce a higher replacement rate (12%-13%) than the fixed-income portfolio (9%). The fixed-income portfolio is therefore outperformed by the other strategies as it is likely to provide a lower return (lower median replacement rate) with a higher risk (lower replacement rate at the fifth percentile).

Figure 4.16. Replacement rates at the median and fifth percentile, by investment strategy, lifelong annuity

As a percentage of the last wage

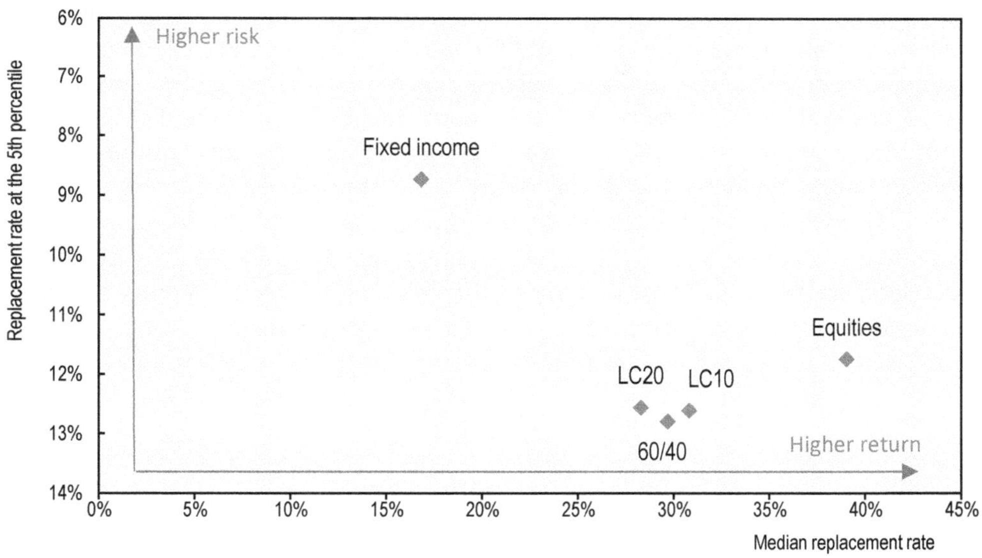

Note: LC10 = Life cycle 10 years; LC20 = Life cycle 20 years.

In most cases, individuals annuitising at retirement would be better-off investing only in equities during the whole accumulation period. Table 4.2 compares the probabilities to obtain a higher replacement rate with each investment strategy compared to the others. For example, the second column shows that the equity portfolio would produce a higher replacement rate with a probability of 87% when compared to the fixed-income portfolio, 81% when compared to the 60/40 portfolio, 76% when compared to the life-cycle strategy reducing the equity exposure 10 years before retirement, and 78% when compared to the life-cycle strategy reducing the equity exposure 20 years before retirement. By contrast, the first column shows that the fixed-income portfolio would produce a higher replacement rate than the other strategies with a probability of no more than 13%.

Table 4.2. Pairwise comparisons of the probability to obtain a higher replacement rate with different investment strategies, lifelong annuity

	Fixed income	Equity	60/40 portfolio	Life cycle 10 years	Life cycle 20 years
Fixed income		87%	90%	90%	91%
Equity	13%		19%	24%	22%
60/40 portfolio	10%	81%		61%	41%
Life cycle 10 years	10%	76%	39%		24%
Life cycle 20 years	9%	78%	59%	76%	

The life-cycle strategy that reduces the equity allocation 10 years before retirement instead of 20 years is more likely to produce higher replacement rates for individuals taking a lifelong annuity. The median replacement rate is slightly higher when the reduction in the equity exposure happens later in the accumulation phase (31% versus 28%, Figure 4.16). Moreover, there is a 76% probability of obtaining a higher replacement rate with the life-cycle strategy reducing the equity allocation 10 years before retirement rather than 20 years. Reducing the equity exposure earlier rather than later reduces the expected return because fixed-income securities become prominent in the portfolio earlier in the accumulation phase and produce lower returns on average.

Investment strategies with some equity exposure are expected to improve replacement rates by a larger margin than the fixed-income portfolio for individuals annuitising at retirement. Figure 4.17 shows the median difference in replacement rates when the fixed-income portfolio produces a higher replacement rate than the alternative strategies (blue bars), and the median difference in replacement rates when the alternative strategies produce a higher replacement rate than the fixed-income portfolio (grey bars). Among the simulations where the fixed-income portfolio produces a higher replacement rate (between 9% and 13% of the cases according to Table 4.2), the fixed-income portfolio only improves replacement rates by up to 5 percentage points, showing that the extent of the loss when having some equity exposure is relatively modest. By contrast, when focusing on the simulations where the investment strategies with some equity exposure produce a higher replacement rate than the fixed-income strategies (between 87% and 91% of the cases according to Table 4.2), having some equity exposure improves replacement rates by 12 to 26 percentage points when compared to the fixed-income portfolio.

Figure 4.17. Median difference in replacement rates when the fixed-income portfolio produces a higher replacement rate than the alternative strategies, and vice-versa, lifelong annuity

In percentage points

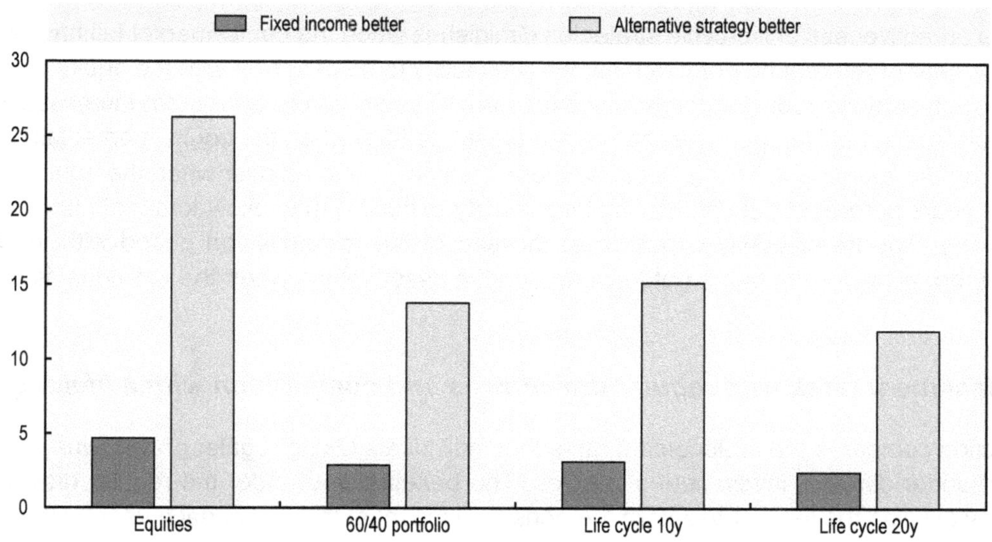

Falls in equity markets towards the end of the accumulation phase affect the replacement rates of the equity portfolio the most. Table 4.3 presents the median replacement rate produced by each investment strategy when considering all simulations, and when only considering the simulations where equity markets fall by at least 10% in the year just before retirement and in the fifth year before retirement. The median replacement rate from a lifelong annuity produced by the equity portfolio falls from 39% to around 30% when equity markets fall towards the end of the accumulation phase. Given that life-cycle strategies have a reduced allocation to equities in the final years of the accumulation phase, the effect of a market fall before retirement is more modest. For example, the replacement rate produced by the life-cycle strategy reducing the equity exposure 20 years before retirement remains at 28% when the equity market fall happens the year before retirement and declines to 26% when the equity market fall happens in the fifth year before retirement. The fixed-income portfolio is not sensitive to equity market movements.

Table 4.3. Impact of equity market falls towards the end of the accumulation phase on replacement rates, lifelong annuity

	All simulations		Equity returns ≤ - 10% the year before retirement		Equity returns ≤ - 10% the fifth year before retirement	
	Median RR	P(Eq better)	Median RR	P(Eq better)	Median RR	P(Eq better)
Fixed income	17%	87%	17%	78%	17%	77%
Equities	39%		31%		29%	
60/40 portfolio	30%	81%	26%	69%	25%	69%
Life cycle 10 years	31%	76%	30%	52%	27%	58%
Life cycle 20 years	28%	78%	28%	59%	26%	61%

Note: P(Eq better) = Probability that the equities portfolio produces a higher replacement rate.

Life-cycle investment strategies are nearly on a par with the equity portfolio when there is a fall in equity markets just before retirement. Table 4.3 shows that the median replacement rate produced by the life-cycle strategy reducing the equity exposure 10 years before retirement (30%) is only one percentage point below the one produced by the equity portfolio (31%) when equity markets fall in the year just before retirement. Moreover, the probability to be better-off with the equity portfolio than with the life-cycle strategy falls from 76% when considering all the simulations to 52% when equity markets fall in the year just before retirement. When comparing with the life-cycle strategy reducing the equity exposure 20 years before retirement, the probability to be better-off with the equity portfolio declines from 78% to 59%.

However, the attractiveness of life-cycle strategies diminishes when the equity market fall happens further away from the year of retirement. For example, the probability to be better-off with the equity portfolio than with the life-cycle strategy reducing the equity exposure 10 years before retirement increases from 52% when the equity market fall happens just before retirement, to 58% when the equity market fall happens in the fifth year before retirement. This is because there is some time to recover when the equity market fall happens five years before retirement. Having large equity exposure may allow to benefit from a potential market recovery. The lower equity exposure at the end of the accumulation period with the life-cycle strategy does not allow for the same potential rebound in asset values when the individual is annuitising at retirement.

4.4.2. Replacement rates with regular drawdowns and comparison with a lifelong annuity

This sub-section compares the replacement rates that individuals taking regular drawdowns would obtain at retirement under different investment strategies. The benefits paid under the regular drawdowns are determined by dividing the level of assets in the pension account at the end of each year by the remaining life expectancy. This payout option illustrates what happens when individuals keep investing their retirement savings during retirement. This sub-section also compares replacement rates between the two payout options, a lifelong annuity and regular drawdowns.

High equity exposure during the payout phase leads to better outcomes when taking regular drawdowns. Figure 4.18 presents the five investment strategies in the risk-return diagram and shows that the fixed-income portfolio and the life-cycle strategies are outperformed by the other two strategies. Having no equity exposure or keeping equity exposure at 20% during the payout phase as in the life-cycle strategies leads to lower median replacement rates and lower replacement rates at the fifth percentile. Given an average life expectancy of 20 years at 65, individuals still investing their assets during retirement would be better-off with higher equity exposures to get higher returns and higher benefits. The probability of obtaining a higher replacement rate with the investment strategies having some equity exposure than with the fixed-income portfolio ranges from 91% (when compared to the equity portfolio) to 94% (when compared to the balanced portfolio).

Figure 4.18. Replacement rates at the median and fifth percentile, by investment strategy, regular drawdowns

As a percentage of the last wage

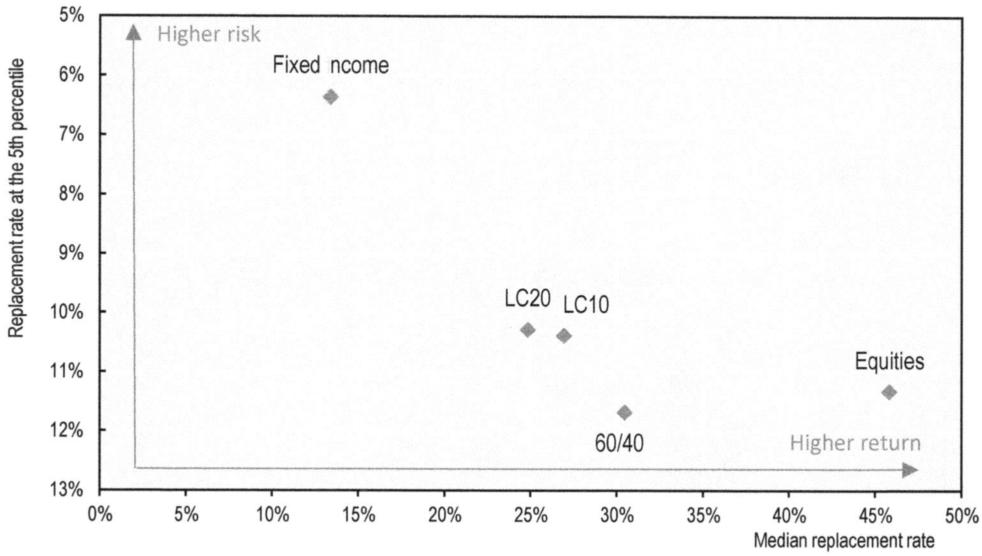

Note: LC10 = Life cycle 10 years; LC20 = Life cycle 20 years.

However, higher equity exposure in retirement also implies a higher volatility of benefits received. Calculating the standard deviation of yearly replacement rates during retirement and taking the median across all simulations results in a volatility of replacement rates ranging from 10% with the fixed-income portfolio to 116% with the equity portfolio (Table 4.4). This means that benefit payments would vary significantly from one year to the next with the equity portfolio. This makes it more difficult for individuals to plan their expenditures as they would be uncertain about how much they would receive each year.

Table 4.4. Volatility of yearly replacement rates, regular drawdowns (%)

	Median standard deviation of yearly replacement rates
Fixed income	10%
Equities	116%
60/40 portfolio	33%
Life cycle 10 years	27%
Life cycle 20 years	23%

Taking regular drawdowns while keeping a high equity exposure during the payout phase tends to lead to higher replacement rates than taking a lifelong annuity. Figure 4.19 compares the median replacement rate and the replacement rate at the fifth percentile when the individual takes a lifelong annuity and when the individual takes regular drawdowns. When the regular drawdowns are associated with the equity portfolio, replacement rates are higher than with a lifelong annuity. When the regular drawdowns are associated with an investment strategy with a low equity exposure (0% or 20%), it is the other way around. Replacement rates are similar between the lifelong annuity and the regular drawdowns when savings are invested according to the 60/40 portfolio. Additionally, the probability for individuals to be better-off with the lifelong annuity than with the regular drawdowns (higher average replacement rate) is 87% with the fixed-income portfolio and 75% with the two life-cycle strategies. This probability falls to 48% with the 60/40 portfolio and 40% with the equity portfolio. The regular drawdowns can only produce higher benefits than the lifelong annuity when the average return of the portfolio between the time of retirement and the time when the individual passes away is higher than the discount rate at the time of retirement used to determine annuity payments. Portfolios with low equity exposures during the payout phase may fail to achieve a sufficient investment return.

Figure 4.19. Comparison of replacement rates between the lifelong annuity and the regular drawdowns

As a percentage of the last wage

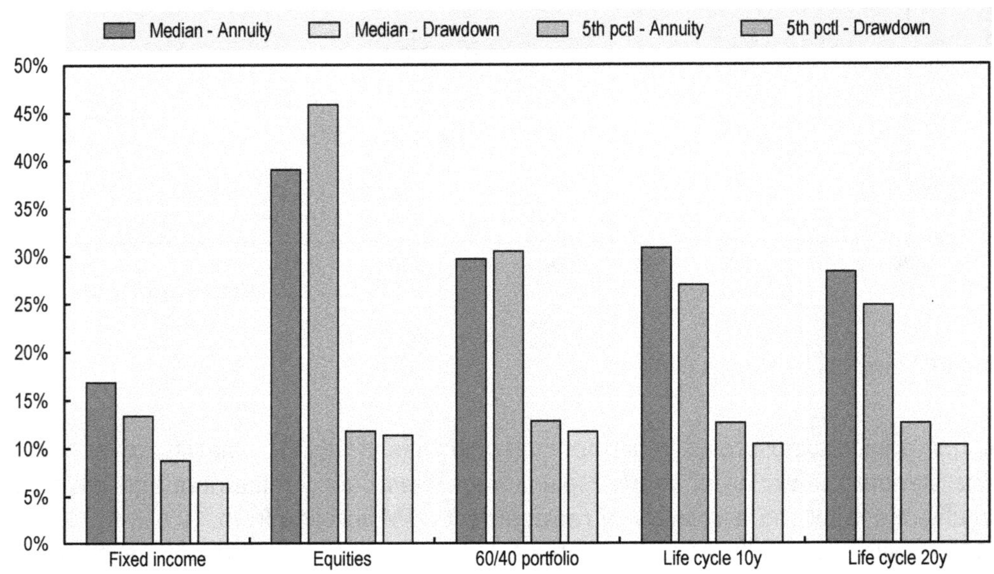

Note: Median = Median replacement rate; 5th pctl = Replacement rate at the fifth percentile.

Table 4.5. Median bequest amount with regular drawdowns

As a multiple of total contributions paid

	Median bequest
Fixed income	0.60
Equities	2.58
60/40 portfolio	1.71
Life cycle 10 years	1.31
Life cycle 20 years	1.22

Individuals taking regular drawdowns may have assets left at the time they pass away and leave a bequest, unlike with a traditional lifelong annuity.[15] The formula used to determine the benefits from the regular drawdowns avoids the risk for individuals of outliving their resources during retirement because the remaining assets are divided each year by a factor always greater than one (remaining life expectancy). However, it also implies that there will be assets left in the account when the individual passes away, and these assets can be passed on to heirs.[16] Table 4.5 shows that individuals taking regular drawdowns would leave a significant bequest. The median bequest amount increases with the equity exposure in the portfolio during retirement.

When combining the sum of pension benefits received by individuals while alive and the bequests, total pension payments tend to be higher when taking regular drawdowns than when taking a lifelong annuity. Figure 4.20 compares total pension payments at the median and the fifth percentile when the individual takes a lifelong annuity and when the individual takes regular drawdowns. Unlike with replacement rates, total pension payments are larger with the regular drawdowns and the difference with the lifelong annuity is larger for investment strategies with higher equity exposure. Overall, the probability for individuals of being better-off with the regular drawdowns rather than with the lifelong annuity, when combining pension benefits and bequests, is equal to 57% with the fixed-income portfolio, 70% with the life-cycle strategies, 84% with the 60/40 portfolio, and 85% with the equity portfolio.

Figure 4.20. Comparison of total pension payments between the lifelong annuity and the regular drawdowns

As a multiple of total contributions paid

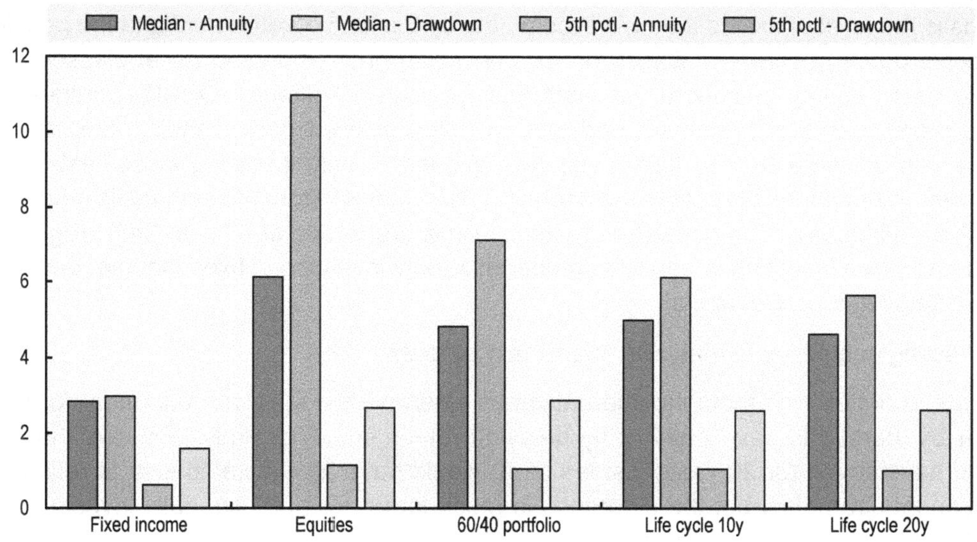

Note: Median = Median total pension payments; 5th pctl = Total pension payments at the fifth percentile.

4.5. Conclusion and policy implications

This chapter argues that investing in equity markets leads to better retirement income outcomes for members of DC pension plans. It assesses whether this is the case in a comprehensive manner by using complementary analyses. The analysis first looks at the current practice and trends of equity investment in DC schemes across a wide range of countries to help understand the relevance of the above policy question. The analysis then assesses whether investing in equities provides higher average investment performance by looking at actual case studies, higher levels of assets accumulated at retirement using historical returns, and higher replacement rates when incorporating capital, labour market and longevity risks using stochastic modelling.

4.5.1. Main findings

Equity investment represents a significant share of the portfolio of DC pension schemes and has been rising steadily over the past 20 years in many jurisdictions. At the end of 2022, the total equity exposure of DC schemes, including public and private equities, represented more than 40% of total investment in 13 out of 38 jurisdictions analysed. By contrast, total equity exposure represented less than 20% of total investment in 7 jurisdictions. Average equity exposures tend to be lower in jurisdictions capping equity investment.[17] Moreover, there has been a general upward trend in the equity exposure of DC pension schemes in many jurisdictions, with an increase of more than 20 percentage points between 2001 and 2022 in 5 OECD countries. Therefore, the policy question to address is whether investing in equities may lead to better retirement income outcomes.

Investing in equity markets would lead to better retirement income outcomes for members of DC pension plans. The analysis shows that higher equity investment usually brings higher average performance when comparing DC pension funds that have different levels of equity exposure within countries or within pension entities. Still, diversification in terms of asset classes and geographical coverage plays a role in investment performance for a given equity exposure. Beyond investment returns, what matters to members of DC pension plans is the level of assets they will accumulate by the time of retirement and the pension benefits they will receive during retirement. Based on historical returns on selected asset classes, the analysis shows that a vast majority of cohorts (at least 80%) across 19 different OECD countries would have accumulated more assets at retirement had they invested at least part of their retirement savings for 40 years in a mix of domestic and foreign equities instead of only investing in domestic fixed income securities (government bonds plus cash and deposits). The analysis from the stochastic model considering uncertain risk variables provides consistent results, with a probability of 87% to 94% of getting a higher replacement rate when investing in equities compared to only investing in fixed income, depending on the investment strategy and payout option.

However, investing in equities comes with three main caveats:

- It leads to better retirement income outcomes when people save for retirement for long periods, either by starting to save early or by delaying retirement. The analysis shows that cohorts that would have saved for 20 years instead of 40 would have accumulated less at retirement with all investment strategies, but the difference is much larger for portfolios fully invested in diversified equities than for other investment strategies. As the length of the contribution period increases, the effect of compounded return becomes more powerful, in particular for portfolios achieving higher average returns. Still, even with only 20 years of contributions, at least 69% of cohorts across countries would have been better-off if they had invested in equities rather than in domestic fixed income.
- It leads to volatile outcomes for individuals and societies. The analysis from the case studies shows that DC pension schemes with higher equity exposures have usually achieved more volatile annual investment returns over the past 7 to 21 years. Additionally, the volatility of replacement rates increases with equity investment, and, during the payout phase, yearly benefits are also more volatile when retirement savings remain invested in equities rather than in fixed income. Individuals, therefore, face more uncertainty regarding their level of pension benefits when investing in equities, making financial planning in retirement more difficult. Uncertainty and volatility also apply at the level of societies, as successive cohorts of individuals are more likely to accumulate different levels of assets at retirement when savings are invested in equities instead of domestic fixed income. Volatile equity returns imply that two individuals born just one year apart could end up with large differences in accumulated assets at retirement despite having the exact same earnings history, contribution rate and investment strategy. Even though such differences could be seen as unfair and hard to understand, they should be nuanced by the fact that both individuals would in general be better-off with a portfolio invested in equities than with any other investment strategy.

- It makes pension benefits sensitive to equity market downturns occuring when people are close to retirement. For example, the analysis from the stochastic model shows that the median replacement rate of the equity portfolio declines from 39% for all simulations to 31% for simulations with a fall in equity markets of at least 10% in the year just before retirement, when assuming that individuals buy a life annuity at retirement. Life-cycle investment strategies can mitigate that risk. By keeping a high exposure to equities during the first part of the accumulation phase and reducing it gradually as the retirement date approaches, life-cycle strategies use the compounded return effect to grow savings and reduce the risk of large losses when accumulated assets are at their peak. The analysis from the stochastic model shows that, while the equity portfolio outperforms life-cycle strategies in terms of replacement rates in more than 75% of the cases, the life-cycle strategies produce higher replacement rates than the equity portfolio with a probability between 40% and 50% when there is a fall in equity markets the year just before retirement. The attractiveness of the life-cycle strategies compared to the equity portfolio diminishes when the equity market fall happens further away from the year of retirement, as there is more time for a market rebound before retirement.

Conservative investment strategies provide only moderate protection to members of DC pension plans. A common approach to address the caveats associated with equity investment is to offer investment strategies that provide more certainty to individuals. The analysis shows that retirement income outcomes are less volatile with a fixed-income portfolio than with investment strategies with some equity exposure. However, most people are likely to be worse-off with portfolios only invested in fixed income and to forego significant pension benefits. Additionally, even when a fixed-income portfolio may be the best option, the difference with other investment strategies may only be moderate, as portfolios with equity exposure may only produce slightly lower accumulated assets and replacement rates in case of negative events.

Finally, there are important trade-offs to consider when investing in equities during the payout phase. The level of equity investments in the payout phase affects the comparison between regular drawdowns and lifelong annuities. The analysis from the stochastic model shows that, when equity exposure does not exceed 20% during the payout phase, people would be better-off taking a lifelong annuity than taking regular drawdowns in at least 75% of the cases. By contrast, there is a 60% probability of getting higher replacement rates when staying invested fully in equities during the payout phase and taking regular drawdowns instead of buying a lifelong annuity at retirement. Therefore, if individuals value flexibility and take regular drawdowns, large investments in equities would increase expected benefits. However, this comes at the cost of higher volatility of benefits and the risk of outliving one's resources, which are risks that lifelong annuities address. Moreover, if individuals take regular drawdowns and withdraw too little during the payout phase or pass away early, they may leave a bequest to their heirs. When considering the sum of all pension payments (benefits while alive plus bequests), the probability of receiving more with regular drawdowns and equity investment than with a lifelong annuity increases to 85%.

4.5.2. Policy implications

Pension regulators should avoid setting frameworks that lead to default investment strategies that are too conservative as equity investment tends to bring better retirement income outcomes. People investing their retirement savings in the default option tend to stay in the default even though it may not match their level of risk tolerance (OECD, 2018[9]). While high exposures to government bonds and low equity investment in the default option may not penalise plan members in the short term in countries where government bonds provide high returns, lack of investment diversification may increase the concentration risk and economic development may reduce future expected returns from government bonds, thereby affecting accumulated assets and pension benefits in the long run.

Countries where DC schemes invest mostly in fixed income should assess the appropriateness of their investment regulations. Investment limits for equity investment may be binding for DC schemes in some countries. Countries should ensure that their investment regulations are not constraining equity investment in a way that could reduce risk-adjusted returns. Similarly, attention should be given to investment limits affecting foreign investment and alternative investments, such as infrastructure and real estate, as they play a role in diversification.

Pension regulators should allow providers to offer life-cycle investment strategies to alleviate the risk of large falls in the level of assets accumulated when people lack the time to benefit from a market recovery. The regulatory framework should allow for innovation in designing the glide path to adapt to the needs of individuals. For example, the reduction in equity exposure may start in the last 10 years before retirement when people are planning to take an annuity, but if they take regular drawdowns and remain invested during the payout phase, the reduction in equity exposure may be smoother and continue into the payout phase as the investment horizon is longer.

Finally, the ideal level and profile of equity exposure is country-specific, and relevant stakeholders in each country should consider following a precise methodology to determine what would be the most appropriate equity exposure for default investment strategies. Default options are important for people unwilling or unable to select their own investment strategy. In some countries, policy makers may want to define a single default investment strategy for the whole population, while in others, policy makers may allow pension providers to define their own default option within a harmonised framework. Selecting an appropriate default investment strategy requires pension providers and policy makers to solve a trade-off between maximising the level of retirement income for plan members and minimising the risk that some plan members may get a retirement income that is deemed too low (OECD, 2020[1]). To solve this trade-off and select a default investment strategy, countries could follow the OECD framework described in (OECD, 2020[1]), which involves five steps: i) pre-selecting the investment strategies to be assessed; ii) assessing these strategies using a stochastic model to reflect the uncertainty of possible outcomes; iii) calculating indicators reflecting their potential riskiness and performance; iv) defining thresholds for risk indicators that reflect the importance given to the downside risk relative to the upside potential; and v) selecting the investment strategy meeting the thresholds for the risk indicators and maximising the performance indicators. While using this framework, pension providers and policy makers should consider the role of DC schemes in the overall pension system, the population's level of risk aversion and the characteristics of the target population for the default option, especially the length of the contribution period, the contribution level, and the payout options they tend to select.

References

Anarkulova, A., S. Cederburg and M. O'Doherty (2023), "Beyond the Status Quo: A Critical Assessment of Lifecycle Investment Advice", *SSRN Electronic Journal*, https://doi.org/10.2139/ssrn.4590406. [3]

Antolin, P. and S. Payet (2011), "Assessing the labour, financial and demographic risks to retirement income from defined-contribution pensions", *OECD Journal: Financial Market Trends*, Vol. 2010/2. [10]

Berardi, A. and C. Tebaldi (2023), "Saving for retirement in Europe: the long-term risk-return tradeoff", *Journal of Pension Economics and Finance*, Vol. 23/2, pp. 272-293, https://doi.org/10.1017/s1474747223000136. [5]

Dunn, R. and M. Berg (2019), "Lifecycle Design – To and Through Retirement", *27th Colloquium on Pensions and Retirement*, https://www.ricewarner.com/wp-content/uploads/2019/12/Rpt-Lifecycle-Design-To-and-Through-Retirement-CEPAR-December-2019-002.pdf. [6]

HMD (2023), *Human Mortality Database. Max Planck Institute for Demographic Research (Germany), University of California, Berkeley (USA), and French Institute for Demographic Studies (France)*, http://www.mortality.org (accessed on 17 October 2023). [11]

Khemka, G., M. Steffensen and G. Warren (2021), "How sub-optimal are age-based life-cycle investment products?", *International Review of Financial Analysis*, Vol. 73, p. 101619, https://doi.org/10.1016/j.irfa.2020.101619. [4]

OECD (2024), *2024 Annual Survey of Investment Regulation of Pension Providers*, https://www.oecd.org/content/dam/oecd/en/topics/policy-sub-issues/asset-backed-pensions/2024-Survey-of-Investment-Regulation-of-Pension-Providers.pdf. [8]

OECD (2020), "Selecting default investment strategies", in *OECD Pensions Outlook 2020*, OECD Publishing, Paris, https://doi.org/10.1787/1c7381db-en. [1]

OECD (2020), "Switching investments in defined contribution retirement savings arrangements", in *OECD Pensions Outlook 2020*, OECD Publishing, Paris, https://doi.org/10.1787/ed47ae07-en. [12]

OECD (2018), "Improving retirement incomes considering behavioural biases and limited financial knowledge", in *OECD Pensions Outlook 2018*, OECD Publishing, Paris, https://doi.org/10.1787/pens_outlook-2018-8-en. [9]

Šebo, J., D. Danková and I. Králik (2020), "In Search of the Optimal Saving Strategy for Pan-European Pension Products", *Financial Assets and Investing*, Vol. 11/2, pp. 54-72, https://doi.org/10.5817/fai2020-2-4. [7]

Siegel, J. (2023), *Stocks for the Long Run: The Definitive Guide to Financial Market Returns & Long-Term Investment Strategies, Sixth Edition*, McGraw Hill. [2]

Annex 4.A. Brief description of the pension funds in the case studies

This annex provides a brief description of the pension funds studied in Section 4.2.

Chile

Every pension fund administrator in Chile offers five different types of funds, from Fund A that can invest 40% to 80% in equities, to Fund E that can invest no more than 5% in equities. Each pension fund administrator must allocate a growing part of investment to variable income securities from Fund E to Fund A. Men older than 55 and women older than 50 can select any Fund except Fund A. Fund B (25% to 60% in equities) is the default option for men and women up to age 35, Fund C is the default option for men aged 36 to 55 and women aged 36 to 50, and Fund D is the default option for men aged 56 and older and women aged 51 and older.

Czechia

Pension management companies in Czechia can offer a range of participating funds with different investment strategies and risk profiles, including the mandatory conservative participating fund. They also manage transformed funds, where participants do not have investment choice but have an annual non-negative return guarantee. In 2013, participating funds were introduced and transformed funds were closed to new entrants. At the end of 2022, 63% of members of pension funds were still in transformed funds.

France

Asset managers provide some of the occupational pension plans available in France. These are the former PERCO plans, now called mandatory or collective company PER plans. Every asset manager offers a choice to plan members between four categories of funds: cash, bonds, equities and diversified. The diversified funds mix the other three categories of funds. These three funds are also the building blocks of life-cycle investment strategies.

AustralianSuper (Australia)

AustralianSuper is the largest superannuation fund in Australia. It is owned by the Australian Council of Trade Unions (ACTU) and the Australian Industry Group (Ai Group), an employer organisation. The entity offers six pre-defined diversified investment options with different risk profiles: Stable, Conservative Balanced, Balanced, Socially Aware, Indexed Diversified and High Growth. The Balanced option is the default.

QSuper (Australia)

QSuper is part of Australian Retirement Trust and is the superannuation fund for employees of the Queensland Government and their family. It offers a range of pre-defined diversified investment options

(Moderate, Balanced, Socially Responsible and Aggressive), as well as a default option following a life-cycle investment strategy (Lifetime). This life-cycle investment strategy is composed of eight funds (Outlook; Aspire 1 and 2; Focus 1, 2 and 3; Sustain 1 and 2). Members' assets are invested in one fund at a time based on their age and their account balance. Assets are transferred to more conservative funds as people reach age 40, 50 and 58 and when the account balance exceeds certain thresholds defined for each age bracket.

PFA (Denmark)

PFA is the largest commercial pension company in Denmark and among the largest in Europe. It is one of the providers of occupational pension plans negotiated by collective agreements. PFA offers four different life-cycle investment strategies with different risk profiles. The four profiles (A to D) vary in their allocation between the high-risk fund and the low-risk fund according to the number of years until retirement. Profile A is the one with the lowest allocation to the high-risk fund, while Profile D is the one with the highest allocation to the high-risk fund.

Alecta (Sweden)

Alecta is one of the providers of occupational pension plans in Sweden and among the largest in Europe. It is the default provider for salaried employees in the private sector. All those born from 1979 onwards are in a DC pension plan. The default option in the DC plan, called Alecta Optimal Pension, is a life-cycle investment strategy based on three funds. Up to age 63, members' assets are invested in a fund with a target asset allocation of 60% in equities, 30% in fixed income securities and 10% in alternative investments (e.g. real estate and infrastructure). Between 63 and 65, the assets are invested in a fund with a target asset allocation of 50% in equities, 40% in fixed income securities and 10% in alternative investments. From age 65 onwards, the assets are invested in a fund with a target asset allocation of 40% in equities, 50% in fixed income securities and 10% in alternative investments.

AP7 (Sweden)

AP7 is the public provider in the Swedish premium pension system. It provides the default investment option. This default option is a life-cycle investment strategy based on two funds, an equity fund and a fixed income fund. The equity fund is invested in global listed and unlisted securities, 99% outside Sweden. The fixed income fund is invested in Swedish fixed income securities. For members in the default option, 100% of the assets are allocated to the equity fund up to the age of 55. From the age of 56, the allocation is annually and linearly rebalanced towards the fixed income fund until reaching an allocation of two-thirds in the fixed income fund and one-third in the equity fund at the age of 75.

Nest (United Kingdom)

Nest is the public provider in the UK's automatic enrolment system. It is the provider of last resort for employers of all sizes. It offers several investment options as well as a range of one-year target date funds, called Retirement Funds, as a default option. The glide path of the Retirement Funds includes three phases during the accumulation phase. The first phase, called the Foundation phase, lasts 5 years and is for people with more than 40 years until retirement. It has moderate exposure to risky assets to promote confidence in savings and minimise the impact of investment shocks that might make younger members stop contributing. The second phase, called the Growth phase, lasts 30 years and aims at outperforming inflation by 3 percentage points a year after charges. The third phase, called the Consolidation phase, is for people within 10 years to retirement. It reduces gradually the allocation to risky assets.

Thrift Savings Plan (United States)

The Thrift Savings Plan (TSP) is a retirement savings and investment plan for US federal government employees and uniformed services members. It offers five individual funds with fixed asset allocations that plan members can mix according to their risk profile. The Government securities investment fund (G Fund) is fully invested in short-term US Treasury securities. The Fixed income index investment fund (F Fund) is invested in government securities, securitised assets and credit instruments. The Common stock index investment fund (C Fund) is fully invested in US equities. The Small cap stock index investment fund (S Fund) is fully invested in small cap US equities. The International stock index investment fund (I Fund) is fully invested in global equities. TSP also offers 10 target date funds, called L Funds, providing a pre-determined diversified mix of the 5 individual funds that evolves as the retirement date approaches.

Annex 4.B. Description of the stochastic model

General assumptions

The baseline assumptions for the stochastic model are similar to those used in Section 4.3 with the analysis based on historical returns. The model assumes an individual joining a DC pension plan at age 25 and contributing 5% of wages each year in employment until retirement at age 65. A 1% annual assets-based fee is charged during the accumulation phase, as well as during the payout phase when savings remain invested.[18] The amount of assets accumulated at retirement is transformed into a stream of income according to the selected payout option. The analysis calculates the replacement rate as the level of retirement income divided by the wage just before retirement. When the level of retirement income varies over time, the average replacement rate is calculated over the retirement period.

The analysis considers the same five illustrative investment strategies as in Section 4.3. The only difference is that the DC plan is assumed to invest only in international securities to avoid referring to a particular country. There are three portfolios with constant asset allocation invested only in fixed income, only in equities, and in a mix of equities (60%) and fixed income (40%). There are two life-cycle strategies reducing the equity exposure linearly from 80% to 20% either 10 years or 20 years before retirement. The relative share of government bonds (88%) and cash and deposits (12%) is assumed to remain constant in the fixed-income part of the different investment strategies.

The analysis considers two different payout options, a lifelong annuity and regular drawdowns. The lifelong annuity pays fixed nominal benefits during the entire remaining lifespan of the individual in retirement. The benefits are equal to the level of assets at retirement divided by the annuity factor. The annuity factor is calculated using survival rates between age 65 and 110, and the government bond yield at the time of retirement as the discount rate. The benefits paid under the regular drawdowns are determined by dividing the level of assets in the pension account at the end of each year by the remaining life expectancy. Given the formula, the individual is ensured to receive benefits during his/her entire remaining lifespan in retirement, although the level of benefits varies and is not guaranteed. In addition, there may be assets left in the pension account to leave as a bequest when the individual passes away. For the regular drawdowns, savings remain invested during the payout phase and the illustrative investment strategies keep the asset mix at the time of retirement constant during the payout phase.

The stochastic model derives uncertainty about financial, labour market and demographic risks by generating 10 000 Monte Carlo simulations. Each Monte Carlo simulation represents one possible realisation of the world for the asset returns, inflation rates, government bond yields, unemployment spells, real wage-growth profiles and remaining lifespan in retirement. This provides the distribution of replacement rates generated by the different investment strategies.

Financial risks

Financial risks, i.e. investment returns, inflation rates and yields on government bonds, affect different stages of the retirement savings journey. Indeed, contributions are taken from wages that grow in line with inflation. These contributions are invested in portfolios mixing three different asset classes that generate different rates of return. Finally, when taking an annuity at retirement, benefits are determined based on a discount rate, which is assumed to be the yield on government bonds at the time of retirement.

The model generates 10 000 simulations of investment returns, yields and inflation rates by drawing random numbers from different distributions. The model assumes that the returns on government bonds and on cash and deposits, the inflation rates and the yields on government bonds are drawn from a normal distribution with mean and standard deviation provided by historical values between 1900 and 2021.[19] The equity returns are drawn assuming a geometric Brownian motion for the underlying equity price, with drift and volatility provided by historical equity returns between 1900 and 2021. Each simulation covers the accumulation phase and the payout phase. Annex Table 4.B.1 presents the moments of the distributions. The model does not intend to reflect financial markets perfectly, but rather to provide a framework to compare the retirement outcomes produced by different investment strategies.

Annex Table 4.B.1. Moments of the distributions for the financial risks (annual basis)

Financial risk	Coverage	Mean	Standard deviation
Returns on equities	Global	9.76%	16.99%
Returns on government bond	Global	5.39%	9.38%
Returns on cash and deposits	United States	3.67%	2.86%
Yields on 10-year government bonds	United States	4.61%	2.48%
Inflation rates	United States	3.00%	4.65%

Note: Treasury bills are used as a proxy for cash and deposits.

The model also assumes correlations between two sets of variables. The correlation coefficients ensure that the value of the different risk variables in each simulation are likely to materialise together and form a plausible realisation of the world. The model assumes that yields on government bonds, returns on government bond, returns on cash and deposits, and inflation are correlated. Using the same historical data as in Annex Table 4.B.1, Annex Table 4.B.2 presents the Pearson correlation coefficients between the four variables. In addition, the model assumes that the risk of unemployment is correlated with the performance of equity markets. The risk of suffering unemployment indeed tends to be lower when the economy is booming, and to increase when the economy slows down or enters into recession, generally with a lag. Moreover, improvements in the economy or higher economic growth may push up returns on equity investment. Therefore, when the economy is doing well, returns on equity investments rise and the risk of suffering spells of unemployment falls, always with a lag, reinforcing the positive feedback cycle regarding the accumulation of income for retirement. The opposite occurs when the economy tanks. To take these patterns into account, the model adds a shock to unemployment rates linked to the performance of equity markets, with a lag. A correlation coefficient of -0.24 is assumed (Antolin and Payet, 2011[10]).

Annex Table 4.B.2. Pearson correlation coefficients

	Yields on 10-year government bonds	Inflation	Returns on government bond	Returns on cash and deposits
Yields on 10-year government bonds		0.26	0.39	0.84
Inflation	0.26		-0.15	0.28
Returns on government bond	0.39	-0.15		0.12
Returns on cash and deposits	0.84	0.28	0.12	

Labour market risks

In addition to financial risks, the model also considers the uncertainty surrounding labour market outcomes. Labour market outcomes, in particular employment and wages, determine contribution levels, and thus the level of assets accumulated at retirement. Contributions to DC pension plans may be discontinued during periods of unemployment and depend on individuals' wages.

In the stochastic model, contributions are calculated assuming a fixed contribution rate of 5% of wages. Wages for all simulations start at USD 22 000 at age 25. This corresponds to the OECD average annual wage in 2021 divided by two to approximate the wage level at the start of the career.[20] Wages then grow in line with stochastic inflation and real wage growth. No contributions are paid in years of unemployment. For each simulation, the model determines whether the individual would suffer any unemployment spell and if so, in which years. The model also builds three different real wage-growth profiles and allocates each simulation to one of the profiles.

Unemployment spells

The model proceeds in two steps to determine stochastically the years of unemployment in the simulations. The first step considers cohort-level unemployment, while the second one considers economy-wide unemployment.

In each cohort, only a certain proportion of individuals will suffer spells of unemployment during their career. On average, only around 40% of individuals in any given cohort suffer spells of unemployment (Antolin and Payet, 2011[10]). Therefore, the model generates only 40% of the simulations with at least one unemployment spell. For the other 60%, the individual will have a full career.

For the simulations where the individual suffers unemployment, the model determines in which years the spells will occur during the career. The economy-wide unemployment rate is the best proxy of the probability of suffering unemployment in any year. The model considers that the unemployment rate varies with age, with younger individuals experiencing higher rates of unemployment than other age groups. Moreover, the unemployment rate shows a large degree of persistence, in particular in European countries. This means that someone unemployed in a given year will have a higher probability of being unemployed the following year.

OECD data show that the unemployment rate in the OECD area declines with age up to approximately 40 years old and remains relatively constant around 5% thereafter (Annex Table 4.B.1). For each simulation where the individual suffers unemployment, the model calculates the unemployment rate by drawing a base rate from a normal distribution with mean 5.04% and standard deviation 0.73%. This corresponds to the observed mean and standard deviation over 2000-22 of the unemployment rates for the age group 40 to 64 in the OECD area. For those aged 25 to 40, the model adds another component that declines linearly to 0 and starts with a draw from a normal distribution with mean 3.71% and standard deviation 0.51%. This corresponds to the observed mean and standard deviation over 2000-22 of the differences in the unemployment rates between the age groups 25-29 and 40-64 in the OECD area. The model then determines whether there is an unemployment spell in each year by drawing from a binomial distribution with probability equal to the resulting yearly unemployment rates.[21]

Annex Figure 4.B.1. OECD area's average unemployment rates by age groups, 2000-2022

In per cent

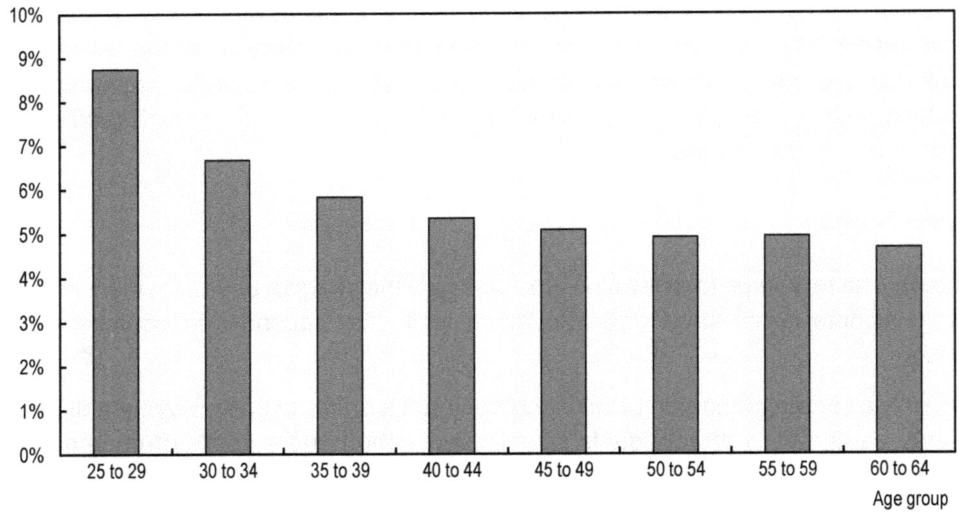

Source: OECD Labour Force Statistics by sex and age.

In addition, the model accounts for the persistence of unemployment. Once the model has determined the unemployment spells following the methodology above, additional spells may be added to reflect the fact that someone unemployed in a year has a higher risk of staying unemployed the next year. Someone unemployed in year N is assumed to have a 75% probability of being unemployed in year N+1 if the unemployment rate as determined before has increased between N and N+1. The probability drops to 50% if the unemployment rate as determined before has decreased between N and N+1 (Antolin and Payet, 2011[10]).

The results are consistent with expectations. Among all the simulations, 64% have no unemployment spells. For those with unemployment spells, the median number of spells is 4 and the average is 5.

Real wage-growth profiles

Labour market risk also originates from the uncertainty surrounding the trajectory of real wages during one's career. Real-wage gains during a career vary across individuals according to their socio-economic situation (e.g. occupation, educational level and income). Labour market studies document that there are three main career paths for real wages. In general, real wages experience the largest gains during the early part of a person's career, with lower gains, even sometimes negative gains, in the latter part. This pattern results in real-wage paths that for some people reach a plateau at the end of their career, while for others, real wages plateau earlier, around ages 45 to 55, and fall thereafter. A minority experience flat real wages throughout their working lives. Annex Table 4.B.2 presents the three profiles of real-wage growth used in the model. The model assumes that 42% of the individuals experience real wages that keep rising during the entire career (high income/education), 55% experience real wages that fall during the second half of the career (middle income/education), while 3% experience flat real wages (low income/education) (Antolin and Payet, 2011[10]).

Annex Figure 4.B.2. Real wage-growth indexes

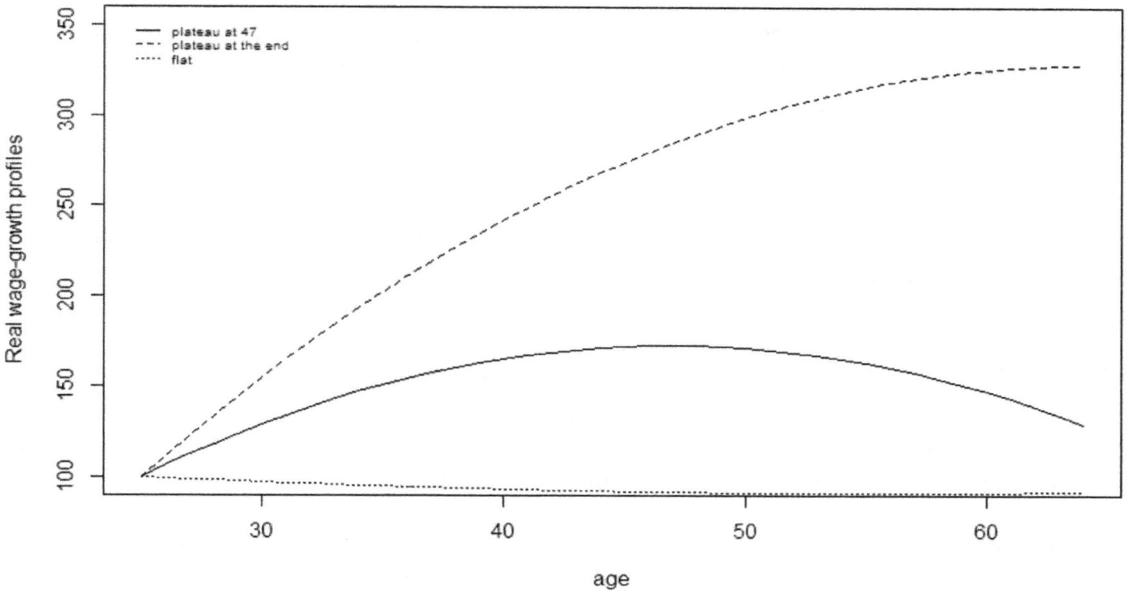

Nominal wages grow with inflation and account for the impact of unemployment. The model assumes that individuals suffering spells of unemployment re-enter the labour market at the nominal wage level they had when last working (i.e. they do not get inflation or real wage growth). However, if inflation or real wage growth declined in between, the last wage is adjusted downward.

Demographic risk

The demographic risk in this model stems from the uncertainty around the number of years the individual may live in retirement (idiosyncratic longevity risk). The model assumes that the individual lives with 100% certainty until age 66, so the retirement period lasts at least one year. At older ages, the possibility of passing away is derived by drawing a random number from a binomial distribution with probability equal to the mortality rate at each age. The mortality rate used for each age from 66 to 110 correspond to the average mortality rate in 2019 across 33 OECD countries (HMD, 2023[11]). The mortality rate is equal to 1 at age 110. The first occurrence of death is used to determine the remaining lifespan in retirement.

Notes

[1] In this chapter, the term "DC pension plan" covers both occupational DC plans and personal plans. In these plans, members can usually select their investment strategy and bear the investment risk.

[2] The 19 OECD countries covered by the analysis are Australia, Austria, Belgium, Canada, Denmark, Finland, France, Ireland, Italy, Japan, the Netherlands, Norway, New Zealand, Portugal, Spain, Sweden, Switzerland, the United Kingdom and the United States.

[3] The performance adjusted for risk or "risk-reward ratio" corresponds to the ratio between the median internal rate of return and the internal rate of return at the fifth percentile.

[4] Annex 4.A describes the case studies and Annex 4.B describes the stochastic model.

[5] Data for the United States come from the Federal Reserve and only cover DC private pension funds (i.e. pension funds for public-sector employees are not included). Data for Australia include a small proportion of defined benefit assets.

[6] In most jurisdictions, the limits vary for different types of pension arrangements.

[7] Frequent switching tends to result in worse net investment performance. Many jurisdictions impose implicit and explicit barriers to switching between investment strategies and pension providers (OECD, 2020[12]).

[8] An analysis of the correlation between equity exposure and average performance using aggregate cross-country data from the OECD Global Pension Statistics database between 2011 and 2022 for 28 jurisdictions does not find a statistically significant correlation coefficient due to country disparities and data limitations, including the relatively short period for analysis (2011-22).

[9] All the data except for France were collected from the websites of pension supervisors (Chile and Czechia) and pension entities. For France, the data source is Europerformance.

[10] In Czechia, although people have access to participating funds with high equity allocations (over 90% for some funds), most people are in conservative funds so the average exposure of members in participating funds was only 7.7% over 2014-22.

[11] In Austria, expressing returns for international securities (equities and government bonds) from USD into national currency leads to very large returns during the years of the First and Second World Wars due to extreme exchange rates. This affects the diversified 60/40 portfolio more than the other investment strategies as foreign investment makes up half of that portfolio.

[12] The analysis considers the same five illustrative investment strategies as in the previous section. The only difference is that the DC plan is assumed to invest only in international securities to avoid referring to a particular country.

[13] There is a 5% probability to get a replacement rate lower than the one at the fifth percentile.

[14] Figure 4.16 shows the y axis in reverse order so that investment strategies producing a lower replacement rate at the fifth percentile are higher in the graph (higher risk).

[15] Some annuity products continue to pay benefits to beneficiaries after the policy holder passes away (e.g. guaranteed period, survivor option). Such annuities pay lower benefits upfront to the policy holder compared to traditional annuities.

[16] Only individuals passing away at the age of 110, the maximum age assumed in the model, have no assets left when they pass away.

[17] See the Annual Survey of Investment Regulation of Pension Providers - OECD for equity investment limits in OECD and selected non-OECD jurisdictions.

[18] The analysis assumes no fees are charged during the payout phase when the individual takes a lifelong annuity. The annuity provider gets a remuneration by investing the assets in a wide range of securities while using yields on government bonds to price the annuity.

[19] Although past performance may not be indicative of future results, historical data is the only available information to project expected returns together with their variability.

[20] In the United States, the median yearly earnings of 25 to 34 years old full-time workers with high-school degree are approximately half the average wage of the population.

[21] The unemployment rate also accounts for a shock linked to equity returns, as explained before.

5 Designing the payout phase for defined contribution pensions to better meet financial needs in retirement

Jessica Mosher

This chapter provides policy makers with guidance on how to design the framework for the payout phase for defined contribution pension plans in a way that considers the heterogenous needs of individuals in retirement. A well-designed framework for the payout of retirement savings in defined contribution plans should consider the role of those savings plans within the broader pension system, as well as how individual and economic circumstances may influence the optimal solution for payout. It should also support individuals in accessing the most appropriate options for their situation at retirement.

Policy makers need to ensure that the framework for the payout of retirement savings for defined contribution plans considers whether the options available to individuals at retirement are suitable for their financial needs. The most appropriate solutions for payout will depend in part on the purpose for which retirement savings will be used, as the financial risks to mitigate will differ depending on this purpose. Mitigating financial risks in retirement is different than doing so during the accumulation of retirement savings, and there is no one-size-fits-all solution that applies to all contexts and individual profiles. The financial risks to mitigate in retirement largely depend on the role of the defined contribution plan within the pension system, as well as individual circumstances and economic context. Payout design needs to consider the heterogeneity of needs in retirement and allow for adequate flexibility to adapt to different situations.

The regulatory framework also needs to consider how to facilitate the matching of financial options at retirement with the individuals who would most benefit from those options. Even when suitable financial options for retirement may be available, individuals may not access them due to a lack of awareness, understanding, or guidance.

This chapter aims to provide policy makers with guidance on how to design the framework for the payout phase for defined contribution pension plans in a way that considers the heterogenous needs of people in retirement. The first section of this chapter presents a framework for assessing financial needs in retirement and describes some of the benchmarks used to do so. The second section looks at how financial solutions can meet these different needs in retirement. The third section discusses approaches to deliver appropriate financial solutions to individuals, along with the benefits and challenges of each. The final section provides policy guidance on designing the framework for the payout phase to account for heterogeneous financial needs in retirement.

5.1. A framework to assess financial needs in retirement

Financial needs in retirement are made up of essential spending, unexpected spending and discretionary spending. The first priority is to have income to cover basic needs and essential spending. Individuals ideally will also have a source of financing to provide security to cover moderate financial shocks and unexpected expenses. Those having remaining resources can use their savings on discretionary spending to enjoy a more comfortable lifestyle (Figure 5.1).

Figure 5.1. Components of financial needs in retirement

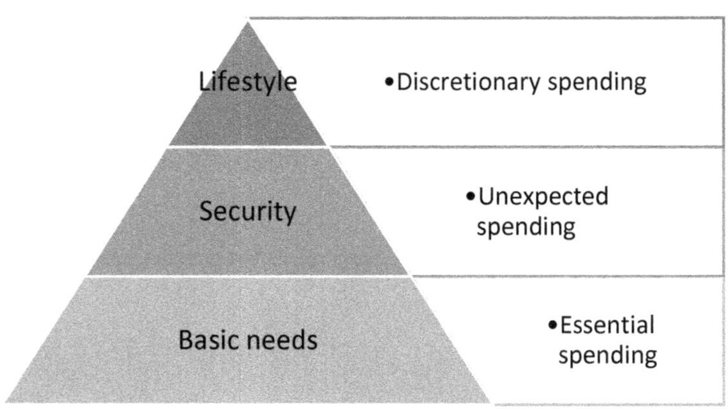

The design of the framework for the payout phase for defined contribution pensions should account for these different needs, as the financial solutions that help meet the different layers are not necessarily the same. Financing for basic needs should be regular and sure. Savings set aside for security will require a certain level of safety and liquidity. Lifestyle needs are likely to require more flexibility and may change over time.

Policy makers need to first assess how much money is required to meet these different needs in retirement in order to understand the expected role of defined contribution plans in financing retirement. Determining the amount of savings needed to finance retirement has to account for how the needs of retirees differ from the rest of the population, as the spending of retirees does not necessarily mirror that of working age individuals. Numerous studies document a decrease in spending following retirement. This is largely attributed to a decline in food and work-related expenses (Olafsson and Pagel, 2018[1]; Agarwal, Pan and Qian, 2015[2]; Velarde and Herrmann, 2014[3]; Luengo-Prado and Sevilla, 2012[4]; Lührmann, 2007[5]; Miniaci, Monfardini and Weber, 2003[6]).

Consumption benchmarks are a useful tool to indicate how much retirement savings people need to finance different lifestyles in retirement. Such benchmarks can help policymakers to determine how much money individuals will need in retirement to cover basic needs, and therefore allow them to calibrate expectations about how retirement savings can best be deployed to meet individuals' financial needs in retirement. They can also allow individuals to have an idea of the lifestyle they will be able to achieve in retirement given the savings they have, or alternatively to adjust their level of savings to achieve their desired lifestyle. Several jurisdictions have developed such benchmarks for their population. For example, the Mexican pensions regulator, CONSAR, calculates the required expenditure to achieve a minimum, moderate, and comfortable lifestyle in retirement. The calculations are based on the National Survey of Household Income and Expenditure (ENIGH) database and provides a breakdown by spending categories.

Benchmarks developed by other jurisdictions recognise that the amount of money needed to cover financial needs in retirement can vary across different types of people, such as whether retirees are single or in a relationship. The Pensions and Lifetime Savings Association (PLSA) in the United Kingdom has defined three categories of living standards in retirement, with different amounts calculated for singles and couples (Table 5.1). The minimum living standard essentially provides only a basic level of income, with very little flexibility for covering other expenses. The moderate living standard allows for some additional security needed to cover irregular expenses. The comfortable living standard involves additional income to cover discretionary expenses to finance a more comfortable lifestyle. The living standards also break down the budget of each living standard category by type of expense (e.g. housing, food, transportation) (PLSA, 2024[7]). The Association of Superannuation Funds of Australia (ASFA) has developed similar retirement standards for Australians, and provides more detailed breakdowns of expenditure by spending categories (ASFA, 2023[8]). In the Netherlands, the National Institute for Family Finance Information (NIBUD) produces reference budgets for singles and couples over the age of 65 (Nibud, 2009[9]).

Table 5.1 PLSA Retirement Living Standards for single retirees

	Minimum	Moderate	Comfortable
Pension income	GBP 14 400 / year	GBP 13 300 / year	GBP 43 100 / year
What standard of living could you have?	Covers all your needs, with some left over for fun	More financial security and flexibility	More financial freedom and some luxuries
House	DIY 100 / year to maintain the condition of your property.	Some help with maintenance and decorating each year.	Replace kitchen and bathroom every 10-15 years.
Food	Around 50 / week on groceries, 25 / month on food out of the home, 15 / fortnight on takeaways.	Around 55 / week on groceries, 30 / week on food out of the home, 10 / week on takeaways, 100 / month to take others out for a meal.	Around 70 / week on food, 40 / week on food outside of the home, 20 / week on takeaways, 100 / month to take others out for a meal.
Transport	No car, 10 / week on taxis, 100 / year on rail fares.	3-year-old small car, replaced every 7 years, 20 / month on taxis, 100 / year on rail fare.	3-year-old small car, replaced every 5 years, 20 / month on taxis, 200 / year on rail fare.
Holidays & Leisure	A weeklong UK holiday. Basic TV and broadband plus a streaming service.	A fortnight 3* all-inclusive holiday in the Mediterranean and a long weekend break in the UK. Basic TV and broadband plus 2 streaming services.	A fortnight 4* holiday in the Mediterranean with spending money and 3 long weekend breaks in the UK. Extensive bundled broadband and TV subscription.
Clothing & Personal	Up to 630 for clothing and footwear each year.	Up to 1 500 for clothing and footwear each year.	Up to 1 500 for clothing and footwear each year.
Helping Others	20 for each birthday and Xmas present. 50 / year charity donation.	30 for each birthday and Xmas present, 200 / year charity donation, 1 000 for supporting family members	50 for each birthday and Xmas present, 25 / month charity donation, 1 000 for supporting family members

Source: Based on PLSA (2024[7]), Retirement Living Standards, https://www.retirementlivingstandards.org.uk/

Financial needs in retirement are likely to vary based on additional factors which benchmarks may need to account for, such as region, housing, and health. The Fin-Ed Centre at Massey University in New Zealand calculates two levels of expenditure based on the actual expenditure levels of retired New Zealanders that vary by household size and whether the retiree lives in a metropolitan or provincial area. The first level is a 'no frills' lifestyle covering basic needs and based on the average spending of the second income quintile. The 'choices' lifestyle allows for more comfort and is based on the expenditure of the fourth income quintile (Matthews, 2023[10]). Another example is the Elder Index developed by the Gerontology Institute at the University of Massachusetts Boston in the United States, which provides an interactive web tool that visually shows the breakdown of necessary monthly expenses by spending category. Calculations vary depending on the county, household size, housing status, and health status (poor, good, excellent) (Elder Index, 2023[11]). The Canadian Elder Standard, developed as an academic exercise, calculated basic income needs that vary by housing (renter, homeowner with or without a mortgage), means of transportation (public transportation or owned car), gender, household size, age (65-74 or 75+), long-term-care needs, and city (MacDonald, Andrews and Brown, 2010[12]).

Consumption benchmarks such as those described above, combined with the expected retirement incomes from other sources, can provide an indication as to what extent retirement savings in defined contribution plans will be used to finance the different types of financial needs in retirement. This can then inform the payout options that should be available for individuals for them to best be able to meet their needs.

5.2. Payout options to meet financial needs in retirement

This section discusses how different payout options at retirement can allow retirees to finance the three different types of spending needs in retirement. It considers consumption needs in light of evidence of what retirees need and want, and discusses the desirable features of options to meet those needs and the circumstances under which alternative options may be more appropriate.

5.2.1. Payout options to meet essential spending needs in retirement

Individuals should ideally have guaranteed lifetime income to be able to cover essential spending needs throughout retirement. Essential spending needs include housing, food, transportation, and healthcare costs. Guaranteed lifetime income products that provide a constant stream of income for life are well suited to cover these needs and are in line with retirees' preferences for a certain level of secure income. Nevertheless, such products may not be appropriate in all situations, and the most suitable option will also depend on context and individual circumstances.

Guaranteed lifetime incomes can come in many forms. The basic product is an immediate lifetime annuity paying a regular guaranteed income for life. Deferred annuities allow for payments to begin at a later date. Payments can also increase or decrease over time, either by a specified amount or indexed to an external variable such as inflation.

Beyond being well-suited to finance essential spending, having a guaranteed income in retirement is also in line with the preferences of individuals. Indeed, the security and safety of retirement income is often a priority for individuals planning for their retirement. A recent survey across 15 European countries showed that security was the most important priority when investing for retirement. Around 80% of respondents chose safety over performance, with women having a larger preference for security compared to men. Additionally, 62% of respondents stated that they preferred an annuity solution in retirement for at least part of their savings, though the majority of individuals still preferred a lump sum over an annuity when shown projections (Insurance Europe, 2023[13]). A survey in the United Kingdom showed that 92% of respondents felt that a guaranteed regular income in retirement was important (Standard Life, 2023[14]). In the United States, having investment options that provide a guaranteed lifetime income was the top improvement identified for workplace retirement plans (EBRI, 2023[15]).

The guaranteed lifetime income that pay-as-you-go public pension benefits provide in many jurisdictions can be sufficient to cover basic income needs. Where this is not the case, guaranteed life annuities can offer the security and certainty of a stable lifetime income to complement the retirement income supplied by the public system.

The extent to which pay-as-you-go (PAYG) public pension benefits are sufficient to cover basic income needs varies across population groups. The self-employed, for example, usually receive lower public pensions than regular employees. Figure 5.2 shows that the median public pension benefit for the self-employed is 78% of that received by regular employees on average across the 15 OECD member countries shown in Figure 4.3, and in Germany they receive only around half of what a regular employee gets.

Figure 5.2. Median public pension of the self-employed relative to employees

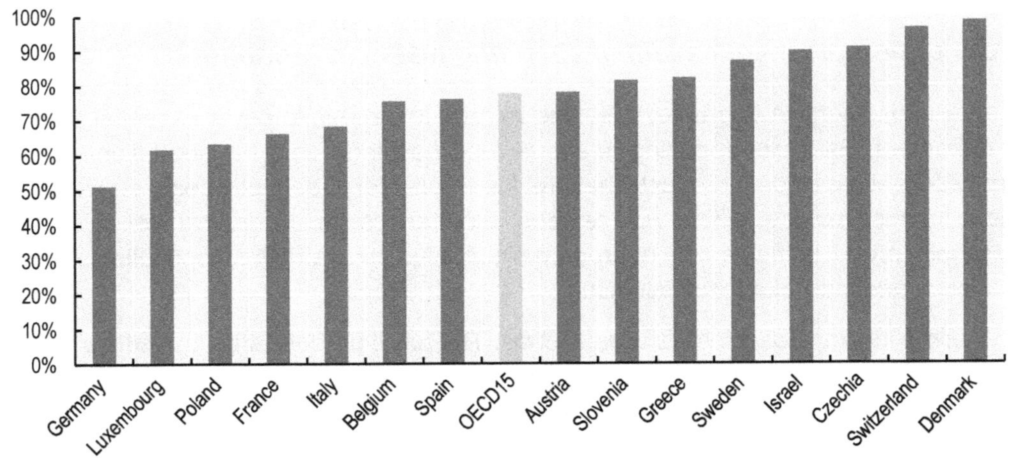

Source: OECD (2019[16]), Pensions at a Glance 2019, https://doi.org/10.1787/07663d56-en

PAYG public pension benefits often have progressive formulas that provide higher relative income replacement rates for low earners. PAYG public pension benefits are therefore more likely to cover low-earners' basic needs compared to high earners.

The time at which individuals claim public pension benefits can also significantly influence the extent to which they are sufficient to cover basic income needs. In some jurisdictions, individuals can increase their benefits by claiming at a later age. The government of Quebec, Canada recently made changes to the rules of the PAYG public pension that facilitate and encourage people to delay the initial claiming of benefits, which could increase the public pension they receive by up to 36% (Laverdière, Hallé-Rochon and Godbout, 2023[17]). In the United States, individuals can increase their public pension benefits by 75% by delaying claiming from age 62 to age 70 (Maurer and Mitchell, 2017[18]). An additional benefit of maximising the amount of public pension benefits is that they generally provide protection against inflation. As such, delayed claiming can be a cost-effective way for individuals to benefit from both longevity and inflation protection for basic income needs, both of which can be more expensive to obtain from a private provider because of the risk exposures involved. In these cases, using retirement savings to finance the first few years of retirement – e.g. via a fixed term annuity or programmed withdrawals – until the public pension is claimed may be a more efficient solution than using the savings to purchase an immediate life annuity.

Inflation protection from PAYG public pension benefits may also eliminate or reduce the need for additional inflation protection to cover basic income needs in retirement. Where additional protection is needed, one needs to consider the value for money offered by inflation-indexed annuities. In principle, a more cost-effective alternative to mitigate inflation risk would be a life annuity that increases by a fixed amount over time, which presents significantly lower risk exposures for providers.

Alternative financial solutions may be better suited for individuals retiring at a different age than the normal retirement age. Those who continue working part-time may not need additional income at the normal retirement age. Individuals retiring earlier than expected – which is often due to job loss, poor health, or caring responsibilities – may not have access to their PAYG public pension at the time they retire and will require an interim solution to meet their basic income needs, potentially via a fixed-term annuity or regular withdrawals from their retirement savings.

The amount of retirement savings that individuals have available also needs to be considered. If savings are not sufficient to purchase a meaningful level of lifetime income, individuals are likely better off taking a lump-sum or drawdown product.

Lifetime income products often lack flexibility and liquidity, making them less suitable for certain individuals. Individuals in very poor health may not benefit from the longevity protection the products offer and may require additional flexibility to cover medical expenses. Individuals entering retirement with high-cost debt may be better off using some of their retirement savings to reduce their debt levels, which would also reduce their basic income needs.

The economic context in which individuals retire may also call for flexibility. Individuals retiring in a low-interest rate environment will require more savings to purchase a given level of guaranteed income. Lifetime income products offering lower or no guarantees could allow them to have higher levels of expected income for a given amount of savings. Individuals retiring after a market crash may be better off waiting until the market recovers to use any savings to purchase a guaranteed lifetime income, rather than locking in their losses as soon as they retire.

Therefore, while guaranteed lifetime income products are normally best suited to meet essential spending needs in retirement, the extent to which retirement savings should finance the lifetime income will depend on the context. The payout options should consider the role of PAYG public pensions in providing a lifetime income, as well as individual or economic circumstances that may require more flexibility.

5.2.2. Payout options to meet unexpected spending needs in retirement

Retirees will ideally be able to keep some of their financial resources aside to use in case they experience an unexpected expense or emergency that cannot be financed using their regularly available resources. Common financial shocks that retirees face relate to healthcare, home repairs, or the loss of a spouse. Funds used for unexpected expenses need to be available and easy to access when individuals need them, and therefore need to be held in relatively safe and liquid assets. The need for retirees to set aside additional savings to cover unexpected expenses in retirement will depend in part on country context, the availability of affordable insurance products, and individual circumstances.

Health shocks are a common reason for people to put aside savings in retirement. In Australia and the Netherlands, for example, a study found that retirees saved primarily to have some precautionary savings for health reasons, and this was a more important motivation for women than for men. Precautionary savings is also higher for those with low liquidity, highlighting the importance of having financial resources that are easily accessible (Alonso-García et al., 2022[19]). The need to save for health shocks, however, also depends on public healthcare coverage. Retirees in Northern European countries tend to spend down their wealth more rapidly than in Central and Southern European countries and the United States. Northern Europe tends to also have higher public healthcare coverage, indicating less of a need for precautionary savings (Nakajima and Telyukova, 2013[20]).

Home repairs are another common financial shock in retirement. One survey of the United States population indicated that over 40% of retirees below age 80 have had an unexpected financial shock, and that nearly a quarter of these shocks were due to major home repairs (Greenwald Research, 2021[21]). A survey in Costa Rica indicated that 61% of those withdrawing a lump-sum from their retirement savings used it for home improvements (SUPEN, 2020[22]).

The loss of a spouse can also be detrimental to a retiree's finances. In a survey of children in the United States with recently deceased parents, one-third felt that the death of one parent had reduced the financial security of the surviving parent, and a quarter reported that the financial situation became much worse (Greenwald Research, 2022[23]). Divorce can also be financially harmful, and can have an even larger negative impact on finances in retirement that the death of a spouse (Greenwald & Associates, 2016[24]). Having a safety-net may help individuals manage their transition following the loss of a spouse.

Nevertheless, a safety net will not be able to absorb all financial shocks, and larger shocks may require alternative means of financing. Where available and affordable, insurance products such as auto, home, and medical insurance can be an effective solution to mitigate larger shocks to the extent that the risk is insurable at an affordable price. Such insurance will be particularly valuable for low- to middle-income households who will have a lower capacity to absorb these types of shocks on their own, but who could potentially afford premiums with their retirement incomes.

However, insurance solutions may not always be available or affordable. Indeed, evidence indicates that long-term care costs and divorce are two of the sources of financial shocks that retirees are the least prepared for. Around 40% of lower-income people in the United States and Canadians report being financially unprepared for long-term care expenses, and 35% unprepared for divorce. These two risks are the most common sources of expenses that retirees are unable to support (Greenwald & Associates, 2016[24]). Most of those over the age of 85 have no realistic view on how they will pay for long-term care (Greenwald & Associates, Inc., 2018[25]). Similarly, among individuals retiring in the United Kingdom around 2022, 31% have no idea how to prepare for long-term care costs, and 27% have no plans to set money aside to do so (abrdn, 2022[26]). One study estimates that 25% of the elderly needing long-term care in Europe would not be able to finance 10% of their expenses even if using all of their financial resources (Bonnet, Juin and Laferrère, 2019[27]).

Homeowners will have an additional financial resource available to them that renters do not, which may also influence the amount of savings that a retiree needs to keep available for unexpected expenses, in particular for health shocks. While there seems to be an aversion to the use of home equity to finance shocks, when it is used retirees tend to use it as a source of financing of last resort in response to the loss of a partner or a large health expenditure. In Europe, changing homes in retirement is most common following a reduction in household members, such as following divorce or the death of a spouse (Angelini, Brugiavini and Weber, 2013[28]). Households in the United States tend to use housing equity as precautionary savings for health risks (Poterba, Venti and Wise, 2011[29]). After health insurance, home equity is the primary resource to finance a health shock (Moulton et al., 2021[30]). One US study showed a significant decline in wealth following the diagnosis of a serious diseases, primarily driven by a reduction in home equity following the sale of a home (Moulton et al., 2021[30]).

Therefore, while safety-nets will not be able to absorb all financial shocks, it is nevertheless important to allow for some flexibility for retirees to set some savings aside to cover moderate unexpected expenses.

5.2.3. Payout options to meet discretionary spending needs in retirement

Retirees should be able to use any additional resources after essential spending and security needs are met as discretionary spending to finance their desired lifestyle. Most retirees with sufficient savings are likely to have regular discretionary expenses to maintain a certain standard of living, as well as occasional discretionary expenses such as holidays or other large purchases. Lifetime income products can be valuable for regular discretionary expenses as they allow people to easily budget their expenditure and avoid underspending. Nevertheless, discretionary spending needs are likely to diverge more across population groups, and therefore the options available should allow for a certain level of flexibility to adapt to different contexts and situations.

People value flexibility about as much as they value security. In the same survey in the United Kingdom showing that over 90% of the population thought a guaranteed income was important, nearly 90% also thought that being able to have flexible access to money was important (Standard Life, 2023[14]). A survey of individuals in the United States revealed that 41% of retired individuals preferred investment solutions to finance their retirement compared to 20% preferring an annuity (GSAM Insights, 2022[31]).

There is also evidence indicating that that regular income is an important factor for financial wellbeing in retirement. Retirees financing more of their consumption through lifetime annuities seem to have higher levels of satisfaction and may remain more satisfied throughout retirement (Panis, 2003[32]). The satisfaction of those not having annuities declined over time. In the United Kingdom, annuitisation has been found to increase life satisfaction as well as consumption levels (Gao, Loewenstein and Wang, 2022[33]). A survey in the United States found that 90% of those who took an annuity reported that their budget was more predictable, that they felt more financially secure and that it was easier to pay for their needs (MetLife, 2022[34]).

Having a regular income also helps people to budget how much they spend in retirement. In the United States, one study showed that those having income from a defined benefit pension plan drew down initial wealth more slowly than those who did not have a defined benefit plan (Siliciano and Wettstein, 2021[35]). This implies that people likely budget their spending based on the annuitised income they receive and spend less of their remaining wealth on discretionary spending.

Indeed, individuals often refer to some reference withdrawal amount to budget their regular spending, even if this level of spending is not optimal. More than half of retirees over the age of 65 in Australia draw down their superannuation account at the minimum required rate (The Australian Treasury, 2020[36]). In the United States, a survey of individuals withdrawing from their accounts indicated that 90% considered that the Required Minimum Distribution rates were important in deciding how much to withdraw, and over half viewed these rates as a good guide for an appropriate drawdown rate (Brown, Poterba and Richardson, 2017[37]). Using such references to budget can lead retirees to not spend down their retirement savings and have a lower standard of living than what they should be able to afford.

Given this evidence, products providing some regular income, whether guaranteed or not, seem quite valuable for individuals to finance their regular discretionary spending and optimise their spending levels over time. Given the heterogeneity of discretionary spending needs, such products could present a wider range of features that allow the individual to increase their expected levels of income while still mitigating some of the risks they face to finance their retirement.

Variable lifetime income products with low or no guarantees could be an attractive solution to increase the amount of expected income that retirees can receive and allow them to have a reference income for budgeting purposes without worrying that they will ever run out of income.[1] However, the income from these products can be subject to volatility making the income payments less predictable. Nevertheless, given that discretionary spending is not strictly necessary, this may be an acceptable trade-off for many retirees. More risk averse retirees may be better off with a product providing a lower level of lifetime income that is guaranteed.

Inflation protection is likely to be less important for products providing discretionary income compared to those meant to cover basic income. Individuals' consumption levels in retirement tend to decline over time across all income levels. The decline in spending varies across spending categories and countries, however. Leisure spending on travel and holidays tend to increase early in retirement before eventually decreasing, particularly for higher-income households (Centro International sobre el Envejecimiento, 2021[38]; Rohwedder, Hurd and Hudomiet, 2022[39]; Crawford, Karjalainen and Sturrock, 2022[40]). One reason that consumption declines with age is that people simply enjoy spending less, implying that it is mainly discretionary spending that declines. One study in the United States found that reported enjoyment from spending predicts spending patterns in all categories, and that enjoyment tends to decrease with age along with spending patterns, even controlling for financial constraints (Rohwedder, Hurd and Hudomiet, 2022[39]). Given these observations, individuals will have less of a need to maintain purchasing power for discretionary spending throughout their retirement.

Drawdown solutions that leave assets invested to regularly withdraw as income can also provide regular cash flow to retirees, with potentially more flexibility than lifetime income products. Nevertheless, these products do not protect individuals against the longevity risk of running out of savings, which may lead them to spend more conservatively than they can afford to. Managed drawdown products where the provider decides the withdrawal amount may be better to optimise income levels in light of investment and longevity risk by dynamically adjusting the payments, though potentially with reduced flexibility. These types of products can also be combined with a deferred lifetime income product to target a more stable income profile and mitigate the risk of eventually running out of assets.[2]

Flexible drawdown products may be best suited for occasional discretionary spending. These allow individuals to decide when and how much they withdraw, so that they can use the money as they need it.

5.3. Approaches to deliver suitable financial options for retirement

Ensuring that suitable options exist for retirees to utilise their savings in retirement does not ensure that they will do so. This is often due to a lack of awareness of options available, a lack of accessible information, or administrative barriers. The rules and regulations of the pension system should aim to overcome these obstacles to increase retirees' take-up of suitable options to finance their retirement.

Even though a large proportion of individuals state a preference for a lifetime or guaranteed income, the proportion of individuals who voluntarily choose such a product is much lower, even when products are readily available. One randomly controlled trial in the United States indicated that over 50% of those having at least USD 100 000 in retirement savings would be willing to purchase a life annuity at prevailing rates, in contrast to only around 12% who actually do (Arapakis and Wettstein, 2023[41]). Similarly, in the United Kingdom, 92% of survey respondents felt that a guaranteed regular income in retirement was important, yet fewer than 10% of individuals accessing their retirement savings for the first time use their savings to purchase an annuity (Standard Life, 2023[14]; FCA, 2024[42]).[3]

One reason for the lack of take-up of lifetime income products is a lack of awareness that these products are available. In the United Kingdom, 32% of people aged 50-69 saving for retirement had not heard of a life annuity, and an additional 21% thought the product was a risky product with volatile income (HM Treasury, FCA, 2023[43]). In the United States, one third of savers were not familiar with lifetime income products (Arapakis and Wettstein, 2023[44]).

Other people have a hard time accessing or understanding information they need to make good decisions. Only 26% of pension savers in the United Kingdom feel that they understand their pension statement (HM Treasury, FCA, 2023[43]). In addition, savers also indicated that the information was not timely or helpful (FCA, 2023[45]). Even when people seek advice to help them make a decision, advisors often fail to discuss lifetime income options with their clients. In the United States, 10% of advisors do not recommend annuities to anyone, and two-thirds of advisors recommend them to fewer than half of their clients (Arapakis and Wettstein, 2023[44]).

Administrative barriers that complicate the process to choose an option for retirement can also impede individuals from choosing the most suitable financial solution. In the United Kingdom, for example, individuals are less likely to make the effort to shop around for a decumulation product compared to an investment product, and have a tendency to stay with their existing providers. Individuals also cited difficulties in contacting their provider for information (FCA, 2023[45]). In the United States, the failure to purchase an annuity may indicate a lack of knowledge of how to go about doing so (Arapakis and Wettstein, 2023[41]).

There are broadly three levels of assistance that can help to overcome the lack of awareness, information, and accessibility around options for the payout phase of defined contribution pensions to help ensure that retirees access suitable products to finance their retirement. The first is a default solution, where individuals will automatically have a payout solution chosen for them. The second is the provision of guidance to give individuals the information and tools needed to make an informed decision on their own and then execute it. The final is financial advice, where individuals can have a personalised recommendation for a suitable financial solution that considers their specific needs and objectives. Each of these options presents different advantages and challenges relating to implementation and ensuring successful outcomes.

5.3.1. Default options

Default options are those that individuals get if they do not actively choose or if they fail to take any action at all. The main benefit of a default option is its effectiveness; because of inertia and other behavioural biases such as choice overload that impede decision-making, the majority of individuals usually end up staying in the default option rather than actively choosing a course of action, even if an alternative may be better suited for their needs. This effectiveness is therefore also a key disadvantage of having a default option. Because it relies on inertia, it perpetuates individuals' disengagement in financial planning for retirement by offering a path of least resistance that may or may not be suitable for their personal circumstances.

The choice to implement a default must be conscious of any potential harm that the option could have, because most people end up in the default. The potential for harm from a default solution for the payout of retirement savings is greater than that for defaults for the accumulation of retirement savings. This is firstly because while lifetime income solutions can be a suitable option for many individuals, they are often irreversible and individuals will not be able to change their mind or adapt in the future if this option is not the most appropriate for their circumstances. Secondly, the variables to consider in retirement are more heterogeneous and complex. Saving for retirement mainly involves deciding whether contributions are affordable and how to employ savings most effectively to maximise the level of savings accumulated at retirement.

The latter consideration can be solved with minimal harm by defaulting individuals into a low-cost investment product with a reasonable long-term investment risk profile such as a lifecycle strategy. While affordability can vary depending on individual circumstances, the solution to address this can be simple and easy to change (i.e. save less). However, financial decisions for payout need to account for uncertainty in future expenses (liquidity risk), short-term investment returns (sequencing risk), and lifespan (longevity risk), which cannot be addressed with a single, simple solution. For example, products providing longevity protection generally do not allow for liquidity, and guaranteed products can lock in any investment losses or low interest rate for life. Identifying an appropriate default solution for payout that is not likely to cause harm is therefore not a simple task, and relying solely on a default option for pension payout may not be ideal.

Nevertheless, default solutions may still be useful in situations where a retiree is likely to be better off with the default than following an alternative path of least resistance. Ideally, a default solution will allow individuals to adapt if they find that the resulting outcome is not appropriate for their needs in retirement. Any default option providing guarantees should consider prevailing financial market conditions to ensure that financial losses or unattractive pricing terms are not locked in for life. Additionally, to the extent possible, defaults should take into account variables that can provide an indication that a certain option is not likely to be suitable.

The irreversibility of lifetime income options makes them problematic as a default option in many cases. Even if many retirees would benefit from a lifetime income, the lack of flexibility could result in substantial harm for certain groups. Examples include those in very poor health who would not benefit from longevity protection and may need their assets available to cover medical expenses, those with high-cost debt who would be better off reducing their debt payments, or those with limited resources who would not be able to receive a meaningful level of income or who may need to retain some liquidity in case of unexpected expenses. Nevertheless, where the other components of the pension system do not provide sufficient longevity protection, lifetime income options as a default may be needed, ideally taking into account the circumstances when this is not likely to be suitable.

There are ways to structure a lifetime income option that allow for some flexibility, though these may not always be sufficient to prevent harm. Many products offer 'cool down' periods that allow individuals to change their mind within a limited timeframe. For example, the Secure Act 2.0 in the United States allows for a cooling-off period of up to 90 days for qualified life annuity products (QLACs). Some products allow individuals to surrender the product before the initial premium has been paid back, but this can be quite costly and can involve high penalties and the opportunity cost of any investment income that the retiree could otherwise have earned. Composite products incorporating a deferred element of lifetime income may be able to more easily allow flexibility. For example, Nest's Guided Retirement Fund in the United Kingdom offers a managed drawdown solution that individuals are free to withdraw from before the age of 85, at which point they will be defaulted into a guaranteed lifetime annuity if they have not yet opted out.

Defaulting retirees into payout options offering guarantees could also cause harm when financial market conditions make it likely that the retiree would receive lower retirement incomes than they otherwise would have. Those retiring following a negative shock to the financial markets or in a bear market are likely to be better off waiting until markets recover to purchase a product with a guarantee to avoid fully locking in any investment losses their savings experienced. Those retiring in a low-interest rate environment would not be able to receive as high a guaranteed income as they may have planned for and may be better off in a product with low or no guarantees to have a higher expected retirement income. Others may be better off delaying claiming public pension benefits and using their savings to finance the interim period. Such circumstances call for more flexibility to adapt to a given context, which may not be possible for a default option to provide.

The application of a default option should also consider any available personal information that could indicate whether a certain solution may or may not be suitable. An obvious variable to consider – and one that is commonly available – is the amount of retirement savings that an individual has accumulated. Nest establishes the default threshold at GBP 10 000, under which individuals cannot access the Guided Retirement Fund. In Singapore, the threshold to be defaulted into a lifetime annuity is SGD 60 000.

Where no personal criteria are used to establish a default, the option likely to cause the least harm is a managed drawdown solution that provides regular payments to the individual depending on the account balance and potentially other factors such as age. This option usually allows for the flexibility to change or adapt if the individual decides it is not suitable for their situation. The default option in Colombia, for example, is a managed drawdown (programmed withdrawal) paying the amount that would be provided if purchasing a life annuity with the account balance in that year. In Costa Rica the default is also a managed drawdown, however payouts are positive investment returns only, which prevents a depletion of assets in retirement but does not optimise the individual's income over their lifetime.

5.3.2. Guidance

Guidance aims to engage individuals in their decision regarding how to use their retirement savings and help them to make the decision themselves. There are various ways to provide individuals with guidance at retirement. Digital tools can help people understand the different options available and the implications of their choices in an interactive way. Choice architecture that is mindful in how options are presented can be employed to nudge people towards choosing a suitable option for their particular situation. Guidance can also be more personalised, potentially leveraging digital tools and/or choice architecture to suggest to individuals which option is likely to be appropriate given their characteristics.

Guidance that aims to engage individuals and provide them with information relevant to their situation is important because generic information about options available at retirement is often insufficient to aid individuals in deciding how to use their retirement savings. A recent survey in the United Kingdom found that 27% of individuals felt that general communication did not help at all with their decision making, with an additional 54% reporting that it only helped a little (FCA, 2023[45]). Another experimental study found that only 14% of individuals made the best decision regarding the amount to withdraw from their pension pot to meet their financial needs and avoid paying higher taxes when given general information about the tax implications of withdrawals from their retirement savings (ABI, 2023[46]).

Digital tools have a large potential to help individuals make better decisions for their retirement because they are generally accessible to most people and elicit the active engagement of individuals in considering their potential options. The individual pension tracking tool in Sweden, Minpension, offers an interactive retirement planning tool to users over the age of 54 that allows them to see the impact of choosing different payout options. The tool has contributed to an increase in the number of people choosing a lifetime income for their retirement (see Chapter 7). Pension providers are also developing tools to help their members choose an appropriate payout solution at retirement. For example, Aviva offers a tool for its Guided Retirement that provides a hybrid payout solution that aims to meet the three layers of needs described in this chapter. The product provides a guaranteed lifetime income account, a flexible account to regularly draw down until the commencement of the guaranteed income, and an accessible, liquid account to use as needed (Rajah, 2024[47]). With the tool individuals can choose what proportion of assets they want to allocate to each of the three strategies and are able to visualise the implications of different allocations. Similarly, Smart Pension offers a digital tool for its Smart Retire solution in both Australia and the United Kingdom that allows individuals to split between the three allocations and makes them think about how much they should put towards each type of need.

Using choice architecture to nudge people towards taking a good decision at retirement for their situation can also be a powerful approach to guide individuals into better payout solutions. Such an approach also seems to be welcomed by consumers. A survey carried out by Scottish Widows found that 38% of respondents preferred to be nudged towards a specific option after responding to a series of questions (Scottish Widows, 2024[48]). Recognising the potential of choice architecture, the Authority for Financial Markets (AFM) in the Netherlands published guidelines for pension providers when designing choice architecture for their members. The guidelines clarify that the AFM expects communications to be aware of behavioural biases to help improve outcomes and not take advantage of consumers. The guidelines also highlight the importance of ensuring that the variables used to distinguish different groups of members are relevant, that the products offered can be reasonably expected to be appropriate, and that individuals are provided with adequate tools to identify their own needs and engage in the decision (Autoriteit Financiële Markten, 2019[49]). The Financial Conduct Authority in the United Kingdom introduced the 'investment pathways' choice architecture, which requires firms to present four options to individuals approaching retirement to help them to align their choice with their objectives regarding how they would like to use their money in retirement. An initial review reported positive results, with a 50% take-up rate by members in the first quarter of 2023 (FCA, 2023[50]).

Personalised guidance aims to get individuals to consider their own situation and highlight the solution that is usually well suited to someone in similar circumstances. Such guidance can feel more relevant and helpful for individuals making decisions at retirement, resulting in better outcomes. One experimental study showed that the proportion of individuals making the optimal decision about withdrawing from their pension account increased from 9% to 64% when the guidance that explained the tax implications of the options was available and suggested an option that would result in lower taxes (ABI, 2023[46]). An example of the provision of personalised guidance is Pension Wise, a free, government-provided service in the United Kingdom that aims to help individuals over the age of 50 decide how to use their retirement savings. Guidance counsellors explain the different options available to individuals along with the tax implications and provide insight about which option might be better given their other sources of pension income, any outstanding debt, their desired retirement age, and preferences around security and flexibility. Users of the service express high levels of satisfaction, with 94% of those accessing Pension Wise in 2019-20 happy with the guidance received (ABI, 2021[51]). Around two-thirds reported that the free guidance helped them to make better financial decisions (Standard Life, 2023[14]).

While the potential to improve outcomes is significant, a major challenge in personalising guidance in a way that can lead to a suggested course of action is that the suggestion can resemble personalised advice, which is normally subject to more stringent regulation. Guidance is usually defined as any information provided that does not explicitly take into account an individual's specific needs or objectives, though it may consider their characteristics. In this sense, it is meant to be relevant for anyone with similar circumstances. However, the line between personalised guidance and personalised advice is not always clear cut.

Because of the blurred distinction between personalised guidance and advice, the regulatory framework can often deter providers from providing personalised guidance for retirement in order to avoid inadvertently crossing the line into personalised advice. Providers of personalised advice are generally exposed to significantly more liability risk if the suggested course of action turns out to be inappropriate for the individual (OECD, 2016[52]). In Australia, personal advice involves the consideration of an individual's objectives, financial situation or needs, or any suggestion where the individual can reasonably assume that this is the case. Many providers therefore feel that the distinction between the two is uncertain and that providers could be held liable if consumers are eventually not happy with the guidance they receive (Levy, 2022[53]). In the United Kingdom, the regulator has attempted to clarify the boundary between guidance and advice, but many providers continue to feel that the distinction is not sufficiently clear. The Association of British Insurers helpfully proposes some key features to distinguish personalised guidance from advice. Namely, rather than providing a recommended course of action, personalised advice can propose a suggested course of action for consideration, highlight relevant variables that need to be considered, reduce the range of options to those most likely to be suitable, nudge individuals towards a specific course of action, and assist them in making use of their existing resources and assets (ABI, 2023[46]). Nevertheless, as the distinction remains difficult in some situations, the FCA is considering alternative approaches to facilitate the provision of personalised guidance. One option being considered is a completely new regulatory framework covering 'targeted support', which would allow providers to suggest a course of action based on limited personal information (HM Treasury, FCA, 2023[43]). Important features of this new framework would include a requirement for providers to determine the type of personal information needed, to ensure that the support is likely to improve consumer outcomes, and to ensure that the individual understands the intended outcome of the solution suggested along with the risks it entails (HM Treasury, FCA, 2023[43]).

Another key challenge to ensure the effectiveness of personalised guidance is a lack of awareness or use of guidance services and tools. Only one-third of retirement savers in the United Kingdom are aware of the free Pension Wise service, and only 14% of people accessing their pension pots over 2019-20 in the United Kingdom used the service (Barrett, 2023[54]; ABI, 2021[51]). In Australia, only 18% of members are aware of digital tools to help them make decisions about their pension (Levy, 2022[53]). Those with small pots may feel that they do not have enough savings to make seeking out guidance or assistance worth it (Kotecha et al., 2020[55]).

However, nudging can also be successfully employed to encourage people to use guidance services and tools. For example, one study increased the number of members taking an appointment with Pension Wise from 3% to 11% by offering the ability to immediately book an appointment (Farghly et al., 2020[56]).

5.3.3. Advice

Financial advice is the most personalised way to ensure that individuals access suitable solutions for their retirement but it is also the most resource intensive to deliver. Individuals taking advice often report positive outcomes, yet not all people are willing or able to seek advice.

Financial advice can often lead to good outcomes in retirement. Individuals are generally positive and confident about their choices when receiving financial advice. In the United Kingdom, individuals feel that the personalisation of advice is the most important value of seeking advice, along with consulting someone who understands their financial situation and having the peace of mind that their financial decisions for retirement are reasonable (AKG, 2023[57]). Around three-quarters of respondents to another UK survey reported that receiving financial advice helped them to better understand complex financial matters and helped them to make better financial decisions (Standard Life, 2023[14]).

For some retirement products, it is clear that financial advice is likely to be the best channel to ensure that the product is suitable given an individual's circumstances. Financial advice is often required for more complex products that may require higher levels of financial capability to determine their appropriateness. This is the case in several jurisdictions, for example, for individuals to obtain a reverse mortgage product (see Chapter 6).

However, individuals may often be reluctant to seek financial advice. Some main drivers of this reluctance are a lack of trust, a lack of awareness, and cost (Barrett, 2023[54]; Kotecha et al., 2020[55]). Around 30% of survey respondents in the United Kingdom reported that they do not seek advice because they do not earn enough, it is too expensive, or they do not have enough savings (Standard Life, 2023[14]).

Cost is a barrier not only for the demand of advice, but also for the supply. Recently, advisors in the United Kingdom have been dropping less profitable clients that they can no longer afford to serve (AKG, 2023[57]).

Digital solutions for personalised advice have the potential to improve the options offered to individuals in a more accessible and cost-effective manner than financial advice provided in person (OECD, 2017[58]). However, individuals seem to be somewhat reluctant to engage solely with a digital platform for advice. In Australia, only 37% of people who recently considered financial advice were open to receiving advice through a digital channel, and 40% felt that it would be more valuable if a person explained the results of the digital tools and recommendations (Levy, 2022[53]). Another survey in the United Kingdom indicated that 35% of individuals preferred in-person support (Barrett, 2023[54]). When asked about whether they would take financial advice from an AI tool, 36% responded that they never would, even if the current technology improves (AKG, 2023[57]). In addition, while digital solutions for retirement savings have grown rapidly, solutions for advice around the payout of pensions have been slower to emerge. Nevertheless, the market for digital advice continues to develop, and this could be a potential option to better match financial needs in retirement with the appropriate products in the future.

5.4. Policy guidelines

Policy makers need to ensure that the regulatory framework allows the design of the payout phase for defined contribution pension plans to adapt to fulfil the financial needs of individuals in retirement. The most appropriate solutions for payout will depend in part on which type of spending the accumulated assets will be used for. The role of assets accumulated in defined contribution plans in financing retirement can vary depending on country context, financial markets, and individual circumstances.

To ensure that payout design is fit for purpose, policy makers first need to determine the role of the assets accumulated in defined contribution plans in financing different needs in retirement in the context of the pension system as a whole and other sources of income in retirement. Given this role, the regulatory framework should allow for the use of appropriate products to meet the corresponding financial needs in retirement, taking into account how these needs may likely vary for different groups of people. It should also consider how to facilitate individuals' decision-making at retirement in choosing or accessing the most suitable product(s) for their particular situation.

5.4.1. Understand the role of defined contribution plans in financing retirement

The role of defined contribution plans in financing retirement will inform the types of products that should be available to individuals at retirement. To determine the intended role of the plans, policy makers first need to understand how much individuals can expect to spend in retirement. Local context and individual circumstances will then inform to what extent assets accumulated in defined contribution plans will be used to finance essential spending, unexpected spending, or discretionary spending.

Consumption benchmarks for retirement are a useful starting point to understand how much retirees will need to spend to achieve different living standards. As a minimum, benchmarks should provide an indication of how much money people need to cover essential spending to finance basic needs such as housing, food, transportation and healthcare.

Benchmarks should account for factors that can have a material impact on the cost of living for retirees. Single retirees, renters, car owners, those in poor health, and those living in metropolitan areas will generally have higher-than-average essential spending needs.

Having a benchmark for basic income needs will allow policy makers to assess to what extent retirement savings will need to be used to complement public pensions and other expected pension benefits to finance those needs, or whether savings are better placed to finance unexpected or discretionary expenses. The sufficiency of PAYG public and defined benefit pensions will vary depending on an individual's situation. Individuals who did not enjoy a full career as a salaried employee are likely to receive lower public benefits. Lower-income individuals, on the other hand, are likely to receive higher relative public benefits.

Once policy makers understand how much income retirees will need to finance their basic needs, they will have a better understanding of the role of assets accumulated in defined contribution pension plans in financing retirement for individuals in different circumstances, which will inform the payout options that retirees should have available to them at retirement.

5.4.2. Consider the financial solutions best suited to meeting different financial needs in retirement

The financial solutions best suited to cover essential, unexpected, and discretionary spending will differ in the risks they should mitigate. The framework for the design of the payout of defined contribution pensions will need to ensure that the appropriate solutions are allowed and available given the expected role of those plans in financing retirement. Figure 5.3 illustrates the risks that need to be mitigated for each type of spending, and the type of solution that is generally well-suited to mitigate those risks in retirement.

Figure 5.3. Illustration of the risks that should be mitigated for different spending needs in retirement and the corresponding type of solutions

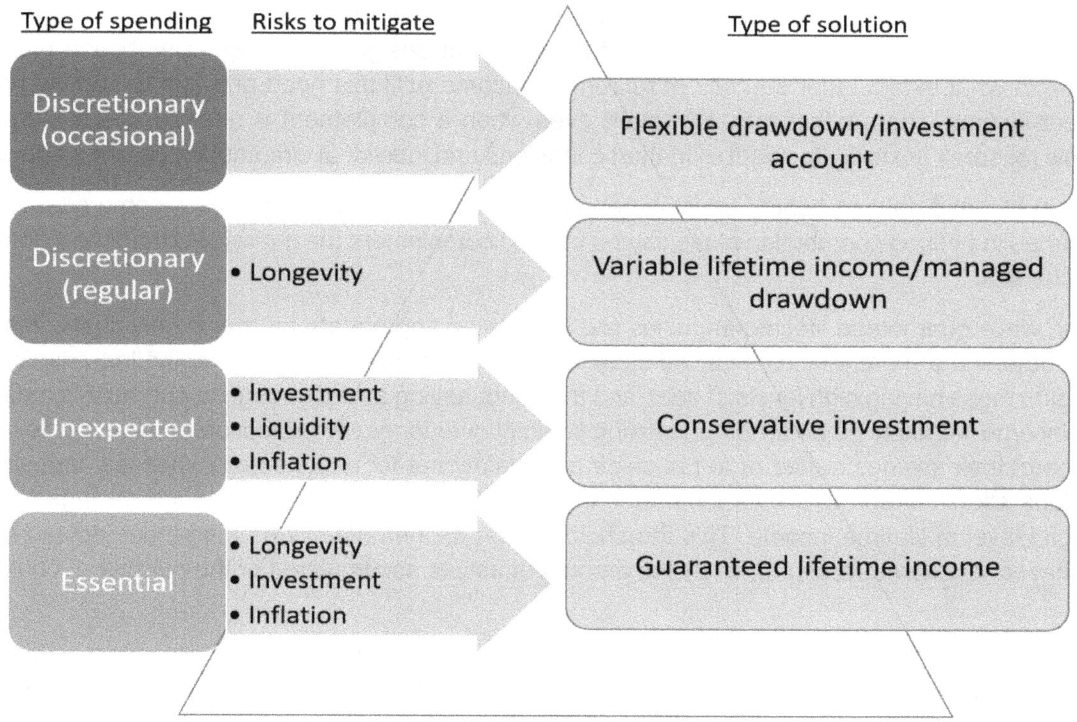

Essential spending to cover basic needs will require a regular, stable source of financing that potentially can keep up with inflation. As such, it should ideally mitigate longevity, investment, and inflation risks. Guaranteed lifetime income products present these features and should be well-suited to financing basic needs for those who need additional income to complement other sources of lifetime income, such as public pension benefits.

Assets used to finance unexpected spending need to be available when the individual needs them. As such, solutions providing this security need to mitigate investment and liquidity risk, and ideally should keep up with inflation to avoid the reduction in value. Assets should be invested in relatively safe and liquid investments where they can continue to earn some return but remain easily available.

Discretionary spending needs are likely to be more heterogenous, but can broadly be broken down into regular discretionary spending to achieve a certain living standard and occasional discretionary spending to finance larger purchases that allow retirees some of the comforts they aspire to. As retirees normally aim to sustain a certain living standard throughout their retirement, products used to finance regular discretionary spending will ideally mitigate longevity risk to allow individuals to optimise their spending over their lifetime without worrying about running out of assets. As discretionary spending is not essential and normally declines with age, investment and inflation protection are less important. With these objectives in mind, variable lifetime income products that offer low or no guarantees can provide a higher expected lifetime income compared to fully guaranteed products. Alternatively, managed drawdown products with a withdrawal rate set at a sustainable level could also be appropriate, potentially combined with a deferred lifetime income product to protect against longevity risk. For the more risk averse, guaranteed lifetime income products could be considered, though at the expense of lower retirement income on average.

Occasional discretionary spending will require more flexibility rather than longevity protection to allow individuals to use their savings as they wish. Flexible drawdowns that keep assets invested are therefore likely to be the most appropriate solution for occasional spending needs.

5.4.3. Ensure essential spending needs are met while considering individual and market circumstances

The minimum objective of any pension system is to ensure that individuals have a sufficient income in retirement to cover essential spending. As such, the payout design for defined contribution plans must recognise to what extent other sources of retirement income fulfil this need and aim to complement this retirement income where necessary. However, even when a complement is needed, the design should also allow for some flexibility to adapt to market conditions and individual circumstances when appropriate.

If PAYG public and defined benefit pension benefits are insufficient to meet basic income needs, assets accumulated in defined contribution plans can be used to complement the guaranteed lifetime income from those schemes.

However, while guaranteed lifetime annuities are likely to be appropriate for many individuals, this option may put others in a more difficult financial situation because of their lack of flexibility. Individuals in very poor health, those having high levels of debt, and those not having saved enough to purchase a meaningful level of income will likely be better off prioritising liquidity over longevity protection to have the flexibility to use some of their savings earlier or to put aside as a safety net for unexpected expenses. Indeed, many jurisdictions allow retirees to take a lump-sum if they have not accumulated enough savings to have a meaningful level of lifetime income. This threshold can be defined directly as retirement income that can be purchased, or alternatively proxied by the amount of assets accumulated or the number of contribution periods.

Unattractive market conditions, such as a market crash or a low-interest rate environment, may also be detrimental if individuals have to lock in a lower guaranteed lifetime income than they otherwise would have been able to obtain. In these cases, individuals may be better off delaying their purchase of a guaranteed lifetime income or considering other types of lifetime income products with variable payments.

The appropriate payout solution may also need to consider how to optimise income over retirement by varying the timing of payments. If individuals are able to significantly increase their public pension benefit by delaying claiming, a better solution may be to use retirement savings as an interim solution for financing retirement until public pension benefits are claimed, particularly in cases where public pensions will likely be sufficient to cover basic income needs if delayed.

While inflation protection for basic income needs is valuable, it may not be necessary if public PAYG pension benefits already mitigate a significant portion of inflation risk for these needs. The benefits of additional inflation protection would need to be weighed against the value for money that inflation-indexed products can offer.

5.4.4. Allow retirees to set aside a portion of their retirement savings to cover unexpected expenses

Allowing flexibility for individuals to set aside a portion of their retirement savings for unexpected expenses goes hand-in-hand with considering how and whether the retirement savings is needed to cover essential spending needs. Payout design for defined contribution plans should allow for the flexibility to keep a portion of savings aside, and recognise when this may be a priority over converting savings into a lifetime income. These needs will be higher in jurisdictions with lower public health coverage and benefits aiming to assist the elderly, as well as for those without housing assets to fall back on.

As such, the payout design of defined contribution plans should allow retirees to keep a moderate amount of assets aside to be used for urgent expenditures. This can be done by allowing retirees to take partial lump sums or by ensuring that a portion of the assets can be kept invested in a relatively safe and liquid investment. Several jurisdictions aim to provide this flexibility by allowing retirees to take a portion of their retirement savings as a lump sum. Such limits are most commonly defined as a percentage of accumulated savings (e.g. Portugal), but can also be defined as a nominal value or as a share of salary (e.g. Ireland). Many jurisdictions allow individuals with balances lower than a pre-defined threshold to withdraw their assets in one go, recognising that having access to that savings would be more beneficial for retirees than having an insignificant level of lifetime income.

5.4.5. Allow for flexibility to meet discretionary spending needs while ensuring the availability of options that provide a regular income

Payout design should allow for sufficient flexibility for individuals to use their remaining savings in a way best suited to their personal situation. Once retirees have sufficient income to finance their basic needs and have set aside funds for unexpected expenses, their remining savings can be used to finance their desired lifestyle.

High levels of retirement savings or voluntary savings in personal plans are most likely used to finance a retiree's discretionary spending. Many jurisdictions recognise the discretionary purpose of retirement savings by allowing savings above a certain threshold to be used as the retiree wishes. In Lithuania, for example, retirees can withdraw savings in excess of EUR 60 000 as they want, though alternative lifetime income options remain available. Most voluntary personal pension plans also allow for significant flexibility in how retirees use their savings, in recognition that the primary purpose of these plans is for individuals to accumulate additional savings to improve their living standards in retirement.

At the same time, options providing regular incomes should be easily available. These solutions can help individuals to budget and spend their savings more optimally over their retirement and avoid the situation where individuals spend less than they could otherwise afford to and constrain their achievable living standards as a result. Lifetime income options are not necessarily available for all types of pension plans in all OECD member countries, though temporary income or drawdown options are normally available.

5.4.6. Establish any default option with care and only when the solution is not likely to cause undue harm

Default options can be very effective in nudging individuals into a specific financial option, but they do not engage people in the decisions about how to manage their retirement savings. This means that people who are defaulted into a particular path are not likely to consider whether that option is the most appropriate one for their particular situation.

Any default option for the decumulation of retirement savings should be implemented in a way that is not likely to cause undue harm to any group of the population. Ideally, it should allow for the possibility for the retiree to adapt if the default turns out to not be suitable for their needs. This implies that life annuities are not appropriate as a default option in most cases because they are irreversible. Features such as cooling off periods or products that provide regular incomes before converting savings into a lifetime income can provide individuals with the opportunity to experience a regular income while still allowing them a window during which to change their mind. Alternatively, managed drawdown products can provide a regular income while allowing retirees to retain the flexibility to adapt the solution at a later point in time.

Ideally, any default option should be flexible and account for market context or other relevant and available information. For example, individuals should not be defaulted into a product that locks in investment losses from which they would have been likely to recover if delaying the transfer of their savings. Similarly, if individuals do not have a significant level of savings, defaulting them into a lifetime income product is not likely to be appropriate.

The implementation of any default option for the decumulation of retirement savings should also make every reasonable attempt to inform savers of their options and engage them with the decision of how to use their retirement savings to make sure they are aware of the consequences if they fail to take any action or decision.

5.4.7. Promote awareness and education about the payout options that individuals have at retirement

There is a need for communication campaigns that highlight the importance of saving for retirement but also that inform people about the possibility for their savings to be used to provide a regular or lifetime income in retirement. Awareness and understanding of the payout options that individuals have at retirement is often inadequate for them to make informed and appropriate decisions about how to use their savings to finance their retirement. This is true even for people who are already saving for retirement. A minimum level of awareness of options leading up to retirement may help people to better engage with and understand the options presented to them at retirement.

5.4.8. Promote the development and use of digital tools to facilitate individuals' comprehension of and access to different options at retirement

Digital tools can be a powerful means to better engage individuals with their choices at retirement by showing the implications of different options on retirement income in an interactive way. Ideally these tools should include personalised data and simulation options that reflect the individual circumstances of users. Pension dashboards, for example, which provide individuals with an overview of their expected retirement incomes, can be used to better engage individuals with their at-retirement planning (see Chapter 7). However, these centralised digital tools often only show potential or expected outcomes on average, and do not necessarily reflect the actual financial outcomes that individuals will have by selecting a specific provider or product.

Digital tools developed by providers can allow individuals to concretely view how specific product options will affect their expected income in retirement based on the actual assets they have accumulated and the specific product options and pricing available. Another advantage of such tools is that they can potentially facilitate the implementation of an individual's preferred solution, which serves to reduce administrative barriers that can prevent a retiree's access to appropriate solutions in retirement.

5.4.9. Leverage behavioural insights to nudge individuals towards appropriate payout options

Behavioural insights can be used to nudge individuals towards payout options that are appropriate for their situation. Well-designed choice architecture can make it easier for individuals to understand their options and to guide them towards the one that best suits their needs and preferences.

Nevertheless, supervisors should ensure that the use of behavioural insights results in good outcomes for consumers and is not used primarily for commercial gain. Nudges can lead individuals to take the path of least resistance and do not necessarily lead to increased individual engagement with financial decisions at retirement. As such, they should be accompanied with tools such as those discussed above that aim to ensure that individuals are aware of their decisions and the implications of those decisions on their finances for retirement.

5.4.10. Encourage and facilitate the provision and uptake of personalised guidance

Personalised guidance can improve financial outcomes for individuals at retirement by suggesting options that are likely to be suitable for an individual with similar characteristics. Personalised guidance still ensures that the individual is informed of all the options available and can therefore take an informed decision of whether or not to follow the suggestion.

However, in many jurisdictions the line between personalised guidance and personalised advice – the latter of which is subject to more stringent regulatory requirements – is not always clear. In principle, personalised guidance does not take into account individual needs or circumstances, only their general characteristics. Nevertheless, in practice this distinction is not always obvious, which can lead to a reluctance of providers to offer any guidance beyond generic information.

One solution could be to set up a publicly funded entity to provide guidance to people approaching retirement. The Pension Wise service in the United Kingdom is an example of this. This solution ensures the objectivity of the guidance. Nevertheless, a key challenge is ensuring that individuals are aware of the service and will take the additional steps required to access it. Procedures that encourage and facilitate taking an appointment at the time when individuals engage with their pension provider can help to promote take-up.

Other solutions aim to give providers more certainty that they are complying with regulatory requirements in providing personalised guidance. Regulators can issue more detailed guidance and clarifications with examples comparing personalised guidance and advice. They can also provide clear steps that providers would need to take to ensure and prove their compliance with the rules in place.

5.4.11. Monitor and support the development of digital solutions for personalised advice

Digital solutions for the provision of personalised advice for retirement have the potential to improve the accessibility of financial advice by reducing the cost of providing it. While many individuals see value in having personalised financial advice and evaluate the advice as having a positive impact on their finances, cost remains a large barrier for many to access the advice.

Digital solutions for financial advice are only beginning to emerge for advice relating to the decumulation of retirement savings, so need further development. In addition, barriers remain to the take-up of such solutions, as individuals often prefer in-person support and are less willing to trust a technology-based solution. Nevertheless, regulators and supervisors should monitor the developments in this space and encourage the development of robust solutions that have the potential to expand the availability and accessibility of financial advice for retirement. Ensuring that these platforms are subject to rigourous security and privacy standards and are adequately regulated will ultimately help to increase the public's trust in digital solutions.

References

ABI (2023), *Consumer research on personalised guidance*, https://www.abi.org.uk/globalassets/files/publications/public/lts/2023/abi-consumer-research-on-personalised-guidance-report-december-23.pdf. [46]

ABI (2021), *Future proofing the freedoms: Supporting consumer decisions about pension withdrawals*, https://www.abi.org.uk/globalassets/files/publications/public/lts/2021/supporting-customer-decisions-about-pension-withdrawals.pdf. [51]

abrdn (2022), *Class of 2022*, https://www.abrdn.com/library/class-of-2022-report.pdf. [26]

Agarwal, S., J. Pan and W. Qian (2015), "The Composition Effect of Consumption around Retirement: Evidence from Singapore", *American Economic Review*, Vol. 105/5, pp. 426-431, https://doi.org/10.1257/aer.p20151005. [2]

AKG (2023), *Research Paper 2023: Future of Advice - State of Flux*. [57]

Alonso-García, J. et al. (2022), "Saving preferences after retirement", *Journal of Economic Behavior & Organization*, Vol. 198, pp. 409-433, https://doi.org/10.1016/j.jebo.2022.04.005. [19]

Angelini, V., A. Brugiavini and G. Weber (2013), "The dynamics of homeownership among the 50+ in Europe", *Journal of Population Economics*, Vol. 27/3, pp. 797-823, https://doi.org/10.1007/s00148-013-0477-5. [28]

Arapakis, K. and G. Wettstein (2023), *Do financial professionals recommend annuities?*, https://crr.bc.edu/do-financial-professionals-recommend-annuities/. [44]

Arapakis, K. and G. Wettstein (2023), *How much do people value annuities and their added features?*, https://crr.bc.edu/how-much-do-people-value-annuities-and-their-added-features/. [41]

ASFA (2023), *ASFA Retirement Standard*, https://www.superannuation.asn.au/resources/retirement-standard/. [8]

Autoriteit Financiële Markten (2019), *Consultation on principles regarding choice architecture*, https://www.bing.com/ck/a?!&&p=9ba57b913d5585d2JmltdHM9MTcwNzc4MjQwMCZpZ3VpZD0zYjI3ZmE2YS1hYWJhLTYxMTQtMzUzYy1lZTRlYWI1MTYwZjkmaW5zaWQ9NTIwMw&ptn=3&ver=2&hsh=3&fclid=3b27fa6a-aaba-6114-353c-ee4eab5160f9&psq=consultation+of+principles+regarding+choice+arch. [49]

Barrett, M. (2023), *Advice Gap Report*, https://thelangcat.co.uk/report/advice-gap-report-2/. [54]

Bonnet, C., S. Juin and A. Laferrère (2019), "Private Financing of Long Term Care: Income, Savings and Reverse Mortgages", *Economie et Statistique / Economics and Statistics* 507d, pp. 5-24, https://doi.org/10.24187/ecostat.2019.507d.1972. [27]

Brown, J., J. Poterba and D. Richardson (2017), "Do Required Minimum Distribution Rules Matter? The Effect of the 2009 Holiday on Retirement Plan Distributions", *Journal of Public Economics*, Vol. 151, pp. 96-109, https://doi.org/10.1016/j.jpubeco.2016.08.010. [37]

Centro International sobre el Envejecimiento (2021), *II Barómetro del consumidor sénior*, https://cenie.eu/es/ii-barometro-del-consumidor-senior. [38]

Crawford, R., H. Karjalainen and D. Sturrock (2022), *How does spending change through retirement?*. [40]

EBRI (2023), *Retirement Confidence Survey*, https://www.ebri.org/retirement/retirement-confidence-survey. [15]

Elder Index (2023), *The Elder Index [Public Dataset]*, http://ElderIndex.org. [11]

Farghly, F. et al. (2020), *The Stronger Nudge: Evaluation Report*, https://maps.org.uk/en/publications/research/2020/pension-wise-the-stronger-nudge#. [56]

FCA (2024), *Retirement income market data 2022/23*, https://www.fca.org.uk/data/retirement-income-market-data-2022-23. [42]

FCA (2023), *Financial Lives 2022: Key findings from the FCA's Financial Lives May 2022 survey*. [45]

FCA (2023), *Investment Pathways: Post-implementation review*, https://www.fca.org.uk/publications/multi-firm-reviews/investment-pathways-post-implementation-review. [50]

Gao, Y., G. Loewenstein and X. Wang (2022), "The Misery of Spending Down the Nest Egg: The Effect of Annuitization on Consumption and Wellbeing", *SSRN Electronic Journal*, https://doi.org/10.2139/ssrn.4180258. [33]

Greenwald & Associates (2016), *Post-Retirement Experiences of Individuals Retired for 15 Years or More: A Report on Twelve Focus Groups an dFifteen in-depth interviews in the United States and Canada*, https://www.soa.org/globalassets/assets/Files/Research/Projects/research-2015-focus-group-report-final.pdf. [24]

Greenwald & Associates, Inc. (2018), *Post-Retirement Experiences of Individuals 85+ Years Old: A Report on Sixty-two In-Depth Interviews in the United States and Canada*. [25]

Greenwald Research (2022), *Life Journey Study: A Report on an Online Survey of 602 Adult Children of Recently Deceased Parents*, https://www.soa.org/globalassets/assets/files/resources/research-report/2022/life-journey-quantitative.pdf. [23]

Greenwald Research (2021), *2021 Risks and Process of Retirement Survey*, Society of Actuaries Research Institute. [21]

GSAM Insights (2022), *Retirement Survey & Insights Report 2022*, https://www.gsam.com/content/gsam/us/en/institutions/market-insights/gsam-insights/2022/retirement-survey-insights-2022.html#section-none. [31]

HM Treasury, FCA (2023), *Advice Guidance Boundary Review – proposals for closing the advice gap*, https://www.fca.org.uk/publication/discussion/dp23-5.pdf. [43]

Insurance Europe (2023), *2023 Pan-European Pension Survey: Key FIndings*, https://www.insuranceeurope.eu/mediaitem/ce4f9788-85f7-4c2b-8f02-a0d0875421a3/Pension%20priorities%20in%20Europe%202023.pdf. [13]

Kotecha, M. et al. (2020), *Pension Freedoms – a qualitative research study of individuals' decumulation journeys*, https://assets.publishing.service.gov.uk/media/5f9800658fa8f543fb7e6c75/pension-freedoms-research-study.pdf. [55]

Laverdière, D., F. Hallé-Rochon and L. Godbout (2023), *Quand débuter ses prestations publiques de retraite : Les avantages de la flexibilité*, https://cffp.recherche.usherbrooke.ca/wp-content/uploads/2023/09/r2023-06-flexibilite_des_regimes-publics_de_retraite_F.pdf. [17]

Levy, M. (2022), *Quality of Advice Review - Final Report*, https://treasury.gov.au/publication/p2023-358632. [53]

Luengo-Prado, M. and A. Sevilla (2012), "Time to Cook: Expenditure at Retirement in Spain", *The Economic Journal*, Vol. 123/569, pp. 764-789, https://doi.org/10.1111/j.1468-0297.2012.02546.x. [4]

Lührmann, M. (2007), *Consumer Expenditures and Home Production at Retirement - New Evidence from Germany*. [5]

MacDonald, B., D. Andrews and R. Brown (2010), "The Canadian Elder Standard – Pricing the Cost of Basic Needs for the Canadian Elderly", *Canadian Journal on Aging / La Revue canadienne du vieillissement*, Vol. 29/1, pp. 39-56, https://doi.org/10.1017/s0714980809990432. [12]

Matthews, C. (2023), *New Zealand retirement expenditure guidelines*, https://www.massey.ac.nz/documents/1554/new-zealand-retirement-expenditure-guidelines-2023.pdf. [10]

Maurer, R. and O. Mitchell (2017), *Incentivizing older people to delay social security claiming*, https://www.econstor.eu/bitstream/10419/162820/1/893662356.pdf. [18]

MetLife (2022), *2022 Paycheck or Pot of Gold Study*. [34]

Miniaci, R., C. Monfardini and G. Weber (2003), *Is there a retirement consumption puzzle in Italy?*. [6]

Moulton, S. et al. (2021), *Economic Security in Retirement: Does Borrowing from Home Equity After a Health Shock Affect Health Outcomes?*. [30]

Nakajima, M. and I. Telyukova (2013), "Housing in Retirement Across Countries", *SSRN Electronic Journal*, https://doi.org/10.2139/ssrn.2328733. [20]

Nibud (2009), *Handbook of reference budgets*, https://www.nibud.nl/about-nibud/. [9]

OECD (2022), "Policy lessons for the design, introduction and implementation of non-guaranteed lifetime retirement income arrangements", in *OECD Pensions Outlook 2022*, OECD Publishing, Paris, https://doi.org/10.1787/1f1cdca9-en. [59]

OECD (2019), "Non-standard forms of work and pensions", in *Pensions at a Glance 2019: OECD and G20 Indicators*, OECD Publishing, Paris, https://doi.org/10.1787/5ffa7926-en. [16]

OECD (2017), *Robo-Advice for Pensions*, OECD Publishing, Paris, https://doi.org/10.1787/8519321f-en. [58]

OECD (2016), "Policy measures to improve the quality of financial advice for retirement", in *OECD Pensions Outlook 2016*, OECD Publishing, Paris, https://doi.org/10.1787/pens_outlook-2016-6-en. [52]

Olafsson, A. and M. Pagel (2018), *The Retirement-Consumption Puzzle: New Evidence from Personal Finances*, National Bureau of Economic Research, Cambridge, MA, https://doi.org/10.3386/w24405. [1]

Panis, C. (2003), *Annuities and Retirement Satisfaction*, RAND Corporation, https://doi.org/10.7249/dru3021. [32]

PLSA (2024), *Retirement Living Standards*, https://www.retirementlivingstandards.org.uk/. [7]

Poterba, J., S. Venti and D. Wise (2011), "The Composition and Drawdown of Wealth in Retirement", *Journal of Economic Perspectives*, Vol. 25/4, pp. 95-118, https://doi.org/10.1257/jep.25.4.95. [29]

Rajah, M. (2024), *Guided Retirement – investing your way to a flexible and secure retirement*, https://www.pensionsage.com/pa/images/30-31_pafeb2024_aviva.pdf. [47]

Rohwedder, S., M. Hurd and P. Hudomiet (2022), *Explanations for the Decline in Spending at Older ages*, https://www.youtube.com/watch?v=zBoOVbsfUVk. [39]

Scottish Widows (2024), *Decumulation: Understanding the needs of the nation*, https://adviser.scottishwidows.co.uk/assets/literature/docs/61266.pdf. [48]

Siliciano, R. and G. Wettstein (2021), "Can the Drawdown Patterns of Earlier Cohorts Help Predict Boomers' Behavior?", *SSRN Electronic Journal*, https://doi.org/10.2139/ssrn.3936006. [35]

Standard Life (2023), *Retirement Voice 2023*, https://lib.standardlife.com/library/uk/Retirement%20Voice%202023.pdf. [14]

SUPEN (2020), *Usos de los retiros totales del ROP*, https://www.supen.fi.cr/publicaciones-del-sector/-/document_library/77Gpun2U3E7K/view_file/51594?_com_liferay_document_library_web_portlet_DLPortlet_INSTANCE_77Gpun2U3E7K_redirect=https://www.supen.fi.cr/publicaciones-del-sector/-/document_library/77Gpun2. [22]

The Australian Treasury (2020), *Retirement income Review: Final Report*, https://treasury.gov.au/publication/p2020-100554. [36]

Velarde, M. and R. Herrmann (2014), "How retirement changes consumption and household production of food: Lessons from German time-use data", *The Journal of the Economics of Ageing*, Vol. 3, pp. 1-10, https://doi.org/10.1016/j.jeoa.2013.12.003. [3]

Notes

[1] Examples of non-guaranteed lifetime income products are discussed in *Policy lessons for the design, introduction and implementation of non-guaranteed lifetime retirement income arrangements* (OECD, 2022[59]).

[2] Numerous composite products offering a financial solution combining withdrawals and retaining funds to purchase longevity protection exist. Some examples include Nest's Guided Retirement Fund, Aviva's Guided Retirement, and Smart Pension's Smart Retire solution.

[3] The FCA reports that in the fourth quarter of 2023, 30 395 individuals out of 367 592 accessing their pension plan for the first time used their savings to purchase an annuity, or 8.3% (FCA, 2024[42]).

6 Home equity release products for the elderly: opportunities and challenges

Jessica Mosher

This chapter provides an overview of the different types of home equity release products available across OECD countries and describes their features and design. It highlights the potential benefits of these products and discusses the need to ensure that adequate protection is in place for users of the products. It also describes some supply-side barriers for the market and measures that can help to mitigate risks for providers.

The home represents a significant portion of total wealth for many households in retirement. A product that allows homeowners to access and use that equity therefore has the potential to significantly improve retirees' standard of living and their financial outcomes in retirement. Additionally, home equity can be a valuable source to help retirees through significant financial shocks that they otherwise might struggle to overcome (see Chapter 5). Nevertheless, the market for home equity release products remains relatively small or non-existent in most OECD countries.

Expanding the availability of home equity release products requires ensuring that the regulatory framework includes adequate protections. There are a number of potential risks to homeowners relating to the design and use of these products. Additionally, several barriers and risks on the supply side remain to be addressed in order for providers to be willing to participate in the market.

This chapter aims to understand the home equity release products for the elderly available across the OECD and the benefits and risks they can pose for both homeowners and providers.[1] The first section provides a general overview of the different types of products. The second section highlights standards that industry groups have developed. The third section compares product features and discusses the implications for homeowners. The fourth section considers supply-side barriers and risks to providers. The fifth section discusses how these products are used to improve financial outcomes in retirement. The final section concludes with a discussion around the implications for the regulatory framework around these products. Annex 6.A summarises the details of products available in the countries covered.

6.1. Overview of home equity release products

Home equity release products have the potential to improve both standards of living in retirement as well as overall well-being for a broad group of retired homeowners. First, they give individuals access to their home equity, which often represents a substantial proportion of their wealth in retirement. Second, they allow individuals to stay in their homes until they die or have to move to a long-term care facility. Finally, they are normally more accessible than traditional home credit products because borrowers are not necessarily required to pass income and credit checks.

Home equity release products are largely based on two models, a loan-type model and a sale-type model. The loan-type is often referred to as a reverse mortgage, which is a loan backed by the home as collateral. There are two types of products that involve a full or partial sale of the home equity. One is a home reversion, which involves selling all or part of the home equity to another party while retaining the right to reside in the home. The other is a sell and rent back scheme, whereby the home is sold to a third party and rented back to retain occupancy.

Several jurisdictions have government-backed programmes that provide home equity release products. However, these programmes do not normally exclude private providers from also offering the products in the market. This discussion encompasses both types of providers.[2]

6.1.1. Reverse mortgage

A reverse mortgage is a lifetime loan using the home as collateral. Borrowers can obtain a percentage of their home value, either upfront as a lump-sum or through periodic payments or withdrawals. Interest accrues on the loaned amount, and the accumulated debt must be paid off when the borrower dies or leaves their home to move to a long-term care facility, usually via the proceeds from the sale of the home.

The main advantage of these products is that borrowers retain ownership of their home and will still be able to pass on the home equity in excess of the debt to their beneficiaries when they die. Additionally, most products do not require any interest or principal payments until the borrower moves out, so the borrower can make full use of the funds loaned to them until the home is sold. The main disadvantage is that their debt continues to accumulate over this period, and can rapidly reduce the excess equity value of the home.

The United Kingdom and the United States are the largest markets globally for reverse mortgages, followed by Australia and Canada. These products exist in some form in nearly all the jurisdictions covered in this chapter.

6.1.2. Home reversion

A home reversion is when the homeowner sells a portion or all of their home equity to a third party in exchange for a lump sum or periodic payments. The home must be sold when the owner moves out of the home or dies, and the third party receives their owned portion of the proceeds.

Unlike with a reverse mortgage, the homeowner does not retain full ownership of the home with a home reversion, though they can still retain a portion of it that can be passed to their heirs. The home equity is normally sold at a discount. However, as this is not a loan, no interest accrues and the homeowner is normally able to obtain a larger sum than they would have with a reverse mortgage.

Home reversions are more prevalent than reverse mortgages in France, Germany, Italy, and Poland (EY, 2020[1]). However, in France and Italy, the contracts tend to be between individuals rather than with a financial institution as the counterparty.

6.1.3. Sell and rent back scheme

A sell and rent back scheme involves the sale of a home, while retaining rights to reside in the home by paying regular fees to the new owner as long as the previous owner continues to occupy the home. The home is normally sold below market value and ownership fully or partially transferred, and there are also models that involve a gradual transfer of ownership.

These types of schemes exist notably in Australia, the Netherlands and the United Kingdom.

6.2. Industry standards

Home equity release products suffer from a bad reputation as people perceive them as products that take advantage of the elderly. This is due to past experience with mis-selling, high costs and the potential to lose one's home (Mayer and Moulton, 2020[2]). This has contributed to a lack of demand for these products, as homeowners do not trust providers, and financial advisors are reluctant to recommend the products for fear of liability.

Industry-formed groups have established standards of good practice for product design to improve their reputation and ensure adequate protection. In the United Kingdom, the Home Equity Council requires that its members offer products that (Equity Release Council, 2024[3]):

- have a cap on the interest rate if variable
- ensure the right of lifetime residency
- allow for the transfer to a comparable property
- include a no negative equity guarantee that the borrower will not owe more than the value of their home equity
- allow for penalty-free repayments.

The European Pensions and Property Asset Release Group has produced similar standards. These include additional points on the competence of intermediaries and the content of product disclosures, as well as consumer protections in the case of early death or insolvency of the provider (EPPARG, 2024[4]).

6.3. Product features and implications for homeowners

Product features and the extent to which regulation imposes requirements for home equity release products vary across jurisdictions. These features include eligibility conditions to access the product, the calculation of the payout received, the calculation of debt owed, contractual rights and obligations, and how to ensure suitability. Many of the rules relating to each of these aspects have implications as to the risks that homeowners may face with these products.

These features are normally more complex and relevant for reverse mortgage products. As such, much of the discussion here will focus on reverse mortgages. However, where applicable, the discussion will also include features of the sale-type products.

6.3.1. Eligibility requirements for reverse mortgages

One advantage of home equity release products for retirees is that the eligibility requirements are generally easier to meet, because these products do not generally require income checks or credit assessments. However, there are certain criteria that individuals must meet. These include minimum age requirements, the property value or type and the individual's relationship to it, and the outstanding mortgage remaining to be repaid. Some jurisdictions also have specific products targeted for a particular use, which may involve additional eligibility requirements.

Minimum age limits are the most common feature of reverse mortgage products, and the regulatory framework often establishes them. The youngest age allowed where limits are formally imposed is 55. This is the case in Canada, Ireland, Korea, and the United Kingdom. A minimum age of 60 is the most common, as in Australia, France, Italy, Japan, Norway and Sweden. The United States requires borrowers in its Home Equity Conversion Mortgage (HECM) programme to be at least 62, and the minimum age in Australia's Home Equity Access Scheme (HEAS) is linked to the minimum age for the public pension. Spain requires that borrowers be 65, though Spain is unique in allowing an exception to the minimum age requirement where borrowers demonstrate 33% disability or dependency. Several jurisdictions have no formal minimum age requirements, including Germany, the Netherlands, New Zealand, Poland, and Sweden, where each provider sets the minimum age for their product.

It is more common that the regulatory framework defines a minimum age for reverse mortgages than for other types of home equity release products. For reverse mortgages, debt can accumulate rapidly over time, and younger borrowers would end up paying a large proportion of their property value in interest. Additionally, younger people are more likely to have access to more flexible and cheaper borrowing options (Financial Conduct Authority, 2020[5]). Indeed, reverse mortgage products can be rather inflexible, and younger borrowers are more likely to experience an unforeseen change in circumstances that require them to repay the loan early, which can be costly.

Reverse mortgage products use the home as collateral, therefore they often require that the mortgage is largely paid off or that the home is owned outright with any mortgage fully paid off. The Housing Pension Programme in Korea (JooTaekYeonKeum, JTYK) requires that the mortgage be fully paid off to qualify for the reverse mortgage. There may also be indirect requirements to own the home outright, through requirements to use the borrowed funds to pay off debt. Reverse mortgage products in Canada generally require that the loan proceeds are used to pay off any outstanding debt and to close any open Home Equity Line of Credit (HELOC). Home reversion in the United Kingdom requires sellers to pay off all debts as well.

There may also be restrictions around the type of property eligible for collateral behind a reverse mortgage. For the US HECM programme, borrowers must occupy the property as a principal residence. In France, the real estate must be used for housing, but residing in the home is not required, and the owner can even rent out the property with the agreement of the lender. The HEAS in Australia allows for the use of any real estate owned in Australia. In Japan, most private lenders often do not allow condominiums to be used as collateral, or impose limits on location and other conditions. In the case of single-family homes, the collateral often only counts the land on which the property sits and excludes the value of the home, resulting in lower possible amounts borrowed (Kojima, 2013[6]).

The eligibility assessment may consider the value of the property. It is common to require a minimum property value, which can also be imposed indirectly through minimum limits on the loan, as is common practice in Sweden. This can exclude lower wealth households from being eligible. The JTYK in Korea actually imposes a cap on the total value of all properties owned. If this exceeds the required threshold, owners have three years to sell the properties in excess of the threshold. This requirement is logical, as selling a property in which you do not reside is a more efficient and cost-effective way to release equity from a property compared to a reverse mortgage.

Borrowers may also be subject to other requirements. Access to the HEAS in Australia imposes residency requirements of ten years of which at least five must be consecutive. While most schemes do not impose income or credit requirements, this scheme also imposes certain asset and income tests related to the means-testing of the first pillar pension. The HECM programme in the United States has required a financial assessment of borrowers since 2015 to ensure that they will be able to cover insurance and taxes owed on the property and for upkeep of the home, which is a requirement to maintain the loan. This was in response to many borrowers maxing out the value of the loan then having to foreclose because they did not set aside funds to cover these costs.

Some jurisdictions have defined specific reverse mortgage products that require a particular use of the funds, which can help individuals with specific financial needs in retirement. In Australia, the Aged Care Loan is a reverse mortgage that aims to aid borrowers to pay for long-term care costs without immediately having to sell their home. The loan is for a maximum term of five years and provides flexibility to seniors who require care to have more time to sort out their finances. Japan also has a reverse mortgage targeted to cover long-term care expenses since 2007. The loan can serve as a mechanism to reduce the assets of the individual and allow them to become eligible for public assistance. France introduced a loan in 2022 targeting low-income households who require home renovations relating to energy use. Local and non-profit agencies in the United States offer single-purpose reverse mortgages at lower rates that must be put toward an approved use. Such targeted programmes can provide an additional source of financing for individuals having specific financial needs in retirement.

6.3.2. Calculation of benefits

The amount of home equity that homeowners can release with home equity release products is typically a function of their age and property value. The product agreement should also define the timing and size of the benefit payments to be made.

Reverse mortgages

The maximum amount that homeowners can borrow with a reverse mortgage is commonly expressed as a loan-to-value (LTV) ratio, so as a maximum percentage of the value of the home. The percentage allowed generally increases with age. This is to mitigate the risk that the outstanding balance of the loan will eventually exceed the property value, meaning that the sale of the home would not generate sufficient funds to fully pay off the loan. Indeed, the United States introduced borrowing limits in 2014 following the financial crisis when property values fell, often below outstanding loan values.

Maximum LTVs vary across countries, but are generally between around 15% for younger borrowers and 50% for older ones. LTVs are usually quite low for younger ages. One product in Sweden and the Spry product in Ireland offer 15% at age 60, and in Australia the maximum LTV for someone aged 65 is around 20-25%. These percentages increase with age up to a maximum of around 50%. Canada imposes a maximum LTV of 55%, which is also the maximum LTV for the only product offered in the Netherlands.

One product in Sweden increases the allowed LTV up to 45% at age 90, while Norway caps the LTV at 49% at age 80. The Spry product in Ireland has a relatively low maximum LTV, at 40% for ages 85 and over.

In addition to age and current property value, other factors can influence the LTV ratio. In Norway, the LTV will depend not only on the current value of the property, but will also consider the housing market and expectations regarding its future appreciation. The sum will also be reduced if the debt is held jointly in a housing cooperative. In the United States, HECM limits also vary by area. The United Kingdom is unique in offering underwritten reverse mortgages, which offer higher LTVs for those in worse health and/or with lower life expectancies. In Australia, maximum loan amounts in the Home Equity Access Scheme are related to the public means-tested pension benefit to which an individual is entitled (age pension). The sum of the public pension and loan payments must be below 1.5 times the maximum rate for the public pension. In Germany, providers can deduct expected maintenance costs from the total amount.

Some reverse mortgage products allow younger borrowers to increase their loan amount at a later stage. In Australia, HEAS borrowers can request an increase in the LTV that corresponds to their age, to the extent that the accumulated outstanding loan amount remains lower than the allowed amount. In Sweden, one product allows borrowers to increase their borrowing limit if their home equity goes up by a minimum amount, for an additional fee.

Several reverse mortgage products also impose absolute minimum and maximum loan amounts. In Canada and the Netherlands, the minimum loan is CAD 20 000 and EUR 30 000, while the maximum amount is CAD 750 000 and EUR 250 000.

Home equity release products can structure payments in a variety of ways. There are generally four ways to pay out the borrowed amounts from a reverse mortgage to the borrowers. The first is a lump sum, where borrowers receive the maximum loan amount all at once. Depending on what the borrowed funds are used for, lump sum payments can be disadvantageous for the borrower because they will owe interest on the entire amount from inception. If they intend to use the funds gradually to finance expenses over retirement rather than, say, pay off debt or finance home improvements, they will end up paying interest on the money that is sitting in their bank. The second option is to pay a fixed annuity, whereby the maximum loaned amount is dispersed over a fixed number of years. This will provide the borrower a regular income and lower the total interest owed, but it will not provide an income for life so they will see their finances decrease after the fixed term ends. The third option is a line of credit, where the borrower can withdraw money against the maximum loan amount as they need it. This minimises the interest paid, because the borrower will not owe interest on funds they have not used. The flexibility, however, may come at an increased cost (i.e. higher interest rates) as the lender will have more uncertainty around the expected cash flows and projected accumulated loan. Finally, the products can pay a life annuity, whereby the lender pays a regular fixed amount until the borrower dies. This is most useful to provide a regular income in retirement and protect the borrower from longevity risk, but again may come at a cost as it also increases the risk exposure to the provider. Table 1.3 summarises the options available.

Table 6.1 Payouts possible from equity release products

Country	Reverse mortgage				Home reversion			Sell and rent back	
	Lump sum	Fixed annuity	Line of credit	Life annuity	Lump sum	Fixed annuity	Life annuity	Lump sum	Fixed annuity
Australia	x	x	x		x			x	x
Canada	x	x	x						
France					x		x		
Germany	x	x			x				
Hungary					x		x		
Ireland	x				x				
Italy	x	x			x		x		
Japan	x	x	x						
Korea	x	x		x					
Netherlands	x	x						x	
New Zealand	x	x				x			
Norway	x	x							
Poland	x	x							
Spain	x	x		x	x		x	x	
Sweden	x								
United Kingdom	x	x	x		x			x	
United States	x	x	x	x					

All reverse mortgage products allow borrowers to take their funds as a lump sum, in full or in part. Some products impose limits on the amount of lump sum. In Australia, the HEAS allows a maximum lump sum of 50% of the public pension benefit over one year. The JTYK in Korea allows a lump sum of up to 50% of the total amount borrowed. Other products impose a minimum lump sum at inception. In the Netherlands, borrowers must take a minimum lump sum of EUR 4 500. In New Zealand, they must take a minimum of NZD 5 000. Lump sums are the only option in Ireland and Sweden.

Fixed annuity payments of borrowed funds are quite common. This is an option for the HECM in the United States, which can be taken only as a fixed annuity or combined with a line of credit. Private products in Japan can also be taken as a fixed annuity or line of credit. In New Zealand, funds can be paid out over ten years. In Korea, borrowers can opt for fixed terms of 10 to 30 years for the Housing Pension. One product in Germany, which is no longer on the market, offered the option of paying a fixed annuity up to the average life expectancy. In Australia's HEAS, regular payments are paid until the maximum loan amount is exhausted. If the borrower opts for a lump sum, their payments are reduced accordingly over the next year. In the Netherlands, the Florius product requires borrowers to set their borrowing duration at inception, over which regular amounts will be paid. Previously, they required that the borrowed amounts be fixed, but they now allow borrowers to make adjustments to the amounts.

Lines of credit are less common, potentially because of the additional uncertainty around the total loan amount and the timing of cash flows.[3] Lines of credit are available in Canada, Japan, the United Kingdom, the United States – where it can be combined with an annuity – and from private providers in Australia, though not through the HEAS programme. There can be minimum limits on the size of each transaction in a line of credit arrangement, as is the case for private providers in Australia.

Life annuities are not commonly offered. This is an option only in Korea, Spain, and the United States. In Spain, borrowers with outstanding mortgages have two options. The first is to receive a capital sum from the lender, and when they eventually manage to pay off their mortgage the lender will pay them a small dividend payment for life. Alternatively, dividend payments can begin immediately and go towards paying off the outstanding mortgage. When it is paid off, the dividends will then be paid to the borrower for life

(Alegria Real Estate, 2021[7]). In Korea, the government acts as the lender, thereby bearing the underlying longevity risk of the transaction.

Home reversions

The standard home reversion product pays the full or partial purchase price of the home as a lump sum. However, some products may distribute the purchase price over time via a fixed term or life annuity. The product offered by Lifetime in New Zealand pays an income over ten years, with an option to extend for another ten years if the seller is under age 90, thereby gradually transferring the home equity to the product provider over time. An alternative model is common in France and Italy, where two individuals enter into a home reversion transaction. With this model, the owner fully sells their home to the buying individual, either via a lump sum or a combination of a lump-sum payment and a lifetime annuity payment, while retaining the right to reside in the home for life.

Sale and rent back schemes

The payments from sell and rent back schemes come in a variety of designs. In Australia, proceeds from the partial sale of the home can be paid out as a lump sum or in instalments. The seller then pays 'rental' fees to the buyer as a percentage of the buyer's equity in the home, which serve to transfer that additional equity to the buyer. As such, the transfer of equity accelerates over time as the payments by the seller increase. In the Netherlands, the Verzilvermijvast product pays 50% of the home value as a lump sum to the seller. The seller then pays 6% of the house value annually. When the seller moves out or dies, Verzilvermijvast makes a final payment of 50% of the difference in the home value. As such, Verzilvermijvast shares the profits and losses from the variation in the home's value with the seller.

Home reversions and sell-and-rent-back schemes can provide rebates in the case that the seller dies or sells their property early, though they are not normally required. Lifetime's home reversion product in New Zealand will reduce the acquired equity accordingly if the home is sold before the ten-year fixed annuity is fully paid out. In both Australia and the United Kingdom, products can provide a rebate to heirs if the seller dies earlier than expected. In Germany, providers may pay a lump sum or a fixed term annuity to compensate for the unused right of residence (Joosten, 2015[8]).

6.3.3. Calculation of debt for reverse mortgages

The calculation of the outstanding debt for a reverse mortgage product depends not only on the amount borrowed and the timing of those payments, but also on the interest rates and any early repayments the borrower makes. Some products may offer equity guarantees to cap the amount of debt that can accumulate.

Interest rates can be fixed or variable. Fixed rates are set at the inception of the contract, and remain constant for the life of the product. This limits the risk to homeowners of increasing the amount of their accumulated debt beyond expectations. Products offered in France, Germany, Italy, the Netherlands, Spain, and the United Kingdom have fixed interest rates. The majority of products in Canada also offer fixed rates. Germany is unique in that providers are not allowed to charge compound interest, so interest is only charged on the initial principal value. This limits the debt that homeowners accumulate over time compared to products that charge compound interest. Variable rates depend on prevailing market conditions. Good practice laid out in the standards set by industry bodies indicate that providers should offer a cap on the interest rate to protect the homeowner from very high interest rate charges that could more quickly erode their remaining equity value. Products offered in Korea, New Zealand, Norway, Poland, and Sweden have variable interest rates, and the majority of products in Australia, Ireland and the United States are variable as well. HECM products in the United States only offer fixed rates for products taken as a lump sum, and variable rates for payments made over time.

Interest rates for reverse mortgages are normally materially higher than rates offered for traditional mortgages. This is to compensate the provider from the additional uncertainty around when they will get their money back and from the risk that the home value will fall below the outstanding loan balance, often referred to as crossover risk. In exchange, however, the homeowner is not normally required to make any repayments on the loan, and reserves the right to reside in the house until death or when they move to a care facility.

Most providers allow borrowers to make early repayments on the loan, albeit often with some fee attached to compensate for the loss of interest accrued. HEAS loans in Australia allow repayments anytime, but private providers often require that the maximum agreed loan be paid out before any voluntary payments can be made. In France, early repayments are subject to a cap on the fees charged.

Some products may require borrowers to make interest payments. This is common, notably in Japan. One product that is no longer offered in Germany presented a unique, though complex, structure requiring repayments to mitigate crossover risk. The loan amount was divided into three parts. The first part was paid to the borrower. The second part was set aside to pay borrowers an income once they had reached their borrowing limit. The third part was used to pay down interest and finance mortgage insurance (Bartsh et al., 2021[9]).

It is common good practice for products to offer no negative equity guarantees (NNEGs). These limit the borrower's liability to the value of their property, effectively meaning that the loan is a non-recourse loan.[4] NNEGs are required in Australia, Canada, France, Italy, Korea, and Norway. In the United States, the government provides this guarantee for HECM loans by purchasing the loan from providers once the balance exceeds 98% of the maximum claim amount (Baily, Harris and Wang, 2019[10]). In the United Kingdom, members of the Equity Release Council are required to provide NNEGs, even though it is not legally required by the state. In Poland, reverse mortgages are also non-recourse even if they do not technically offer an NNEG. After the borrower's death, the home is transferred to the lender to sell, who is then required to reimburse the heirs the excess of the sale proceeds over the outstanding loan balance. In the other jurisdictions the NNEG is available for some products, though not mandated, except in Germany where providers do not currently offer it and in Spain where it is not available.

While the provider normally guarantees a non-recourse NNEG itself, a few jurisdictions differ. In the Netherlands, the only product available offered by Florius provides a conditional NNEG. The guarantee holds only when the house is sold at full market value. In the case that the house must be sold for less, the heirs will still owe the difference between the market value and the selling price. In the United Kingdom, the Equity Release Council provides the NNEG insurance, which the providers finance directly. In the United States, it is the homeowner who explicitly bears the cost of the insurance for a HECM loan, which is 2% up front and 0.5% annually. The insurance is provided by the government and ensures that the borrower will receive their funds if the lender is unable to make payments. Similarly in Korea, borrowers of JTYK loans must pay a premium to the government for the NNEG. In Japan, the Reverse60 programme provides homeowners with the option to have a non-recourse loan, in which case they must pay a higher premium and the risk is insured by the government. Private providers in Japan rarely offer a NNEG.

The no negative equity guarantee is an important feature from a consumer protection standpoint, as the combination of compound interest and the risk of declines in the housing market mean that the crossover risk is material. The risk that the home value falls below the outstanding loan balance could leave beneficiaries with significant debt to repay even after the sale of the home used as collateral. Indeed, several jurisdictions, including Australia and the United States, mandated NNEGs following the collapse of the housing market during the financial crisis, which led to numerous cases of debt exceeding home values. Following the mandate, Australia noted conservative loan values offered to homeowners (ASIC, 2018[11]).

The NNEG limits the loss of equity to the value of the home, but some providers also offer an equity guarantee to ensure that the borrower will retain a certain percentage of equity in their home. This can be a valuable feature, particularly where individuals may rely on their home equity to finance the costs of long-term care. The Australian Securities and Investments Commission estimated that 63% of reverse mortgage borrowers in Australia were at risk of not having enough equity remaining in their home by age 84 to pay for aged care (ASIC, 2018[11]). Equity guarantees are available in Australia, the Netherlands, and New Zealand.

6.3.4. Contractual rights and obligations

The contractual terms of the product must lay out the various rights and obligations of the homeowner and the conditions to terminate the product. These include the costs and fees that the homeowner must cover, their right to exit the contract, the obligations to maintain the property, rights for lifetime residency and tenancy protections, the ability to transfer the contract to a new property, the delay allowed to transfer owed funds to the provider, and insolvency protection for the homeowner.

Although equity release products normally do not require ongoing payments, there are normally upfront costs that the homeowner must bear. However, the transaction itself can incorporate some of these costs by adding them to the loan value or reducing the benefit transferred, so homeowners do not necessarily feel the full initial costs of the product. Homeowners are normally obliged to cover all costs relating to the establishment of the contract. This often includes an initiation fee, an ongoing servicing fee, and any third-party charges such as the valuation of the property, inspections, and the like. The United Kingdom requires reverse mortgage borrowers to engage an independent solicitor to complete all the legal work, and in France, they are required to consult with a notary. Some jurisdictions may have restrictions in place to limit the level of fees that providers charge, as is the case for HECM loans in the United States for the origination fee and servicing fees. Origination fees are capped at USD 6 000.

Several countries require that providers give homeowners time to change their mind about signing the contract. Such cooling-off periods are normally around 30 days, and are required in Canada, France, and Poland.

Conditions of the contract normally require homeowners to meet all tax obligations, insurance premiums (e.g. fire, flood), and ensure the normal maintenance of the home. These requirements help to prevent avoidable depreciation of the property value, which would present an increased risk to the provider of not receiving their expected funds. Not fulfilling these obligations can be grounds for early termination of the contract and the forced sale of the home. A few countries have specific measures in place to enforce this upkeep. To apply for a HECM loan in the United States, borrowers must demonstrate that they have sufficient funds to cover the expected costs. In Germany, funds can be put aside for this purpose. In Sweden, homeowners must allow for regular inspections to ensure the upkeep and maintenance of the home. Apart from failing to upkeep the home, other reasons for early termination of a reverse mortgage contract in Canada include using the money for something illegal or lying on the application. In Poland, any decline in property value that is the fault of the resident can trigger the termination and early repayment of the loan. In Japan, some private providers require repayment if the value of the property falls below the outstanding loan amount, even if this is a result of market fluctuations outside of the homeowner's control. This last example clearly presents a serious risk for borrowers of being kicked out of their homes. Australia introduced a measure to protect homeowners in breach of contract that requires providers to speak directly with the borrower and provide them with a notice period before enforcement proceedings to obtain the loan repayment.

The ability to continue to reside in one's home for life is one of the big draws of equity release products for the elderly, and indeed standard practice is to provide a lifetime residency guarantee. However, this is not always the case. In New Zealand, there is no requirement for reverse mortgage providers to offer such a guarantee. In the United Kingdom, only the members of the Equity Release Council are bound by its standards, which include that providers ensure the right of lifetime residency. Sell and rent back schemes in the United Kingdom do not provide a right to lifetime residency, and in Australia schemes that gradually transfer the equity to the provider may not necessarily allow residents to stay in the home if their retained equity falls to 0%.

While the homeowner taking out the equity release product normally has the right to lifetime residency, this is not necessarily the case for spouses or other residents of the home. Typically, the people who are on the title of the home will be included in the right to lifetime residency. However, if only one spouse is on the title, the other spouse will not automatically be covered, and in most jurisdictions, there is no obligation for any tenancy protection for other residents in the home. This presents a large risk that surviving spouses could get kicked out of their home when the spouse holding the contract dies. To compound this risk, minimum age requirements usually apply to the youngest age on the contract, so someone with a younger spouse may not even be eligible to apply. In the past, this has occasionally led to the poor advice to remove the younger spouse from the title to be eligible to obtain the product. To address this risk, Australia requires that providers of reverse mortgages that do not include tenancy protections provide a warning to homeowners about the potential consequences, but they also found that this warning was not necessarily effective. Private providers in Japan tend to use trusts, which allows surviving spouses to stay in the home and continue to make use of the reverse mortgage. Since 2014, HECM loans in the United States have provisions in place to cover eligible non-borrowing spouses.

Usually, the contract terminates when the homeowner dies, moves to a care facility, or sells the home. At this point, any outstanding loan must be paid off, or the proceeds from the sale of the home to which the provider is entitled transferred. However, some jurisdictions allow individuals to transfer their reverse mortgages to their new property when they sell their home, providing that it meets the same requirements that the original home met, including the property value. This is possible in Canada, Ireland, and the United Kingdom.

Normally, providers allow for a certain period of time following the exit of the property to sell the property (and/or repay the loan). This is usually around 12 months. However, the grace period may differ depending on the cause of the exit. In Canada, the delay allowed may be longer in the event that the resident moves to a long-term care facility.

A final reason for the termination of a contract can be the insolvency of the provider. Most jurisdictions do not have protections in place to make homeowners whole in the event of a default. Where this does exist, the government acts as the guarantor. This is the case for HECM loans in the United States and the JTYK in Korea.

6.3.5. Ensuring suitability

Many jurisdictions have established measures to help to ensure that adequate protections are in place and that the product is suitable for the individual taking them.[5] Equity release products are very long-term and complex products which can provide a sizable payment to homeowners, with comparatively little direct cost for them or ongoing payment obligations. It can therefore be difficult for homeowners to fully understand the potential consequences that the product could have for them twenty or thirty years in the future, and for them to assess the potential risks.

Disclosure is one approach to promote understanding, though alone it is generally not sufficient. Australia requires reverse mortgage providers to disclose home equity projections using the government's MoneySmart calculator and a warning of the risks if the product does not offer tenancy protection. The United States requires fee disclosures.

Legislation may also require providers to take steps to assess whether the product may be suitable for the borrower. The enhanced responsible lending obligations introduced in Australia include a requirement for the provider to assess the future needs of the borrower, not only their current situation, to make sure they are aware of the long-term consequences that the product could have on their financial situation. Providers are also subject to maximum LTV limits for the product to be considered as suitable. Since 2015, lenders for the HECM programme in the United States must make a financial assessment of borrowers to ensure they will be able to meet ongoing costs relating to the care and upkeep of their property. The United Kingdom requires providers to take 'reasonable steps' to ensure that the product is suitable. However, the Financial Conduct Authority found that this assessment is often treated as a box-ticking exercise (Financial Conduct Authority, 2020[5]).

A particular concern with these products that target elderly individuals is that they are at higher risk of having cognitive decline and may not be capable of fully understanding the product and its implications. To mitigate this risk, the United Kingdom requires that an independent solicitor certify that the person making the decision to take the product is competent to do so. Providers in France face marketing restrictions, and are prohibited from using certain tactics such as door-to-door sales that the elderly could be vulnerable to. The higher potential for cognitive decline also raises the risk of elder abuse, where relatives or other people close to the individual may convince them to enter an equity release agreement in order to take advantage of the financial gains they will subsequently receive. ASIC found that providers in Australia were not doing enough to watch for signs of elder abuse. These signs include repayments being made by an adult child, money transfers to a non-borrower, money transferred to a child, the involvement of children in the application process, non-borrowers affirming that they received the required financial advice, or any file notes indicating abuse by a sibling. Nevertheless, providers often have indirect safeguards in place, including limiting the power of attorney where non-borrowers may benefit, and only disbursing money into the borrower's account (ASIC, 2018[11]).

Some jurisdictions go further in ensuring suitability and require that potential borrowers of reverse mortgages to obtain counselling or financial advice. Independent financial advice is required in Canada (in some provinces), New Zealand, Spain and the United Kingdom. While not required, some providers in Australia and the only provider in the Netherlands require financial advice. Japan and the United States take a lighter touch, requiring a meeting with a counsellor to explain considerations around eligibility and suitability, and other options that may be available to the individual. Such information sessions do not provide advice, rather they aim to ensure the homeowner is sufficiently informed. A requirement to obtain financial advice may not always be sufficient, however, to ensure the suitability of a product. The FCA found that advisors in the UK receiving a request for the required advice from an individual wanting the product did not sufficiently challenge the individual regarding whether the product was suitable for them (Financial Conduct Authority, 2020[5]). In Australia, advisers have been reluctant to provide guidance about equity release products for fear of liability, given the prevailing negative perceptions around the products (ASIC, 2018[11]).

An important consideration in assessing suitability is the potential impact to means-tested benefits and taxes owed that the payout from these products could have. Equity release payouts can affect an individual's eligibility for means-tested benefits in Australia, Sweden, and the United Kingdom because the means-test considers home equity differently from liquid assets. ASIC found that providers in Australia were not providing sufficient warnings to individuals about the potential impact on their public pension benefits (ASIC, 2018[11]). Taxes owed are another consideration. While payouts from reverse mortgages are not normally taxable as they are treated as loans, home reversions can incur additional capital gains tax. However, some jurisdictions do provide tax benefits for equity release products. Korea provides a tax credit for reverse mortgages that reduces the borrower's property tax by 25%. Italy provides exemptions from stamp duty and property tax. In Ireland, Spain, and the United Kingdom, home reversion payouts are exempt from tax. In the United Kingdom, reverse mortgages can reduce inheritances taxes owed when the individual dies, as this tax considers wealth net of debt.

6.4. Supply side barriers and risks

There are many barriers for providers to enter and stay in the equity release market. As a result, markets tend to be very small and concentrated in most jurisdictions. Some of these barriers include capital requirements, as well as the various risk exposures from these products including property prices, interest rates, longevity, and reputational risk. Several jurisdictions have introduced government-backed programmes to address these supply-side barriers.

In many jurisdictions, the equity release market remains very small and concentrated among a few providers. In Australia, two competitors wrote 80% of the market during 2013-2017 (ASIC, 2018[11]). Similarly, two providers dominate the New Zealand market. and there is only one product available in the Netherlands, offered by Florius Verzilverhypotheek. In Germany, there were only 200 reverse mortgages outstanding in 2015 (Bartsh et al., 2021[9]). HomeEquity Bank was the sole seller of reverse mortgages in Canada until recently.

One reason for the small number of providers is the high barriers to entry that companies face, particularly with respect to the required capital. Starting in the business requires a very large amount of upfront capital, which the provider will not normally receive back until decades later. Lenders can have difficulty to access wholesale funding. Indeed, the availability of funding has been the largest challenge for providers in the equity release market (EY, 2020[1]). This has also led existing providers to terminate their business. For example, Seniors Money in Ireland could no longer raise funds during the financial crisis, and had to stop writing new business. Another barrier relating to capital is that such products require more Tier 1 capital, which can be a disincentive for providers to enter the market (ASIC, 2018[11]). Where the provider is subject to risk-based capital regimes, requirements to protect them against such long-term risks can be expensive.

Providers entering the market also have numerous risks they need to manage and mitigate, one of the most significant being the uncertainty in property prices. For sale-type products, a drop in home values will reduce their profits once they are able to sell the home. For reverse mortgages, a drop in home values increases the risk of crossover, where the accumulated loan value could exceed the proceeds obtained from selling the home. For products with a no negative equity guarantee, this would result in a loss for the providers or for the institution or entity insuring the guarantee. Indeed, several providers stopped business following the financial crisis when property values dropped. There were 20 lenders in Australia before the crisis, and now there are only 3 (Knaack, Miller and Stewart, 2020[12]). The market in Ireland significantly shrunk after the crisis as well, and completely dried up in Hungary. In the United States, many reverse mortgage loans triggered the no negative equity guarantee during the crisis, and the Department of Housing and Urban Development, who insures the programme, had to raise premiums and reduce borrowing limits as the HECM programme was running on a loss.[6] While widespread shocks to the housing market are difficult to mitigate, providers generally address normal risk levels through eligibility requirements and due diligence on the housing type, its construction, as well as its location.

Providers also face moral hazard with respect to homeowners' willingness to ensure the maintenance of their home value. The elderly may be less engaged in the maintenance and upkeep of their homes, particularly when they will have no financial gain from doing so. Reverse mortgage providers usually include provisions requiring that the occupant of the home maintain its upkeep as a condition for keeping the loan, which mitigates this risk. Where a no negative equity guarantee is offered, providers need to also mitigate the moral hazard that the heirs will sell the home at a discounted rate, for example to a relative, which would result in losses to the provider. The Netherlands mitigates this risk by requiring that the home be sold at market value for the no negative equity guarantee to apply. However, this puts additional risk on the heirs, who may not be able to sell at market value within the window in which the lender requires repayment.

Interest rate risk is also a factor reverse mortgage providers need to mitigate. Providers face a contradictory problem with respect to setting the interest rate for their products. On one hand, higher rates increase the crossover risk that the accumulated debt will exceed the value of the home. On the other hand, higher interest rates also compensate providers from bearing this risk, so they need to balance these two considerations. More recently, low interest rates have also reduced profitability of writing these products. Providers can also face basis risk between the mortgage rate and their financing rate, particularly when one rate is variable and the other fixed. This risk can be mitigated with interest rate swaps, however.

Providers of home equity products face significant uncertainty regarding future cashflows because equity release products are for the lifetime. As such, providers cannot be sure as to when the home will be sold and they will recoup their investment. Lifetime annuities as a form of payment increase the longevity risk that providers face, because not only will they risk waiting longer than expected to receive repayment, but they would also have to make payment for a longer period of time. As a result, very few providers offer lifetime annuities as a form of payment.

Licensing requirements for providers to be able to offer equity release products may also explain the lack of lifetime annuity options as a form of payment. These products are typically offered by banks or credit agencies, whereas often only insurance companies are licensed to provide lifetime annuity payments. As such, either the provider would have to be an insurance company or partner with an insurance company.

Finally, providers entering the market need to be very careful about managing reputational risk and how they communicate about these products. Given the past issues relating to a lack of protections, such as the no negative equity guarantee, and high costs, the public's perception of these products tends to be negative and there is a lack of trust of providers. Reputational risk is compounded by the fact that these products tend to be difficult for the general public to understand, and therefore can be seen as products that take advantage of the elderly, particularly when there is no remaining home equity at the end of the contract. Such situations can also lead to disputes with heirs. This has been a problem in Italy, for example (Hoekstra et al., 2018[13]). To mitigate the risk of disputes, the United Kingdom keeps the assessment from the independent solicitor on file as proof that the homeowner was competent in choosing to select the product. In Japan, most providers require the use of a trust which allows them to avoid dealing with any heirs in the termination of the contract.

Several jurisdictions have developed government backed equity release programmes given the challenges to develop a private market. Australia Government's Home Equity Access Scheme is provided by Services Australia and the Department of Veteran Affairs. The programme provides a reverse mortgage up to a limit linked to public pension eligibility, and is paid fortnightly until the allowed loan amount has been fully paid out. Some municipalities in Hungary offer a home reversion equity release scheme which pay a lump sum and monthly lifetime payments in exchange for homes (Hoekstra et al., 2018[13]). Japan's Reverse60 programme offers retail reverse mortgages to homeowners that are underwritten by the Japan Housing Finance Agency and which pay a lump sum. Korea introduced its JooTaekYeonKeum (JTYK, Housing Pension) in 2007 through the Korea Housing Finance Corporation, which provides lifetime monthly payments to the reverse mortgage borrowers. The Home Equity Conversion Mortgage (HECM) was created in 1988 in the United States. Loans from this programme are available through any Federal Housing Administration (FHA) approved lender and are insured by the government. The HECM programme services over 90% of the reverse mortgages in the American market (Baily, Harris and Wang, 2019[10]).

6.5. The use of home equity release products in retirement

Home equity release products have the potential to benefit retirees in many situations. Common uses for the funds generated from these products include paying off debt, covering large punctual expenses such as home repairs, general improvement in living standards, and as a funding of last resort particularly for long term care needs.

Home equity release products can be beneficial for individuals retiring with high outstanding debt. Indeed, a common use of funds obtained from an equity release product is to pay off or manage debts. This is the case in the United Kingdom as well as Japan where homeowners use them to refinance their loans (Financial Conduct Authority, 2020[5]; Rethink Tokyo, 2022[14]).

Home equity release products could also be a good way for individuals to finance necessary punctual costs that they may not be able to budget for with their regular income or savings in retirement. Home improvements, for example, are another common use for these products. France has a product specifically targeting those with lower means who would like to use the funds for home improvements (Rialland, 2023[15]). In the United Kingdom, the FCA found that equity release products could be a helpful solution to help individuals to finance early or gradual retirement (Financial Conduct Authority, 2020[5]). These products could be a source of bridge financing to help people manage the period during which they may not have access to all their eventual sources of income in retirement.

Home equity can also simply be a means to improve living standards more generally. HECM loans have a high penetration among the low-income groups in the United States (Knaack, Miller and Stewart, 2020[12]). In contrast, in Korea JTYK loans are more common among individuals in high-rise housing, which tend to be owned by wealthier individuals (Clow, 2020[16]). In Italy, people view these products as an option to improve living standards where income is not sufficient to meet basic needs, rather than as a means to simply live more comfortably (Fornero, Rossi and Urzi Brancati, 2015[17]). Equity release products could be particularly helpful for the single elderly and surviving spouses, especially women, who have on average fewer financial resources in retirement and may have seen their retirement incomes decrease following the death of their spouse. Indeed, in the United States nearly two-thirds of HECM borrowers are single, with around 70% of those being women (Knaack, Miller and Stewart, 2020[12]). Some have suggested that line of credit reverse mortgage products could be a way for retirees to manage sequencing risk. Specifically, individuals could rely on the line of credit during periods of negative returns to avoid locking in their losses and harming their future retirement income potential (Pfeiffer, Salter and Evensky, 2012[18]).

Housing is often used as a source of financing of last resort to help in covering financial shocks that individuals are not able to easily absorb, such as long-term care or divorce. Australia has a product targeted specifically to those needing long-term care to aid individuals to manage their finances during the transition to a long-term care facility and allow for more time for these individuals to sell their homes. Home equity release products also have the potential to be a means to absorb larger shocks when continued residence in the home is required or desired. In the event of divorce, for example, one partner could stay in the home, while the other partner could put the proceeds from the equity release product towards a second home.

Nevertheless, where housing equity is needed as a financing of last resort, the use of equity release products for other purposes could result in a lack of funding to help people when they have no other options, as is often the case for long-term care. This was a concern ASIC raised in the Australian market, where it found that a significant portion of individuals having reverse mortgages risked not having sufficient funds to pay for the average upfront cost of aged care (ASIC, 2018[11]).

Home equity release products also tend to be rather inflexible, which may make it more difficult for individuals to adapt their finances to changing circumstances. This risk is higher for younger borrowers who have a longer period of time over which their circumstances could potentially change.

These products can also impede downsizing. If the individual wishes to sell their house and purchase another, they would not have as much home equity available to do so. A more efficient solution to release home equity would be to downsize as early as possible and obtain the excess capital directly without going through an equity release product, which could still be obtained at a later stage if needed.

While equity release products have the potential to help people meet their financial needs in retirement in certain circumstances, many people are not aware of these products, and even if they are, numerous barriers for uptake remain. First is the poor reputation of these products and prevailing lack of trust in the financial providers who offer them. Individuals may be reluctant to enter a reverse mortgage contract due to debt aversion, as many have spent most of their lives paying off their mortgage and may not feel comfortable taking on the debt again. People often have emotional attachments to their homes, which may diminish their willingness to enter a home reversion, or to accept that they would have less – or potentially no – home equity to leave to their heirs. Access to financial advice is also a challenge in many jurisdictions, and individuals who could benefit the most from these products may not seek them out or be able to obtain advice. When they can access advice, advisors may be reluctant to advise these products for fear of regulatory liability.

6.6. Conclusions

Home equity release products can be a useful means for many retirees who own their homes to increase their financial resources in retirement. Nevertheless, the regulatory framework around these products needs to ensure their suitability and control for the potential risks to homeowners while also considering the need for providers to manage their risks. This section summarises some implications for the regulatory framework around home equity release products based on the international examples discussed. These observations relate to the profile of homeowners who are most likely to benefit from these products, ensuring the suitability of the product, good practices in product design and contractual terms, and the supply-side challenges to offer these products.

6.6.1. Homeowners who could benefit from equity release products

Home equity release products can be a valuable additional source to finance individuals' needs in retirement, but they are not suitable for every situation. Products should target individuals who would be most likely to benefit from them.

Home equity release products are most beneficial for older individuals who would like to continue living in their current home for the rest of their life. As such, equity release products are not likely to be suitable for those who plan to downsize at some point, as they can limit the flexibility to change homes and would reduce the value that people would get from the sale of their property. Younger retirees are more likely to have a change in circumstances that could require them to change homes, making the suitability of an equity release product more uncertain. Additionally, reverse mortgages are relatively more costly for younger retirees because the debt accumulates over a longer period of time, reducing the amount of equity they are able to release with the product.

Equity release products can be particularly valuable for homeowners who need additional financial resources in retirement. Using home equity to pay off outstanding debt can reduce essential income needs in retirement. Home equity can also help retirees to absorb expenses that they may not be able to afford otherwise, such as home repairs. It can also provide individuals with a source of financing of last resort to support extraordinary expenses such as long-term care or divorce.

Home equity release products are better suited for those who do not prioritise leaving their home as a bequest to their heirs. These products reduce the home value that can be left to heirs, either by increasing the debt that heirs will need to pay off or by reducing the owned equity in the home, thereby reducing the value of the bequest.

6.6.2. Ensuring suitability

The regulatory framework should include measures that help ensure that the products are suitable for the homeowners accessing them. These include requirements for advice or guidance, required disclosures of relevant information, and the possibility for homeowners to reflect on whether their decision is the right one.

Several jurisdictions require the involvement of an independent professional for an individual to acquire a home equity release product to help to ensure that the product is suitable. The role of these professionals can be to ensure that the individual understands the product and its financial implications, to assess whether the product is suitable given the individual's financial situation, or to verify the competence of the individual to make an informed decision in their own best interest. These professionals can also serve to flag any sign of potential elder abuse, where a family member or acquaintance may be pressuring the individual to take an equity release product in order to take advantage of them.

Product disclosures should ensure that individuals are aware of the financial implications of taking a home equity release product and have the information needed to be able to assess whether the product is suitable for them. Good practice for disclosures for reverse mortgages is to include projections of the accumulated debt and home value to help individuals understand how much excess home equity would remain in the future. Disclosures should also be sure to highlight any potential tax owed from the proceeds of the equity release product, as well as the impact it could have on other means-tested benefits that retirees receive.

Some jurisdictions require that equity release products allow for a cooling-off period to give individuals the time to reflect on their decision on their own time and change their mind about taking the product if they decide that it is not right for them. The duration of these periods is typically around 30 days.

6.6.3. Good practices for product design

While home equity release products have the potential to improve retirement outcomes for certain groups, they can also present significant risks to homeowners. The regulatory framework should aim to mitigate these risks and minimise any potential harm. Industry groups have already come up with numerous good practices in product design that regulatory frameworks can borrow from, and international experience provides additional examples of product features that can be beneficial for homeowners.

Home equity release products should provide tenancy protections that allow for individuals to remain in their homes for their remaining lifetime. Indeed, this is one of the main draws of home equity release products, and prevents people from losing their home in old age. Ideally, declared spouses should also be granted the right to lifetime residency, even if they are not on the contract for the equity release product or on the title of the home. If these protections are not granted, spouses could lose their home without having any means to relocate to a new home. Simply disclosing the consequences of not having tenancy protections for spouses is not always effective at getting people to understand them. A couple of jurisdictions take measures to allow for this protection, either through the use of trusts or specific provisions in the regulation.

Other product features limit the debt that borrowers of reverse mortgages accumulate, including interest rate caps, limits on the debt owed, penalty-free repayments, and allowing for multiple disbursements of funds. Where interest rates are variable, industry good practice is to introduce a cap on the interest rate to limit how much debt can accumulate over the borrower's lifetime. A very important product feature to protect borrowers is the no negative equity guarantee (NNEG), which makes the loan non-recourse by preventing the lender from requiring heirs to pay back debt in excess of the home value. An equity guarantee is a similar feature that is available in some jurisdictions, and guarantees that the owner retains a minimum percentage of equity in their home. This feature is useful where home equity can be an important source of financing for long-term care needs, and prevents borrowers from exhausting their available home equity and losing that source of financing of last resort for significant financial shocks. Industry standards also allow for penalty-free repayments if borrowers choose to reduce their debt levels by repaying part or all of their reverse mortgage. Finally, another useful feature is to allow individuals to receive their payments over time rather than only as a lump-sum. This prevents debt from accumulating on a sizable lump-sum that individuals may not need immediately, and instead allows for a disbursement of payments over time as income or as a line of credit for borrowers to use as needed.

6.6.4. Good practices for contractual terms

The contractual terms of home equity release products should ensure that homeowners will have adequate protections and will be treated fairly regarding the receipt and repayment of funds.

Some jurisdictions ensure that homeowners are guaranteed to receive the amounts they are contractually entitled to even if the provider goes insolvent. This is normally insured by a government-backed guarantee, and this protection can involve an explicit premium.

Individuals should also be treated fairly in the event that the provider enforces any payments due to a breach of contractual terms. Before enforcing payments or foreclosure on the home, providers should engage with individuals and attempt to remedy the situation, and failing this they should provide a notice period before commencing any enforcement proceedings.

When payment to the provider becomes due, either because of death or permanent departure from the home to a long-term care facility, providers should allow for sufficient time for the sale of the home and the fulfilment of contractual obligations. Family members managing the estate normally have around 12 months to manage selling the home, and the grace period can be extended in the event of departure due to long-term care needs to allow more time to sort out the financial situation of the occupant.

6.6.5. Supply-side challenges

While product design needs to limit risks to homeowners, measures also need to be in place to allow providers to effectively mitigate their own risk exposures. These risks include moral hazard, crossover risk, and the length of time until the home is sold.

Providers are exposed to moral hazard because individuals have less incentive to ensure the upkeep and maintenance of their home if they will not benefit financially from doing so. This could lead to a deterioration in the home value, reducing the price at which it can be sold and thereby increasing the risk that providers incur a loss. One way to mitigate this risk is to ensure that homeowners have sufficient resources to finance required maintenance, insurance payments, and property tax. Approaches taken to mitigate moral hazard include requiring adequate financial resources for an individual to qualify for the equity release product, requiring that a certain amount of the funds be set aside for maintenance and upkeep, or requiring that home occupants allow for regular home inspections to ensure the home is adequately cared for.

A key risk exposure for providers of reverse mortgages is the crossover risk that the accumulated loan balance exceeds the market value of the home. For non-recourse loans with NNEGs, this would result in providers not getting full repayment of the loan. Some jurisdictions require an explicit premium for a third party to cover this risk. Another measure to limit risk exposure is to limit the amount that individuals can borrow as a function of their home value and their age. Limits are lower for younger borrowers, say 15% of the home value of someone aged 60, increasing up to around 50% for older borrowers aged 80 and over. Such limits reduce the risk that debt will accumulate to a level exceeding the value of the home.

Imposing a minimum age to access a home equity release product reduces somewhat the uncertainty around when the provider will be repaid by reducing the expected duration of the product. A minimum age of 60 to access equity release products targeting the elderly is common.

Nevertheless, other risks to providers remain, and supply-side challenges can go beyond the regulatory framework around equity release products. For example, financing and capital requirements are a major barrier to entry, which can result in a concentrated and uncompetitive market.

Authorities could consider the introduction of a government-backed programme to ensure the availability of access to good-value products to homeowners where the supply of home equity release products is lacking and where authorities feel such products could improve financial outcomes in retirement. Several jurisdictions taken this approach. However, uptake remains low and further consideration is needed to promote retirees' awareness of and demand for home equity release products to capitalise on the assets they have available to them in retirement.

References

Alegria Real Estate (2021), *Reverse mortgage in Spain: how does it work?*, https://alegria-realestate.com/en/articles/reverse-mortgage-in-spain-how-does-it-work. [7]

ASIC (2018), *Review of reverse mortgage lending in Australia*. [11]

Baily, M., B. Harris and T. Wang (2019), *The unfulfilled promise of reverse mortgages: Can a better market improve retirement security?*, https://www.brookings.edu/wp-content/uploads/2019/10/ES_20191024_BailyHarrisWang-1.pdf. [10]

Bartsh, F. et al. (2021), *Is There a Need for Reverse Mortgages in Germany? Empirical Evidence and Policy Implications*, EconPol. [9]

Clow, C. (2020), *Wealthier Koreans More Likely to Have Reverse Mortgages in that Country, Data Suggests*, https://www.housingwire.com/articles/wealthier-koreans-more-likely-to-have-reverse-mortgages-in-that-country-data-suggests/#:~:text=The%20figure%20has%20been%20steadily%20declining%20since%20then%2C,country%20than%20they%20are%20in%20the%20United%20States. [16]

EPPARG (2024), *Standards*, https://epparg.org/standards/our-standards/. [4]

Equity Release Council (2024), *Our Standards*, https://www.equityreleasecouncil.com/about/standards/. [3]

EY (2020), *2020 Global Equity Release Roundtable Survey*, https://epparg.org/wp-content/uploads/2021/01/2020-Global-Equity-Release-Roundtable-Survey.pdf. [1]

Financial Conduct Authority (2020), *The equity release sales and advice process: key findings*. [5]

Fornero, E., M. Rossi and M. Urzi Brancati (2015), "Explaining why, right or wrong, (Italian) households do not like reverse mortgages", *Journal of Pension Economics and Finance*, Vol. 15/2, pp. 180-202, https://doi.org/10.1017/s1474747215000013. [17]

Hoekstra, J. et al. (2018), *Integrating Residential Property with Private Pensions in the EU*, https://repository.tudelft.nl/islandora/object/uuid:7a493e86-ea33-4951-820a-fa98dbf2c04e?collection=research. [13]

Joosten, A. (2015), *Equity Release Products: Analysis for the Netherlands*, Netspar. [8]

Knaack, P., M. Miller and F. Stewart (2020), *Reverse Mortgages, Financial Inclusion, and Economic Development: Potential Benefit and Risks*. [12]

Kojima, T. (2013), "How to make reverse mortgages more common in Japan", *Nomura Journal of Capital Markets*, Vol. 4/4. [6]

Mayer, C. and S. Moulton (2020), *The Market for Reverse Mortgages among Older Americans*, https://repository.upenn.edu/cgi/viewcontent.cgi?article=1695&context=prc_papers. [2]

OECD (2012), *G20/OECD High-Level Principles on Financial Consumer Protection 2022*, OECD Publishing, Paris, https://doi.org/10.1787/48cc3df0-en. [19]

Pfeiffer, S., J. Salter and H. Evensky (2012), "Increasing the Sustainable Withdrawal Rate Using the Standby Reverse Mortgage", *Journal of Financial Planning*. [18]

Rethink Tokyo (2022), *Reverse 60 home loans see 41 percent lending increase*, https://www.rethinktokyo.com/news/2022/02/26/reverse-60-home-loans-see-41-percent-lending-increase/1645816254. [14]

Rialland, M. (2023), *Le Prêt Viager Hypothécaire et les Prêts Avance Mutation et Rénovation*, https://www.moneyvox.fr/credit/viager-hypothecaire.php. [15]

Annex 6.A. Country details

This annex provides some details of home equity products available in the countries included in this chapter.

Australia

The minimum age to access an equity release product is 65. There are four types of products available in Australia:

- ***Reverse mortgage*** – Individuals borrow money against their home in exchange for a lump sum, income stream, or line of credit. The loan must be repaid when they sell, move out, or die. Individuals can obtain around 20-25% of their home equity at age 65. Homeowners have the option to repay early, and to protect a portion of their equity in case they will need it in the future to cover long-term care costs. NNEGs are required.
- ***Home reversion*** – Individuals can sell their home partially or in full in exchange for a lump sum. There is usually an upfront fee of around AUD 2 000, plus transaction costs. Homeowners may have the option to buy back the sold share, and products can provide a rebate to heirs if the owner dies earlier than expected.
- ***Equity release*** – Individuals sell a portion of their home in exchange for a lump sum or instalment payments. They then pay fees as a proportion of the sold equity, which are paid through an additional transfer of equity. As such, fees paid/equity transferred increases over time. The individual may have the right to stay in the home when they retain 0% equity only if the contract allows it.
- ***Government's Home Equity Access Scheme*** – This is a government-sponsored reverse mortgage programme provided by Services Australia and Dept of Veterans Affairs. The loan is secured against any real estate in Australia. Individuals must be eligible for the Age Pension, and have resided in Australia for ten years, of which five consecutive. The maximum loan amount is based on age and real estate value, but individuals can request an increase at a later age if the outstanding loan value remains below the maximum loan for that age. The loan pays a non-taxable fortnightly payment. The sum of the Age Pension and the loan payment must be less than 1.5 times the maximum rate for the Age Pension. Since 2022, individuals can also opt for a lump sum representing up to 50% of the total loan payments over the next year, which would reduce the fortnightly payments accordingly over the year. Individuals can repay the loan at any time, and must cover all legal costs relating to the transaction. All loans have a NNEG.

In 2012 Australia introduced enhanced responsible lending obligations for reverse mortgages. These requirements included:

- an assessment of the needs of the borrower
- maximum LTV ratios for the loan to be considered suitable
- the disclosure of home equity projections from MoneySmart's calculator, an information statement, a tenancy protection warning, and annual account statements
- an obligation to speak directly to the borrower in the event of a breach of contract, providing a notice period before enforcement proceedings commence.

Some lenders require financial advice, but it is not mandated.

Canada

Individuals must be at least 55 years old to qualify for a reverse mortgage. They can borrow up to 55% of the value of the property, subject to a minimum of CAD 20 000 and a maximum of CAD 750 000. A cooling-off period is mandatory, as is a NNEG. Borrowers are required to pay off any outstanding debt and to close open HELOCs. Financial advice is required in some cases. Proceeds can be paid as a lump sum, in instalments, or as a line of credit. The grace period to pay back the loan will depend on if the owner leaves the home because of death or long-term care. Borrowers can pay back the loan early, subject to any applicable fees.

France

Reverse mortgages were introduced in 2006. Cooling-off periods and NNEGs are required, and there are restrictions around how the products can be marketed. Homeowners are required to consult a notary. Early repayments are subject to fee caps, and interest rates are fixed.

In 2022, a new reverse mortgage product was introduced for low-income households to have finances to make renovations to improve energy consumption. Only two lenders currently offer this product.

Germany

Reverse mortgages were introduced in 2009.

NNEGs are not required. Reserves are set aside to cover the costs of property maintenance. Payments can be made as a lump sum or in instalments.

Home reversions remain more popular than reverse mortgages, but both markets are small. In 2015, there were less than 1 000 outstanding home reversions, and only 200 reverse mortgages (Bartsh et al., 2021[9]).

Hungary

The market for reverse mortgages dried up following the financial crisis.

Some municipalities have home reversion programmes where they pay residents monthly payments for life in exchange for their home (Hoekstra et al., 2018[13]).

Ireland

Spry Finance is the main provider of reverse mortgages. Their product has a minimum age of 60 and offers a NNEG. Borrowers must hire a solicitor. Proceeds are paid as a lump sum. They can transfer the loan to a new property. The loan must be repaid 12 months after moving out of the property.

Italy

A 2015 Decree defined a reverse mortgage and established the minimum age of access at 60. NNEG is required. Borrowers can make early repayments.

Home reversion agreements between two individuals are more common than reverse mortgages.

Japan

The Reverse60 programme in Japan is a government-sponsored programme where loans written at the retail level are insured by the Japan Housing Finance Agency. Financial counselling is required, and the minimum age is 60. Borrowers must pay premiums, which are higher when homeowners opt for the NNEG. Proceeds are paid as a lump sum.

Private providers also offer reverse mortgages, but few have NNEGs and repayment can be triggered if property value declines.

Korea

Korea introduced the government-sponsored JooTaekYeonKeum (JTYK, Housing Pension) in 2007. The programme is insured through the Korea Housing Finance Corporation. The minimum age is 55, and the owner's mortgage must be paid off. Borrowers can receive lifetime monthly payments, or take instalments over 10 to 30 years, or have a lump sum of up to 50%. Rates are variable, and borrowers must pay NNEG premiums.

Prior to the introduction of the JTYK, private providers offered reverse mortgage products, but they only paid lump sums and did not mitigate any risks for the homeowner.

Netherlands

There is currently only one reverse mortgage product in the Netherlands, offered by Florius Verzilverhypotheek. The minimum age is 67 (increased from 60 more recently), the maximum LTV is 55%, subject to a minimum of 30 000 and a maximum of 250 000. Borrowers are required to receive financial advice, need to choose the duration over which they will borrow funds in advance, and are required to take a minimum lump sum of EUR 4 500 at the contract's inception. They can make adjustments to the amount of instalment payments. There is a NNEG conditional on selling the house at market value within 12 months, otherwise the heirs must pay back the difference.

New Zealand

Reverse mortgages were introduced in New Zealand in 2003. Products are not required to offer tenant protection, lifetime occupancy guarantees, or NNEGs. Interest rates are variable. Individuals can choose to have a minimum equity guarantee, and are required to take a lump sum of at least NZD 5 000 at the commencement of the contract, otherwise payments can be made in instalments. Borrowers are required to take independent financial advice.

The provider Lifetime introduced a home reversion product to the market in 2023, the first product of this type to be available in New Zealand. In exchange for a partial sale of the home equity, individuals receive payments in instalments over ten years, with the option to extend by ten more years if they are under age 90. Lifetime occupancy is granted.

Norway

Reverse mortgages, or Seniorlån (Senior Loans) require a minimum age of 60, and have a maximum LTV of 49% at age 80. Proceeds can be paid as a lump sum or in instalments. NNEGs are required.

Poland

Reverse mortgages have been regulated since 2014. A 30-day cooling-off period is required. Heirs have 12 months to pay off the loan, otherwise the property title is transferred to the lender. The lender must pay back any excess of the sale price over the outstanding loan amount.

Home reversions are more prevalent, and pay life annuities.

Spain

Reverse mortgages have been regulated since 2007. The minimum age is 65, unless the individual demonstrates at least 33% disability or dependence. Payments can be made as a lump sum, or as a fixed or lifetime annuity. Borrowers must receive financial advice. There are no NNEGs. Interest rates are fixed.

Borrowers with outstanding mortgages have two options. The first is to receive a capital sum from the lender, and when they eventually manage to pay off their mortgage the lender will pay them a small dividend payment for life. Alternatively, dividend payments can begin immediately and go towards paying off the outstanding mortgage (Alegria Real Estate, 2021[7]).

Sweden

Reverse mortgages were first introduced in 2005. There is no requirement for a NNEG. Proceeds are paid as a lump-sum, and borrowers must allow regular inspections to verify the upkeep of the property. Interest rates are variable.

United Kingdom

The minimum age for an equity release product is 55.

Reverse mortgages and home reversions are both regulated by the FCA.

Payments from reverse mortgages can be lump sums, regular instalments, or a line of credit. Providers that are members of the industry body the Equity Release Council (ERC) are required to abide by their standards, which include capping variables rates, right to lifetime residency, right to change properties, NNEG, and allowance for early repayments. Adhering providers pay the ERC a premium to insure themselves against the risk of crossover. Homeowners are obliged to obtain financial advice from an independent FCA-certified advisor, and hire an independent solicitor to carry out the legal work and ensure that they are competent to make the decision to take the product.

Providers of home reversion must take reasonable steps to ensure that the product is suitable. Homeowners must cover costs relating to administration, valuation, and the solicitor. Products may provide a capital protection where heirs receive a rebate if the owner dies much earlier than expected. Owners are obliged to pay off any outstanding mortgage with the proceeds.

United States

The Home Equity Conversion Mortgage (HECM) programme was created in 1988. Loans are available through Federal Housing Administration (FHA)'s approved lenders and are insured by the government. Over 90% of the reverse mortgages in the United States are from the HECM programme.

Homeowners must be at least 62, occupy their home, and have sufficient funds to pay taxes, insurance, and home maintenance costs. They must also pay the mortgage insurance premium of 2% up front and 0.5% annually to cover provider insolvency. Origination fees are capped, as are the monthly servicing fees which are added to the loan's balance. Payments can be a paid as a lump sum, instalments, life annuity, line of credit, or a combination of these options. The loans are non-recourse. Fixed rates are offered for lump sum payments, otherwise the rate is variable. Before entering the agreement, individuals must meet with an HECM counsellor to discuss eligibility, suitability, and other options to raise funds. The session is not meant to provide guidance, but rather to make sure the individual has sufficient information to make an informed decision.

Fee disclosure and counselling requirements were introduced in 1998. In 2015, rules changed to require the financial assessment of borrowers.

Notes

[1] The scope of the products discussed are those that intend for the product to be used as a source of financing in retirement. The chapter focuses on the products available in 17 jurisdictions where these types of products are available: Australia, Canada, France, Germany, Ireland, Hungary, Italy, Japan, Korea, the Netherlands, New Zealand, Norway, Poland, Spain, Sweden, the United Kingdom, and the United States.

[2] See Annex 6.A for details of the specific programmes by jurisdiction.

[3] Reverse mortgage lines of credit differ from the Home Equity Line of Credit (HELOC) products offered in many jurisdictions in that borrowers are normally required to pay interest on HELOC's and must reimburse the credit within a given time frame.

[4] A non-recourse loan does not allow the lender to pursue any compensation above the value of the collateral.

[5] In line with the G20/OECD High-Level Principles on Financial Consumer Protection (OECD, 2012[19]).

[6] Not all HECM products are Department of Housing and Urban Development (HUD) insured loans. Only HECM loans insured by HUD are Federal Housing Administration (FHA).

7 Individual pension dashboards: Design, development and operation

Jessica Mosher

This chapter presents good practices and lessons for the design and development of individual pension dashboards that provide users with information on their accumulated pensions. These lessons draw from the numerous international examples of such dashboards described in the chapter.

Individual pension dashboards that provide individuals with information on their accumulated pensions are expanding globally and have the potential to greatly improve communication to individuals about the retirement incomes they can expect.[1] These platforms can offer an accessible and user-friendly format to engage individuals with their retirement planning and provide a comprehensive picture of retirement preparedness across different sources of retirement income. In addition, they can serve to make the operations and management of pensions easier and more efficient, and potentially provide relevant stakeholders with information to monitor the system's success in delivering adequate pensions.

This chapter looks at some of the individual pension dashboards that have been developed or are being developed to improve retirement planning and the delivery of pensions.[2] The first section summarises some of the different functionalities of these dashboards depending on the objectives for their development and use, and briefly describes their functions. The second section focuses on the design and content of dashboards, while the third section discusses operational considerations in their development. The fourth section discusses the importance of the continued evolution and monitoring of the success of the dashboard. The final section concludes with good practices and policy considerations for the development of individual pension dashboards relating to each of these elements. Annex 7.A details the elements included in each of the examples discussed in this report.[3]

7.1. Introduction to individual pension dashboards

Individual pension dashboards can have multiple functionalities. A key functionality is to provide individuals with a centralised point of access to view their accumulated pensions and have information about how much retirement income they can expect to have. Some platforms may also allow individuals to manage their retirement savings accounts and make contributions, transfers, or change investment strategies. Others may cater to the needs of multiple stakeholders, taking advantage of the technical infrastructure to facilitate back-office administration, such as tracking employer contributions, or to provide a source of data on a system's coverage, participation, and results. Table 1.4 summarises the key functionalities of the dashboards described in this chapter along with the scope of pensions included.

Table 7.1. Summary of the scope and functionality of individual pension dashboards

Jurisdiction	Platform	Pillars covered	Functionality
Australia	myGov	2	Information, Limited account management
Belgium	Mypension.be	1, 2	Information, Data
Chile	Pension Simulator	2, 3	Information
Croatia	My Pension (Moja Mirovina)	1, 2 (3 planned)	Information
Denmark	PensionsInfo	1, 2, 3	Information
Estonia	Minu Pension	1, 2, 3	Information
Germany	Digitale Rentenübersicht	1, 2, 3	Information
Hong Kong, China	eMPF	2, ~3	Information, Data, Account management, Administrative functions
Ireland	PensionsVault	2, 3	Information
Israel	Pension Clearing House	2	Information
Latvia	Government Services Portal	1, 2	Information, Limited account management
Mexico	AFORE Movil	2	Information, Account management
Netherlands	Mijnpensioenoverzicht.nl	1, 2	Information
Norway	Norsk Pensjon	1, 2, 3	Information, Data
Slovak Republic	Orange Envelope	1,2,3	Information
Spain	Plataforma Digital Común	2 (partial)	Information, Data
Sweden	MinPension	1, 2, 3	Information
UK	Pensions Dashboard	1, 2, 3	Information

Source: See Annex Table 7.A.1 for the references for each of the platforms.

The functionality offered by an individual pension dashboard is linked to the purpose for which it is developed in the context of the design of the pension system. Several OECD countries have developed individual pension dashboards to provide a centralised source of information for individuals to see the pensions that they have accrued from multiple sources on a single platform. These platforms can also aim to help people understand what they need to do to increase their expected retirement income, thereby nudging them to change their investment strategy, save more and/or retire later. These dashboards often include information on accrued rights from public pensions (Belgium, Croatia, Denmark, Germany, Latvia, the Netherlands, Norway, Sweden, the United Kingdom), though not all also include information from voluntary personal pensions (Belgium, Croatia, Latvia, and the Netherlands currently do not). Some dashboards include information only on asset-backed pensions (Australia, Chile, Ireland, Israel, Mexico, Spain). In Spain, the platform currently only covers a subset of occupational pension funds.

Dashboards providing information to individuals about their defined contribution pension plans may also allow individuals to manage their accounts. The main purpose of the AFORE Movil application in Mexico is to increase pension coverage by facilitating the account management for members. In addition to providing information on account balances and performance, the app allows individuals to open an account, make contributions, change pension providers, and name their beneficiaries. In Australia, the myGov platform provides more limited functionality, but does allow individuals to consolidate their accounts and make transfers between providers. The Government Services Portal in Latvia allows users to request to change providers.

Digital platforms can also be used as a means for data exchange. The dashboard in Belgium is used to deliver statistical data, as well as to automate and optimise data flows to pension providers and improve their processes. In Norway, the pension dashboard also serves as a means to exchange data with the government so that the government can have the same information on its own website, and to provide data to Statistics Norway. Providers can also request data from the platform to include on their own websites. In Spain, the platform being developed for the new publicly-promoted occupational pension plans will provide supervisory bodies with a source of data on how the system is functioning.

Dashboards can also integrate all these functionalities. This is the case with eMPF in Hong Kong, China, which was developed with a view to allow members to view their retirement savings account information, but also to open a new account and make contributions and other transactions. The platform will also be used to manage the administrative functions of providers and will be a source of data for supervisors to monitor the system.

The content and design of the dashboard is driven by its purpose, even if the main functionality of the platform is only to provide information. In Belgium, for example, the dashboard has a legal mandate to increase the transparency of the system and allow individuals to access their personal information regarding their pensions. As such, the tool is primarily informational and does not aim to support decision-making for occupational pensions.[4] The dashboard in Sweden, however, aims to provide information to improve decision-making, and thereby incorporates tools to help people understand the implications of different decisions they could make. In the United Kingdom, one aim in the ongoing development of the dashboard is to provide individuals with sufficient information to make informed decisions following the Pension Freedoms, though the focus to do so will likely be more on guiding users towards independent financial advice rather than providing elaborate projection tools. Subject to certain rules, projections and additional modelling tools may be included but will not allow the user to execute transactions directly from the dashboard. Dashboards can also aim to address the challenge of lost pension accounts that savers have forgotten about. For example, the United Kingdom's dashboard will automatically show all of the user's pension accounts in one place, even those they may not have been aware they had, though the platform will not allow the consolidation of a user's accounts. However, digital platforms can also facilitate the consolidation of an individual's accounts, as in Australia, where users can easily consolidate their accounts on the platform in addition to viewing them in a single place.

7.2. Design considerations for the content of individual pension dashboards

The scope, content and format of the interface through which users access their dashboard can have a significant influence on their use of and engagement with the platform. The design of the dashboard therefore needs to be carefully considered. The IOPS Good practices for designing, presenting, and supervising pension projections include good practices on both the content and format of pension projections shown on these platforms, and highlight many of the good practices discussed through the examples provided in this chapter (IOPS, 2022[1]).[5]

7.2.1. Scope

Ideally, individual pension dashboards would include information relating to all sources to finance retirement that users may have available to them.[6] Including both public pay-as-you-go pensions as well as asset-backed pensions would allow individuals to see how much they can expect to have in total, and thereby more easily assess what actions they would need to take to achieve their desired retirement outcomes.

Nevertheless, the process and calculations needed to integrate public pensions and asset-backed pensions, as well as mandatory and voluntary plans, normally differ. The integration of the public and private sources of retirement income may need to be considered separately at the initial stage. Indeed, many European countries only have dashboards showing information on accrued rights for the public pension (Austria, Czechia, Finland, France, Italy, Lithuania, Malta, Poland, Portugal), with several planning to add information on asset-backed pensions (EIOPA, 2021[2]). Belgium's Mypension.be started with information on the public pension only, and later added information on occupational pensions. The information for these two different sources of pensions are updated at different frequencies, with the public pension updated once every three months, and the occupational pension updated only once per year. Additionally, the platform currently shows the pension from the two sources separately rather than aggregated. The dashboard in Latvia also shows pension entitlements from the public pay-as-you-go and defined contribution pensions separately. The rules of the public pension can also make a personalised calculation more complex than for asset-backed pensions, particularly where the public pension is means-tested against other sources of income in retirement, as in Denmark for example.

Data quality can also differ between pension sources. In Sweden, it took the dashboard longer to obtain good quality data from the public pension than it did from private providers. However, prior to implementation, the need for agreement on standards regarding the format in which private providers submit the data can take longer, as in the United Kingdom.

Personal voluntary pensions can also be more challenging to integrate into a dashboard. This is the case especially where financial accounts are not automatically linked to a common national ID number, because they are more dispersed and not connected through a single employer or provider. While Belgium's Mypension.be originally intended to integrate personal pensions, it has not yet done so.

7.2.2. Content

Individual pension dashboards often automatically link to an individual's pensions so they can see their consolidated information simply by logging in. Some dashboards also allow users to add additional accounts or financial resources that may not be automatically linked, as in Chile and Sweden. Sweden even allows users to input information regarding their housing assets. Denmark and Norway invite users to contact their pension providers if one of their accounts does not show up in the dashboard. Denmark and the Netherlands allow users to include their spouse's pension accounts in the dashboard to facilitate household retirement planning. Other dashboards – typically those that are privately developed without government involvement – require that users manually link their pension accounts to the dashboard, as in Estonia, Ireland, and the Slovak Republic.

The minimum information provided by dashboards is the amount of pensions accrued at the time of the request. This amount is stated in terms of accumulated assets for asset-backed individual retirement savings, or as pension income for public benefits or asset-backed defined benefit plans.

Most dashboards also include an estimate of expected pension income at the statutory retirement age to provide individuals with a general idea of how much they can expect to get. One exception is the myGov platform in Australia, whose primary objective is to help individuals find all their superannuation accounts and to consolidate smaller accounts, rather than helping them to have a view on how much they will have at retirement. Australia provides a retirement income calculator as a separate service on the Moneysmart site. Similarly, Latvia provides a pension calculator on its My Pension (Mana Pensija) site where individuals can manually input their accumulated pensions for each source to receive an estimate of future retirement income.

Some dashboards also show static projections for retirement income under different assumptions. The dashboards in Chile, the Netherlands and the Slovak Republic show expected retirement income under good and bad investment scenarios, as will Belgium's in 2026. Dashboards in the United Kingdom will show both currently accrued values and projected values that assume that the current level of contributions will continue until retirement. They will only show the information submitted by the providers and will not allow the user to manipulate the information to model different scenarios or projections.

Many dashboards also include a calculator function where users can adjust certain parameters to see how this could impact their expected retirement income in addition to static projections of retirement income. The most common parameter that platforms allow users to change is retirement age, as this is the simplest parameter, and it allows users to see how much they can get depending on how much longer they will work. Belgium, Chile, the Netherlands and Sweden also allow users to modify their employment characteristics, such as hours worked or salary. In addition to a simple calculator with these basic parameters, Norway provides an advanced calculator where individuals can see the impact of their marital status, which affects the public pension benefit, of taking partial retirement while continuing to work, and of any employment outside of Norway. Chile also allows users to include spouses and/or dependent children in the calculation. Denmark is considering allowing users to vary the age at which they begin taking different types of pensions to accommodate partial retirement plans. The Netherlands, where pension assets must be split with ex-spouses, allows people to see the impact that a divorce has on their pension. Belgium is considering including the impact of taking parental leave on retirement income calculations. While most calculators only allow the adjustment of parameters that individuals can control, the Minu Pension app in Estonia allows users to see the impact of different investment return scenarios. Sweden's MinPension includes a more detailed retirement-planning feature available to users over the age of 54 to calculate the impact of different retirement ages and the retirement income options possible. While it does not allow users to implement the strategy chosen, it does provide information regarding the steps that users need to take to do so.

Most dashboards show a single estimated income at retirement in real terms, so that individuals can compare the estimate with their current salary. A main shortfall in this approach is that individuals do not see how their purchasing power may erode over retirement. Sweden is considering how to provide this information to users.

Many dashboards provide additional information that can be useful to users beyond the minimum requirements of providing basic information about pensions accumulated and expected retirement income. Several provide details about the amount of contributions that individuals have made into their plans. This is normally shown on a per-plan basis, with some dashboards like the Orange Envelope in the Slovak Republic tracking the amount and date of each contribution made. Other dashboards show estimated benefits both gross and net of tax, which can be useful for users to get a sense of how much disposable income they will have in retirement. Denmark provides information on the tax treatment for each source of retirement income, indicating whether the income is tax exempt or the percentage at which it will be taxed. Details regarding survivor or disability benefits are also commonly shown, as these types of benefits are often linked to individuals' pension plans.

A few dashboards, mostly those having the objective in part to support investment or provider choice, provide information on investment returns and the fees charged by providers. For example, Australia allows users to select up to four funds to compare their performance and fees. The platform also classifies funds as performing or underperforming based on their relative net investment returns over the last nine years. Latvia's My Pension website also provides users with comparable information on fees and performance of defined contribution pension plans, though this is separate from where users can find information on their own account.

While no dashboard currently includes information relating to the Environmental, Social and Governance (ESG) characteristics of pension investments, both Norway and Sweden are actively considering how to integrate this aspect in the future.

Many dashboards provide additional functionality beyond the provision of information on the platform. The most common feature is the ability to download a summary of the information for individuals to share with their financial advisor. In Denmark, for example, the file can be transferred directly from the platform to the provider.

Other functionalities facilitate administrative tasks for the user. The platform in Belgium allows users to opt for email communications about their pension, and to track the administrative status of their requests and their communications with their provider. Ireland's PensionsVault allows users to store all their pension documentation. Israel and Sweden allow users to request a power of attorney. Mexico allows users to open a new pension account and to register their beneficiaries.

Other platforms also allow for more detailed management of pension accounts. Australia's MyGov allows users to consolidate pension accounts, change providers, and apply for compassionate release of their funds. Mexico's AFORE Movil allows users to make voluntary contributions, change providers, and withdraw voluntary contributions. Estonia's Minu Pension also allows for contribution payments and transfers between funds.

7.2.3. Format

The format of the digital platform and how information is presented to users is extremely important to engage users and make sure they understand the information provided and make use of the platform as intended.

Employing a layered presentation of information is useful to avoid information overload, where individuals are presented with more information than they can process, and to highlight the most important information that users need to know. The first layer presents the key information about pensions, namely how much users currently have and their expected income in retirement. The interface then allows individuals to click to drill down to more detailed information regarding the breakdown of the summary figures by type of pension or by plan, and then to the specific details of each plan. With this approach, individuals can choose to look for additional information if they have the time and willingness to do so. This avoids deterring those who just want to have a quick overview of their accrued pensions and who would be more likely to be overwhelmed by a large amount of information. PensionInfo in Denmark, for example, allows users to expand information on the type of pension payment to show the different plans, and then to see additional details for each specific plan.

Ideally, accrued pensions are communicated on an aggregate basis as well as broken down by source of pension. This would allow individuals to have a full-picture view of how much income they can expect in retirement and to plan accordingly. Nevertheless, a few dashboards, such as the ones in Belgium and the Slovak Republic, present the pay-as-you-go public and asset-backed pensions on separate tabs. This is something that Belgium would like to change, to show both pension sources in the same place on the dashboard.

Dashboards may better achieve their goals if they avoid using technical vocabulary that most individuals would not normally use, and rely on simple and relatable terms. Terms like 'lump-sum' or 'annuity' may not be commonly understood. Instead, terms or phrases that make the meaning of these technical terms more obvious are more likely to be effective at getting people to understand the information presented. Denmark's dashboard refers to lump-sums as a 'once and for all' payment, and annuity income as 'over a number of years' or for 'as long as you live'. One of Israel's private dashboards uses the term 'payments' instead of contributions. The dashboard in the Slovak Republic explains the percentiles of the simulations of future investment performance as 'optimistic/sunny days scenario', 'neutral/ordinary days scenario', and 'pessimistic/rainy days scenario'.

Visuals can also help individuals to better understand the information being presented. Pie charts are often used to show the breakdown of accrued pensions by type of pension or plan. Several dashboards, such as in Denmark and Sweden, show the breakdown of expected income in retirement as bar charts, which also show the development of the pension income received over time from each source. Users can also slide an indicator for retirement age up and down to immediately see the impact of advancing or delaying retirement. Additionally, Sweden indicates an individual's life expectancy by a small triangle for them to visually see how long they can expect to receive their income in retirement on average.

In recognition that some individuals are more visual while others prefer to see numbers presented in a table format, several dashboards also provide the option of seeing one or the other. Norway's dashboard shows a table below the figure depicting the same information on the amount of expected retirement income each year by source.

Visuals can also help individuals to better understand difficult concepts. Slovakia's Orange Envelope shows a traffic light to indicate whether users can expect a decrease in their standard of living based on the expected replacement rate. Green means they will have a replacement rate of at least 65%, whereas red implies a replacement rate of under 50%. Denmark uses an ice cream cone analogy to explain the impact that inflation can have on the purchasing power of retirement income, with the number of scoops of ice cream you can get decreasing over time. The Netherlands uses a navigation metaphor to help people understand the concept of uncertainty in investment outcomes. Chile presents optimistic and pessimistic scenarios around the expected outcome at different retirement ages in both absolute terms and visually on a bar chart.

Several dashboards also aim to convey how an individual's income will change in retirement compared to their current salary. The Slovakian dashboard communicates an expected replacement rate, which is the ratio of expected retirement income over current salary. However, many individuals have difficulty understanding percentages. Other dashboards therefore tend to use visuals or absolute references to convey the change in income. Sweden shows the individual's income by age before and through retirement, so users can see the change in income at retirement and over time. Denmark and Norway indicate the current salary level with a line added to the graph of retirement income which allows individuals to easily compare what they can expect to get compared to what they have now. The Netherlands provides the user with an absolute value of the difference between their current income and their future retirement income, which can be a more relatable figure for them as it is more easily comparable to their current spending and budget.

Other features can nudge individuals towards information to help them improve their retirement outcomes. Sweden's dashboard has a tool that users can use to compare their expected retirement income with other users in the country with a similar profile. Users then get asked how they feel about this information, and can click the corresponding happy, neutral or sad face. If they click the sad face, they will be directed to information on how they can improve their retirement outcomes. Sweden found that rather than make people worried, providing information on how they could improve their situation kept them engaged.

Design needs to also consider the format in which individuals will access the platform. While mobile apps have the benefit of connecting with a wider proportion of the population, the smaller screen size can make it difficult to design an interface that can effectively communicate all the information available.

Nevertheless, certain formats can be more or less effective at engaging different groups of the population. Initially, Sweden found that the dashboard's main users were those with high interest in and knowledge of pensions already, namely higher income males who have financial advisors, which was not the demographic group targeted with the platform. Sweden introduced simplifications in the format and seamless logon to the dashboard to better target low-interest groups. It also found that it could improve engagement by tailoring the content for different groups, not necessarily the format. For example, it created a retirement planning tool for those approaching retirement.

Different age groups also tend to access the dashboards in different ways. Younger people are more likely to access the platform via a mobile app. In the Netherlands, 40% of users access the dashboard from their mobile, and these users also tend to be younger. Younger people generally tend to be less interested in the details of their pensions. Indeed, the majority of people who consult the pension dashboards tend to be over the age of 45. This also highlights the importance of layering the information on the dashboard so that younger, less engaged users can quickly access the information most interesting and useful for them. Sweden found that younger people were less likely to drill down into the details of their pension plans. Middle-aged people were more likely to access the platform via a web search, so it also added more information signposting to the platform on its website to target information for these individuals. Chile found that younger users have less knowledge about the pension system and had more difficulty in filling out required information for the projections, whereas older individuals had a harder time navigating the tool and finding the definitions of the terms used (Antolin and Fuentes, 2012[3]).

Differences in usage are also observed by gender. Sweden found that women tended to use the dashboard for longer but with less frequency, and showed more hesitancy in making decisions with the information.

7.3. Operational considerations for the development of individual pension dashboards

There are numerous operational aspects to consider when developing an individual dashboard for pensions to ensure its efficiency, cost-effectiveness, security, and proper functioning. These include the mandatory or voluntary nature of the participation of pension providers, the ownership and operation of the platform, the governance structure, the financing of the platform, the digital architecture, and the platform's promotion. Table 7.2 summarises the main operational aspects relating to the development of the digital platforms referenced in this report.

Table 7.2. Summary of the key operational aspects of individual pension dashboards

Jurisdiction	Platform	Year established	Pillars covered	Initiative	Participation	Number of providers	Ownership	Governance	Financing	Centralised database
Australia	myGov	2013	2	Public	Via tax office	~100	Public	Public	Public	Yes
Belgium	Mypension.be	2010	1, 2	Public	Mandatory	212	Public	Public	Public	Yes
Chile	Pension Simulator	2012	2, 3	Public	Mandatory	7	Public (+ Private)	Public	Public	Yes
Croatia	My Pension (Moja Mirovina)	2024	1, 2 (3 planned)	Public	Mandatory	4	Public	Public	Public	No
Denmark	PensionsInfo	1999	1, 2, 3	Private	Voluntary	100	Private	Public-Private	Private	No
Estonia	Minu Pension	2019	1, 2, 3	Private		5	Private	Private	Private	Only for 1st pillar, if requested
Germany	Digitale Rentenübersicht	2023	1, 2, 3	Public	Mandatory	~450	Public	Public-Private	Public	No
Hong Kong, China	eMPF	2024	2, ~3	Public	Mandatory	13	Public	Public	Public	Yes
Ireland	PensionsVault		2, 3	Private	Manual input		Private	Private	Private	
Israel	Pension Clearing House	2012	2	Public	Mandatory	~100	Public owned outsourced to private	Public	Members	Yes
Latvia	Government Services Portal		1, 2	Public	Mandatory	9	Public	Public		
Mexico	AFORE Movil	2017	2	Public	Mandatory	10	Public-Private	Public	Public	
Netherlands	Mijnpensioenoverzicht.nl	2011	1, 2	Public-Private	Mandatory	~200	Public-Private	Public-Private	Private	No
Norway	Norsk Pensjon	2008	1, 2, 3	Public-Private	Voluntary	100	Private	Public-Private	Private	No
Slovak Republic	Orange Envelope	2019	1, 2, 3	Private	Manual input	5	Private	Private	Private	Yes
Spain	Plataforma Digital Común	2024	2 (partial)	Public	Mandatory	5	Public	Public	Public	Yes
Sweden	MinPension	2004	1, 2, 3	Public-Private	Voluntary	~30	Private	Public-Private	Public-Private	Yes
UK	Pensions Dashboard	2026	1, 2	Public-Private	Mandatory	~3 000-4 000	Public (+ Private)	Public (+ Private)	Private	No

7.3.1. Participation of pension providers

Individual pension dashboards owned by the government seem more likely to require mandatory participation from private providers. This is the case in Belgium; Chile; Hong Kong, China; Croatia; Germany; Israel; Latvia; Mexico; the Netherlands; Spain; and the United Kingdom. However, digital platforms that are owned by the private sector, but where the government is involved in the governance of the platform – such as in Denmark, Norway, and Sweden – have succeeded in achieving high coverage through voluntary participation, though this usually involves pressure from the government and significant initial support from the industry's largest players. In Denmark, PensionsInfo began as a private initiative, and initial coverage was only 10%. Nevertheless, more providers joined in each year, reaching 30% coverage in 2007, at which point political pressure was used to encourage the abstaining providers to join to avoid mandated participation. PensionsInfo now covers 99% of the market in Denmark. Norway has succeeded in obtaining 99% coverage for occupational pension funds for private-sector workers, with only small providers not participating. In contrast, Mijnpensioenoverzicht in the Netherlands began as a voluntary collaboration between the government and the three largest players, but participation by all players was eventually mandated.

The number of pension providers likely plays a larger role in whether or not participation needs to be mandatory. A large number of providers makes it more difficult to agree on the common data standards necessary to facilitate the operation of the digital platform. Countries having over around 100 providers are more likely to require mandatory participation. Germany, the Netherlands, and the United Kingdom, where participation is mandated, have around 450, 200 and 3 000-4 000 providers, respectively, compared to around 100 for Denmark and Norway and only around 30 for Sweden. Despite the relatively small number of providers in Hong Kong, China, of 13, they mandated participation because the providers were initially reluctant to change their administrative processes and adopt the new common platform. In Spain, only providers approved to offer publicly promoted occupational pension funds are required to connect to the platform, which is viewed as a way to ensure the quality and accessibility of pension information for the participants of plans connected to these funds.

Private providers can nevertheless have incentives to participate voluntarily because of the benefits that this can have for their members. In Sweden, providers can use the dashboard to discuss with their members about their pensions in a more engaging and comprehensive way, and at lower cost than they could do by developing a tool on their own. In Norway, providers can get the data from the dashboard to present it on their own portals for their customers. In Denmark, individuals can obtain their provider's contact details from the dashboard and contact them directly to obtain information even if this provider does not participate in the dashboard. In this way there is also pressure from peers and members for providers to participate in order to remain competitive and offer quality services.

7.3.2. Ownership and operations

The ownership and operations of pension dashboards can involve public or private entities, or a combination of both with varying levels of participation. Dashboards that are owned and operated by public sector institutions are also often managed by existing public institutions. The myGov platform in Australia, which provides information and consolidation abilities for Australians' superannuation accounts, is owned and operated by the Australian Taxation Office. Chile's Pension Simulator is operated by the Chilean Superintendence of Pensions, but the development of the platform was outsourced to external providers, and providers are allowed to develop their own pension simulator as long as they follow the specifications required by the regulator. Spain's Common Digital Platform is owned and managed by the Social Security Office, while Croatia's My Pension platform is managed by the Central Registry of Affiliates (REGOS). The individual pension dashboard in Latvia is accessed via the government portal which provides a wide range of public services to the population.

Alternatively, publicly owned dashboards can instead rely on specialised public or semi-public institutions to manage operations. Such models can promote the independence of the platform and reduce the risk of conflicts of interest. Mypension.be in Belgium is jointly owned by three public entities: the Federal Pension Service, the National Institute for Social Security of the Self-employed, and Sigedis. Sigedis is a non-profit entity funded by the government that provides the technology-based solutions for all operational aspects involving individual data, including database management and data collection. In Germany, the independent entity managing the pay-as-you-go public pension, Deutsche Rentenversicherung, created the division Zentrale Stelle für die Digitale Rentenübersicht (ZfDR), to fulfil its legal mandate to develop and operate the dashboard. The publicly provided Pensions Dashboard in the UK is being developed by the Money and Pensions Service (MaPS), which is an independent body of the Department for Work and Pensions, though providers will also be able to develop their own versions of the dashboard. MaPS expects to outsource many of the technical aspects of operations to tendered providers. The eMPF platform in Hong Kong, China will be built and operated by a fully owned subsidiary of the Mandatory Provident Fund Schemes Authority (MPFA). The initial development of the platform will be outsourced to an external contractor, who will transfer operations back to the eMPF once the platform is successfully up and running.

Several dashboards are managed via a public-private partnership. Public-private partnerships facilitate co-operation among the stakeholders and have the benefit of involving private providers who will be required to provide data to the dashboard and already have the experience and know-how of managing their data. Such partnerships can also lead to cost efficiencies by leveraging the knowledge and capabilities of the private entities. The AFORE Movil application in Mexico was developed by the pension regulator CONSAR and is operated jointly with the private sector. Nevertheless, most public-private ventures tend to rely on external service providers for much of their development and operations. In the Netherlands, the Pension Regulator Foundation has legal authority from the government to run the Mijnpensioenoverzicht dashboard, but the functions of the dashboard are largely delegated to external providers, who include a pensions consultancy, a digital provider, and a specialised creative communication provider. In Sweden, MinPension is run by a not-for-profit subsidiary of Insurance Sweden but is run as a consortium with the public Swedish Pensions Agency and is jointly financed by both institutions. MinPension, which has 14 staff, works with many external IT providers to develop and run the platform, but is considering bringing some of this expertise in-house due to the lack of pensions knowledge in the IT institutions. The Pension Clearing House in Israel is publicly owned, but its operations are fully outsourced to private entities.

Dashboards that are owned and developed fully by private pension fund associations can either run operations in-house or outsource them to external providers. PensionsInfo in Denmark is owned and operated by Insurance & Pensions Denmark, the industry association. The Norsk Pensjon dashboard in Norway, which is jointly owned by the largest life insurance companies, has only four staff, and therefore outsources all operations.

Other dashboards that have been developed independently of the government are generally fully owned and operated by the private entity responsible for their development. This is the case for the Minu Pension app in Estonia, the PensionsVault service being developed in Ireland, and the Orange Envelope dashboard in the Slovak Republic.

While most dashboards developed with government involvement result in a single access point through which all individuals go to consult their pension information, Israel and the United Kingdom allow private providers to also develop dashboards relying on the same data architecture. In Israel, the government provides the Pension Clearing House, through which all providers are mandated to submit any request for information. Individuals can request their information directly through the clearinghouse, which is fully operated by a private company winning the tender from the government, or through a privately-owned platform that connects to the clearinghouse to obtain the requested data. In the United Kingdom, the public dashboard will be run by the Money and Pensions Service (MaPS), but private institutions will also be able to develop dashboards that connect to the same digital architecture. In both Israel and the United Kingdom, the intention is that individuals will be allowed to choose the service that best suits their needs and preferences.

7.3.3. Governance structure

The governance structure of dashboards that are fully publicly owned is often also public, though it can sometimes involve the private sector in an advisory role. In Belgium, the dashboard is jointly governed by the three entities owning the platform, though the Federal Pension Service tends to take the lead as it manages the aspects related to the public pension. In addition, the social partners and the Minister for Pensions contribute to the development of the high-level vision relating to communication. In Israel, while the operations are fully managed by the private company Swiftness Ltd. who has the exclusive mandate to manage the clearinghouse, the company is supervised and controlled by the Insurance and Savings Capital Markets Authority. In Spain, the Social Security Office governs the Common Digital Platform. In the United Kingdom, the Money and Pensions Service (MaPS) will be in charge of the governance of the public dashboard, in part because it will be in charge of making any changes to the data standards affecting all providers so representation by the private sector could present a conflict of interest. Nevertheless, the United Kingdom does expect that there will be a sub-committee that will include private sector representatives to discuss data standards and make recommendations to the governing body. In contrast, the governance of the dashboard in Germany includes both public and private sector representatives, with a steering committee that includes representatives of consumer protection organisations, the Federal Ministry of Labour and Social Affairs and the Federal Ministry of Finance, as well as representatives of all three pension pillars. In addition, the Steering Committee regularly consults with five advisory bodies composed of technical experts in relevant fields.

Where the dashboards are at least partly owned by the private sector and the government has been involved in their development, both the public and private sectors are normally represented in the governance structure. In Denmark, where the industry association Insurance & Pensions Denmark owns the dashboard, two ministries are represented on the board of directors which is made up of 11 people. In the Netherlands, the dashboard is run by the Pension Regulator Foundation, which is made up of representatives from the pension and insurance associations as well as the Social Insurance Bank. The Dutch Ministry of Social Affairs is an observer at all Board meetings, and sub-committees advise the Board on the topics of communication, IT, and pension schemes. In Norway, where the dashboard is run by a private industry-owned entity, the Board is made up of three representatives from pension providers and two independent members, while the social partners, government, and other stakeholders are represented on the advisory board. In Sweden, the Board includes representatives from the Swedish Pensions Agency, the National Government Employee Pensions Board, as well as representatives from the private sector.

7.3.4. Financing

The private sector often fully finances the dashboard, even when the government has been involved in the initiative to develop it. In the Netherlands, the dashboard is financed through annual fees paid by the pension providers in proportion to their membership size. In Norway, providers finance the dashboard on a per-request basis, with half of the proceeds coming from providers sending data to meet individual requests, and the other half coming from providers making requests to obtain data for their own platforms. In Denmark, providers pay an upfront fee when joining the dashboard and then an additional fee paid on an annual basis. In the United Kingdom, the public dashboard will be financed by a levy on the financial services industry, and providers of private dashboards will pay an application fee as well as an annual fee that intends to cover the costs of supervision.

It is uncommon for costs to be shared between the public and private sectors. However, the MinPension dashboard in Sweden is financed equally by MinPension and the Swedish Pension Agency, and operates as a consortium.

It is also uncommon for costs to be borne by members, as publicly managed dashboards are normally free to access. In Israel, however, members pay a small application fee as a function of the frequency with which they would like to receive their information.

Fully public initiatives are normally entirely financed by the public sector. The eMPF platform in Hong Kong, China is a public initiative, and as such is financed by the government. Initial set up costs are around USD 630 million, a relatively large amount given the broad scope of the platform and its multiple functionalities.[7]

Not all public bodies have a dedicated budget for the set-up and operations of their digital platform, however. For example, in Spain the Common Digital Platform is financed from the general budget of the Social Security Office.

7.3.5. Digital architecture

The implementation and design of dashboards must consider three key issues relating to their digital architecture: the standardisation of data formats, data protection, and data storage.

Data standardisation

Having common standards for the submission of data is crucial for a dashboard to operate efficiently and to provide accurate information to individuals. This requires all providers to agree upon common data standards and the format in which they will send their data to the platform.

Agreeing upon the common data standard can take time but is necessary for the success of the dashboard. In Sweden, it took between two and five years for providers to send consistently good data, highlighting the importance of establishing robust information standards from the beginning.

Having existing standards for the information shown on pension statements or for pension projections can facilitate agreement between providers. This was the case in the Netherlands, where providers had already issued standardised statements and projections. Denmark also had existing standards and a methodology for pension projections. As a result, it did not need to mandate any data standards, and it considers new standards as optional until all providers are able to adapt to them. In contrast, given the large number of providers in the United Kingdom, data standards had to be mandated and all providers are obliged to comply with the standards established by the MaPS. Because of the possibility of multiple dashboards, the United Kingdom also had to agree on design standards to set out the minimum requirements for the information that digital platforms must show in order to ensure consistency in the information presented across the dashboards.

In submitting the data, there also needs to be a unique way to link pension accounts to the individual. National identification numbers are a convenient way to easily do this. Where these IDs are also already linked to financial accounts in the country, this can also ensure that the individual will automatically be able to see all their accounts, even if they had previously lost track of them or forgotten about them. In Australia, the dashboard is housed in the tax office and linked to the tax ID of individuals. In Denmark, national IDs were already connected to all financial accounts, which made it very easy to link the data to the dashboard. In contrast, the Netherlands relied upon individuals' names and birthdays when it first started its dashboard, but eventually linked accounts with individuals' social security number. The United Kingdom plans to rely on individuals' characteristics, as financial accounts are not necessarily linked to ID numbers.

Data protection

Identity verification is a crucial aspect of data protection, as it will ensure that the information that is being sent has been requested by the individual to whom it belongs. Digital platforms therefore need to have a secure log-in requirement to verify the identity of the person requesting the information. The AFORE Movil app in Mexico allows users to verify their identities through facial recognition. The United Kingdom incorporates an identity service that confirms the ID of the individual requesting the data through the platform. People in Belgium can connect to their platform with an electronic ID card. In Germany, members need to have a digital German ID, which may have deterred some people from registering as it represents an additional administrative barrier for access (Serenelli, 2023[4]). By contrast, in Latvia users have a range of options to verify their identity: they can use one of five qualified means of electronic identification, or alternatively use the same identification details they use with their provider. In Israel, individuals can request a unique code from the digital platform that they can communicate to someone such as an advisor to give them power of attorney to request data from the digital platform on their behalf.

There are normally additional requirements for providers to ensure the data used by the dashboard is secure. In Denmark, individuals wishing to share their data via the platform with their provider or other financial intermediary may only do so if the provider is a member of the industry association and that they comply and abide by relevant laws such as the EU's General Data Protection Regulation (GDPR). Providers must also have a secure login to their own sites. In the United Kingdom, providers must abide by a code of connection and guarantee minimum standards with respect to data security.

To comply with data protection laws such as GDPR, dashboards may require explicit individual consent for the provider to transfer their data to the platform. Sweden and the United Kingdom both require individual consent from people using the dashboard. Denmark requires consent if individuals wish to transfer their information from the platform to their provider or another financial intermediary. Norway requires a signed agreement between the platform and the provider to exchange data and information. In contrast, members accessing the platform in Spain must do so using an electronic certificate that a security platform with everyone's IDs would provide, though users can also use other means of identification such as a mobile key, permanent key, or PIN key.

Minimum standards for data security are necessary where multiple dashboards are allowed. In the United Kingdom, a governance register will ensure that digital platforms meet the required security and performance standards.

Data storage

There are two main approaches to store data for dashboards. The first is to have a centralised database where providers send their data and to which the dashboard directly connects. Dashboards in Australia; Belgium; Hong Kong, China; Israel; Spain, and Sweden rely on a centralised database. The second approach is to offer live access to the databases stored by the providers. For this approach, when an individual connects to the dashboard, it queries the databases for all providers to find the plans belonging to the individual and returns the information for plans matching the individual's ID to the dashboard for consultation. Once the individual logs off, their personal data is deleted. This is the approach taken in Croatia, Denmark, Germany, the Netherlands, Norway, and the United Kingdom. However, in Germany individual users may choose to store their data for up to five years after their last login.

Having a centralised database is easier and less costly to implement, but it can present a larger risk for data security because all the data is stored in one place. This is why Denmark eventually changed its initial approach of having a centralised database to one with live access. Sweden is also moving towards a less-centralised hybrid model, where larger providers are beginning to provide data in real time.

Having a centralised database can also increase the delay to update data on the platform. While live-access structures return updated information in real time, data has to be uploaded to the centralised database at regular intervals. In Belgium, data relating to the public pension is updated less frequently than for occupational pensions. In Israel, providers send the data only when requested by the user. They are required to send the data within three business days, but in practice they are able to send it within four hours.

Nevertheless, centralised databases do have some advantages. They can make it easier to use the data for purposes other than providing information to individuals. In Belgium, for example, the law explicitly allows the data to be used for other studies. Another advantage of a centralised database is that it ensures the availability of data when individuals request it, because it is not dependent on the technical availability of the sources of data.

7.3.6. Promoting awareness and use

Individuals need to be aware of the possibility of accessing their pension information through the dashboard and make use of its functionalities for such a platform to achieve the objectives of developing it. In Mexico, the pension regulator runs regular communication campaigns to get people to use the AFORE Movil app. In Hong Kong, China, the MPFA ran awareness campaigns leading up to the launch of its platform, which will be followed by marketing campaigns that will aim to educate and train the population on the dashboard in addition to promoting its use.

The channel of communication used may also need to consider the type of user targeted. In Sweden, those with low knowledge and interest in pensions were targeted via telephone or employer meetings rather than via internet channels that work better for those more inclined to find out about their pension.

The entity managing the dashboard may not necessarily have a budget to promote it to potential users. In these cases, providers themselves can play a significant role in encouraging their members to access the platform. Providers can have a natural incentive to do so. In Sweden, the dashboard is a useful tool for providers to consult with their customers about their retirement planning, and it is much cheaper for them to refer to the common dashboard rather than develop one themselves. In Denmark, Pensions & Insurance Denmark does not have any budget for marketing, but the dashboard is promoted by both banks and providers, in part because banks request information on pensions for mortgage applications. Belgium and the Netherlands have made it mandatory for providers to signpost the dashboard in the statements they provide to members. Providers in Chile who have not developed their own pension simulator are required to provide a link directly to the regulator's simulator.

Employee representatives can also play a role in promoting the awareness of the digital platforms as a way to assist in the retirement planning of their membership. In Sweden, unions promote the dashboard to their members.

7.4. Evolution and monitoring of individual pension dashboards

The development of an individual pension dashboard is often an ongoing endeavour, with improvements to the platform made gradually over time in response to feedback and observations about what could be working better or what may be missing. The dashboard's development is often informed through the monitoring of metrics that indicate usage, engagement, and ultimate improvement in retirement outcomes that indicate to what extent its design has been successful in achieving its objectives.

7.4.1. Continued development

The development of an individual pension dashboard can be a long and iterative process. Many countries have gradually improved their dashboards as they learned from experience and identified aspects not considered in the original design. In Sweden, 95% of the initial platform was discarded and rebuilt after two years as the dashboard did not achieve the desired objectives. In 2017, the dashboard also underwent large changes to its interface to improve user experience. With respect to projections, more complex tools, namely a dynamic retirement income calculator where individuals can change input assumptions, and a retirement planning tool available for those aged over 54, have gradually been added. In Denmark, the PensionsInfo website has been upgraded five times with gradual improvements. The digital platform in

Belgium has gradually expanded coverage and improved personalisation, content, and the format of the interface over time. The Common Digital Platform in Spain is starting very simply, initially showing only contributions and assets accumulated. However, a projection tool on the platform to show expected future retirement incomes is expected to be developed. In Germany, the dashboard started operating as a pilot project where providers could connect voluntarily and test the portal with citizens interested in doing so. The regular operation of the dashboard began in December 2023 on a voluntary basis, though providers have since been required to connect to the platform.

7.4.2. Impact assessment

The performance of the dashboard should be regularly monitored so that improvements can be made to increase user access, engagement, and ultimately improve retirement outcomes. It is important to monitor the use of the dashboard by age, gender and income to assess its success in promoting inclusiveness. Women, young adults, and lower income groups tend to be the groups with most difficulties in engaging with pensions.

User testing is a useful approach to determine how to improve the content and format of platforms to better engage different groups. Sweden is continuously testing to improve the user experience of its site. Denmark also does a lot of user testing, with one of the next objectives being to improve how the impact of purchasing power is presented. EIOPA did some user testing in Italy, Spain and Romania to assess comprehensibility and engagement, and notably found that consumers tended to prefer bar charts to donut charts in showing the breakdown of their expected retirement income (EIOPA, 2021[5]). Chile has conducted experiments to test how users respond to personalised information, showing that this had a short-term effect of increasing voluntary savings (Fuentes et al., 2023[6]).

Impact assessment can also include looking at how the information provided in the dashboard is working to improve retirement outcomes for individuals. For example, the AFORE Movil app in Mexico succeeded in increasing the number of accounts for voluntary savings and facilitated the opening of retirement savings accounts for independent workers new to the system. In Sweden, the dashboard has significantly increased the proportion of people reporting that they feel they can make well-informed choices about their future pension. It has facilitated retirement planning by showing people how they can take different pensions at different times in line with their needs, and more people are now working longer as part-time employees. The dashboard has also led to more people opting for life annuities, perhaps because the dashboard shows how retirement income can change over time.

7.5. Good practices and lessons for the development of individual pension dashboards for pensions

This section presents good practices and lessons for jurisdictions looking to develop an individual pension dashboard to facilitate individuals' access to information about their pensions and their expected future retirement income. These are derived from the examples discussed in this chapter and cover all aspects of development from the initial conception of what the dashboard aims to achieve, through to its design, development and impact assessment.

7.5.1. Purpose and functionality

The purpose of an individual pension dashboard should be clearly defined and its functionalities established to achieve that purpose.

Individual pension dashboards should provide functionalities in line with a clear purpose and objective

The purpose for the establishment of the dashboard and the objectives it aims to achieve should guide its functionality and content. Dashboards intending to improve the provision of information and increase awareness about pensions and retirement income should ensure that the information included is relevant and useful for the targeted user groups. Those intending to aid in decision making should provide tools for users to understand the implications of their decisions. Dashboards intending to make the management of pensions more accessible and efficient should allow users to initiate transactions from the platform and/or facilitate the exchange of data.

7.5.2. Content and design

Individual pension dashboards should include content that is relevant and useful for individuals' retirement planning and should present information in a way that is easily understandable and effective in engaging users.

Dashboards should automatically include all sources of retirement income where possible and relevant

Public pensions, occupational pensions, and personal pensions should ideally automatically be included in dashboards aiming to provide information to individuals about their retirement and to help improve their retirement outcomes. This will allow individuals to have a full view of the retirement income they can expect to receive and the different sources that will contribute to it. Including public pensions in addition to asset-backed pensions will be particularly important for individuals to have a holistic view of their situation.

Nevertheless, it may not be possible to include all sources of pensions from the outset, and many jurisdictions have included additional sources over time. For pensions that cannot be included automatically, as is often the case for personal pensions, the dashboard may allow users to manually add this information themselves.

Dashboards should provide an estimate of future retirement income in real terms

It is important to show users an estimate of future retirement income to provide a relatable indicator of financial preparedness for retirement. Showing only the amount of assets accumulated is not useful information for an individual to assess whether they will have enough money to finance their retirement. Nevertheless, where contributions and/or accumulated rights to pension plans are relatively low, it may be advisable to also show the projected level of assets accumulated because the achievable level of lifetime income may be relatively small and could discourage people from making additional savings. Real values are preferred for retirement income estimations so that individuals can more easily compare with their current salary and spending levels, even if this estimate is not perfect.

Projections should convey the uncertainty around estimations

Future projections should include clear indications that the values provided are only estimates and that the actual figures could be different depending on investment returns, other assumptions, and how the economy ultimately evolves. One way to do this is by presenting several estimates of future retirement income, for example a good scenario and a bad scenario in addition to the expected scenario. Alternatively, there could be an estimate that excludes any future contributions as well as one that shows the expected amount if individuals continue contributing at the same level.

Retirement income calculators are a useful tool to aid decision-making

Retirement income calculators can be an effective tool to engage users and help them to understand how the decisions they make can affect the level of expected income they can have in retirement. They allow users to adapt assumptions themselves to see how different parameters can change expected outcomes. At a minimum, calculators should allow users to change their retirement age and contributions, but more advanced versions can also allow people to adjust parameters such as investment returns or employment.

Retirement income should, where possible, be shown over time and not only at the point of retirement, and should reflect the different payout options available

It is useful for people to see how their retirement income could change over time and the impact of the different options they have to withdraw their retirement savings. This may also help them to understand the value of taking their savings gradually as income rather than as a lump sum.

Additional variables affecting retirement outcomes are also useful to include

Additional variables that are relevant and useful for members could include investment performance, asset allocations, fees charged by the providers, tax treatment, and survivor or disability benefits. Basic information about their plan and the contact details of their provider is helpful for users to be able to follow up with questions or issues regarding their plan.

Allowing users to download a summary of the information presented can facilitate the use of the information for retirement planning

Many dashboards allow users to download a summary of their pension information included on the platform to use for their broader financial planning in consultation with a financial advisor. Some platforms even allow individuals to send the summary directly to their financial advisor through the platform. This feature can encourage and facilitate the active use of this information to plan for their retirement.

Information should be presented using a layered approach

Presenting information in a layered approach makes the information more accessible to individuals and allows them to engage at the level of detail they are interested in without being overwhelmed with too much information from the beginning. This involves presenting the key information first, and then allowing users to drill down for additional details. For example, the initial information shown can be the assets accumulated or total expected income in retirement. This can then be broken down by the source of income (public pension, occupational pension, etc.), and then users can drill down into the details of each plan.

Technical vocabulary and jargon should be avoided

The information shown needs to be simple and understandable. Many users do not understand technical terminology commonly used for pensions (e.g. annuity, lump sum), and are not likely to engage with information that they find difficult to understand.

Visuals can aid user understanding and engagement

Along with simple vocabulary, visuals can help people to understand difficult concepts. For example, showing a graph with retirement income by source over time allows people to see when their income is expected to increase or decrease, and the income they can expect over their lifetime. Other visuals can help people understand if they are on the right track with their retirement planning (e.g. traffic light) or the impact of inflation over time.

Including information on what people can do to change outcomes is important to positively impact retirement planning

Estimates of future retirement income should be accompanied by references explaining the steps that people can take to change their outcomes. Providing users with information on their situation is only a first step and will not necessarily be sufficient to improve retirement outcomes. People will not necessarily know what to do with that information to increase their expected retirement income. With this additional information, people who find that their expected finances in retirement are not in line with their needs or expectations would then know concretely what they could do to improve it.

User testing is important to understand the most effective formats to engage different types of people

Testing the format and functionality of the dashboard with real users is important to ensure that the platform will be useful and fit for purpose to achieve its goals. User testing can allow developers to see which formats are best at engaging people and helping them to understand the information that the dashboard provides. Such testing can ensure that users are able to easily navigate the dashboard and use the tools provided. The dashboard should also be accessible for different types of people with various objectives of using the platform, which can vary with age, gender, or knowledge of pensions, for example. Testing should also consider the device from which users will access the dashboard to make sure the content is still readable and usable.

7.5.3. Development and operations

Numerous practical aspects are involved in the development of individual pension dashboards. These relate to how to organise various stakeholders to support, develop and manage the platform, how to ensure the accuracy and security of data provided to the platform, and how to promote awareness and use of the platform by the population.

Mandating pension providers to connect to the dashboard is effective in ensuring broad and timely coverage

Broad coverage of providers is important to ensure that the dashboard will be useful for users and in turn to ensure that they will continue to access and make use of the platform. The most effective way to ensure broad and timely coverage is to make providers' participation mandatory. Nevertheless, even if required to connect, providers will still need sufficient time to develop the necessary infrastructure and processes to do so. As such, it may be preferable to allow for voluntary participation initially and allow more time for providers to comply with mandatory participation.

However, where the largest players strongly support the dashboard, voluntary participation may be sufficient to achieve broad coverage. Once the dashboard is viewed as a valuable tool for members and/or employers to access information about the pension system and pensions, providers will be more incentivised to connect their pension funds on their own. They may even be pressured by their members to do so, so that the members will be able to easily access all their pension accounts in one place. Additionally, as more providers connect, competitive pressure should encourage the remaining providers to connect as well.

Nevertheless, voluntary participation is less likely to be successful where there is a large number of providers or where initial support from the private sector is lacking. Mandating participation may also be the preferred approach when the government owns the platform to justify the investment and ensure its success, and to avoid the reputational risk of a failed project.

The management of publicly owned dashboards by independent public or semi-public entities can mitigate potential conflicts of interest and ensure the appropriate expertise

It is common for specialised institutions to be in charge of managing the operations of publicly-owned dashboards. This can reduce conflicts of interest in the advancement of the dashboard because the mandate of the entity includes the development and management of the dashboard in the interests of the members and the other stakeholders of the system. It can also allow for the integration of more specialised knowledge in-house, rather than having to outsource all the required activities.

Single access points can simplify the promotion of the dashboard, but may not appeal to all potential users

Most individual pension dashboards operate with a single access point where users can log in to access their personalised space. This allows for simple communication campaigns that guide potential users to the particular website or app for the dashboard, and can educate users on how to use the dashboard. With this approach, there may be less confusion about how to access and use the dashboard because there is only one place to go and a single user interface to learn. However, users can be heterogenous in their preference regarding how they engage with their pensions. They may rather prefer to access such information through their financial provider's website if they are more used to managing their finances from there. They may also prefer different formats or tools that alternative access points may offer. Nevertheless, where multiple access points are allowed, it is important that all are subject to minimum standards for the quality and consistency of information provided.

Multiple stakeholders should be involved in the dashboard's governance

Public-private governance models have the advantage of promoting coordination between the different stakeholders involved in the system and making sure the views of the different parties are represented. However, it can also come with challenges, as the interests of the two sides may not always align. This can lead to disagreements around decisions that need to be made around the priorities for the development of the dashboard, and potentially slow decision-making.

Alternatively, public governing bodies can consult sub-committees or advisory bodies in the decisions they make to ensure that they consider the views of different stakeholders. Such bodies can include private-sector representatives. This can also ensure that they have the input of relevant experts in taking decisions.

Dashboards should have a clear source of financing and a dedicated budget

The way in which the platform is financed should be aligned with its purpose and objectives. Having a dedicated budget allocated to the development and operation of the digital platform can avoid potential conflicts with other priorities of the entity or institution in charge of managing the platform. Such conflicts could prevent additional financing to develop and improve the platform.

Providers of data to the platform need to conform to a minimum set of common data standards

Data standards should be established from the outset. To the extent possible, existing standards should serve as a basis for the format of data to be fed to the platform. This can include, for example, the format used for pension statements or standards used for pension projections. Data standards will more likely need to be mandated where the industry does not already follow a common standard and where there are a large number of providers in the market.

Unique identifiers are required to link pension accounts to individual users

The simplest approach to link users and accounts is to rely on individuals' national ID numbers. However, pension accounts are not always linked to these numbers in all jurisdictions. In these cases, it is more challenging to establish a unique identifier, and several variables including full names, birthdays, and potentially other characteristics need to be used to link an individual's accounts to their personal space on the platform. Several jurisdictions rely on electronic identification numbers, which an individual may need to separately apply for. This additional step can nevertheless be a barrier for the take-up and use of the platform for those less inclined to do so.

Data protection measures are crucial to safeguard the security of individual data

Data providers and intermediaries must comply with applicable data protection laws. Often, providers must demonstrate that they comply and uphold data protection standards on their own platforms. Dashboards that process individuals' data should verify the identity of the user to allow access to the data. They also often require individual consent before the data is accessed. This can be done when users register or sign into the dashboard for the first time, or when they request to perform certain transactions.

The choice between a centralised database and a live-access model needs to consider cost, security, service objectives and data needs

Pension dashboards can access the data shown to users either via a centralised database where all relevant data is stored, or through a live-access model where the dashboard obtains data from providers in real-time when the user logs in, and then subsequently deletes it. Live-access models are more complex and costly to implement, however they also offer more security because the data is not being stored in a single place. However, centralised databases can allow for the data to be used for other purposes such as the monitoring of the system and can ensure the data is available when requested.

Legislating the authorised use of data stored in a centralised database can facilitate its use to improve policy

A centralised database offers a valuable opportunity as a source of data for governmental, statistical or academic studies. Legislating the authorised use of data provides a legal basis for it to be used by the government and other stakeholders for studies about the pension system. Such studies can help to identify areas of success or improvements needed in the system and inform policy measures to improve retirement outcomes in a targeted manner.

Communication plans are crucial for the success of dashboards

Communication should involve awareness campaigns targeting potential users to inform them how they can access the platform and what information they will be able to find on it. The channels of communication should consider the most effective medium for the type of user targeted.

Additionally, communication is imperative for managing expectations and raising awareness around the dashboard. Communication with media outlets and the public can keep them up to date on the progress of the dashboard and avoid unrealistic expectations. The lack of a sound communication plan can backfire as the public's expectations may be unrealistic, which could lead to challenges to move forward if the initial platform falls below those expectations.

Users will need to understand that the initial version of the platform is only a first step, and that the dashboard will continue to improve over time. Otherwise, they may have high expectations and be disappointed with the little amount of information that the dashboard may initially provide, and they will be reluctant to consult the dashboard again in the future.

Pension providers can be useful to help promote dashboards

Communication budgets are often limited and may not be sufficient to finance an effective communication campaign for all potential users. As such, pension providers can be useful advocates for dashboards, and it is often in their interest to promote them to members. A well-designed dashboard is an easy and more cost-effective way for them to engage members with their retirement savings, and to potentially encourage them to save more. Beyond the voluntary promotion by providers, they could also be required to provide information on how to access the dashboard on their own websites and include this information in their communications to members.

7.5.4. Evolution and monitoring

The development of individual pension dashboards is a long process involving improvement over time and the monitoring of usage and retirement outcomes to ensure they are effective in achieving their objectives.

The development of a dashboard should establish clear objectives with a timeline of milestones to achieve them

Many dashboards begin in a simple manner, but there needs to be a clear view on how the platform should develop going forward and what other information and functionalities it will include. It is also important to establish a timeline in which to achieve those objectives.

Having a clear plan to develop the platform will have numerous benefits. First, users can know what changes to expect going forward and adapt their expectations accordingly. They can potentially also be given the opportunity to provide feedback about what worked for them, what they did not like, or what may be missing to improve the platform going forward. Second, having explicit milestones will provide incentives to continue the development of the platform, rather than maintain the initial simple version. Finally, if the participation of providers is not mandatory, a clear plan will help them to understand the potential added value of the platform in the future, and they will be more likely be willing to work towards connecting to it voluntarily as an additional benefit for their members.

Measurable metrics should be used to assess the impact of the dashboard given its objectives

Metrics can provide an indication of whether the dashboard is successful in achieving its objectives and its impact on the desired outcomes within the pension system, and if something may need to be adjusted. It is important to link metrics to the objectives and the timeline of milestones to achieve. Access to the platform is a useful metric to determine the extent to which the platform is actually used by stakeholders. Access can be measured through the proportion of users logging into the platform, the frequency with which they do so, or the duration of their visit. Other metrics can provide an indication of any positive impact on desired outcomes. If the dashboard aims to provide information, it should ideally improve users' knowledge and understanding of pensions. Additional metrics could be whether contributions change, whether members consolidate their accounts, or how people tend to withdraw their money. Regardless of the metric used, it is important to consider the impact for different demographics to determine whether the platform is effective in engaging and improving outcomes for different types of people.

References

Antolin, P. and O. Fuentes (2012), "Communicating Pension Risk to DC Plan Members: The Chilean Case of a Pension Risk Simulator", *OECD Working Papers on Finance, Insurance and Private Pensions*, No. 28, OECD Publishing, Paris, https://doi.org/10.1787/5k9181hxzmlr-en. [3]

EIOPA (2021), *Technical advice on pension tracking systems - impact assessment*, https://www.eiopa.europa.eu/system/files/2021-12/technical_advice_pts_impact_assessment.pdf. [5]

EIOPA (2021), *Technical advice on the development of pension tracking systems*, https://www.eiopa.europa.eu/system/files/2021-12/technical_advice_pension_tracking_systems_for_publicationfinal.pdf. [2]

Fuentes, O. et al. (2023), "Personalized Information as a Tool to Improve Pension Savings: Results from a Randomized Control Trial in Chile", *Economic Development and Cultural Change*, https://doi.org/10.1086/720718. [6]

IOPS (2022), *Good practices for designing, presenting and supervising pension projections*, https://www.iopsweb.org/IOPS-Good-practices-for-designing-presenting-and-supervising-pension-projections-2022.pdf. [1]

Serenelli, L. (2023), "German government to make pension funds join dashboard", *IPE magazine*, https://www.ipe.com/news/german-government-to-make-pension-funds-join-dashboard/10070133.article?utm_campaign=1543686_20.11.23%20ipe%20daily%20news&utm_medium=email&utm_source=IPE&dm_i=5KVE,X346,C5E85,42YZM,1. [4]

Annex 7.A. Summary of elements included in individual pension dashboards

Annex Table 7.A.1. Comparison of the content of individual pension dashboards

Country	Platform	Pillars covered	Accounts shown	Assets accumulated	Expected retirement income	Retirement income calculator (dynamic projection)	Contributions	Tax	Survivor/disability	Investment performance	Fees	Plan /provider information	Other functionality
Australia	YourSuper Comparison	2	Automatic	Yes	No	No	Yes	No	No	Yes	Yes	Yes	Consolidation, transfers between funds; compassionate release
Belgium	mypension.be	1, 2	Automatic; Manual additions possible for missing accounts	Yes	Yes	Retirement age; salary; job; hours worked	Yes	Yes	Yes	No	No	Yes	Can sign up to receive pension communications by email; track communication with provider

Chile	Simulador de Pensiones	2, 3	Automatic	Yes	Yes	Retirement age; salary; voluntary contributions; other savings; investment strategy; withdrawals; spouse and dependent children	No	Yes	No	No	No	No	Email of results
Croatia	Moja mirovina	1, 2 (3 planned)	Automatic		Yes	Retirement age; salary; investment return; economic growth;							Download results
Denmark	PensionsInfo	1, 2, 3	Automatic	Yes	Yes	Retirement age	Annual contri-butions per plan	Yes	Yes	No	No	Yes	Download pdf or send directly to advisor
Estonia	Minu Pension	1, 2, 3	Manual input	Yes	Yes	Investment return	No	No	No	Yes	No	Yes	Can make contributions and transfers
Germany	Digitale Rentenüber-sicht	1, 2, 3	Automatic	No	Yes	No	No	No	Yes	No	No	Yes	Can export to advisors
Ireland	Pensions Vault	2, 3	Manual input	Yes	Yes	Yes							Storage of pension documents; connect with advisor
Israel	Swiftness	2	Automatic	Yes	Yes	Yes	Yes		Yes			Yes	Power of attorney requests; Download report
Latvia	Services Portal	1, 2	Automatic	Yes	No	No	Yes	No	No	No	Admi n only	Yes	Request to switch providers

Mexico	AFORE Móvil	2	Automatic	Yes	Yes	Yes	Yes	No		Yes			Open account, register beneficiaries, change providers, make contributions, withdraw voluntary contributions
Nether-lands	Mijnpensioenov erzicht.nl	1, 2	Automatic; can also add partner's pension	Yes	Yes; also in good and bad investment scenarios	Retirement age, salary change, divorce	No	Yes	Yes			Yes	Download pdf
Norway	Norsk Pensjon	1, 2, 3	Automatic	Yes	Yes	Salary, retirement age; advanced calculator with marital status, partial retirement, and work abroad	No	No	Yes	No	No	Yes	Download pdf
Slovak Republic	Orange Envelope	1, 2, 3	Manual input	Yes	Good – average – poor investment scenarios		Monthly contri- - butions per source	No	Yes	Yes	Yes		
Spain	Plataforma Digital Común	2 (partial)	Automatic	Yes	Planned	Planned	Yes	No	No	Planne d	No	Yes	Download pdf
Sweden	MinPension	1, 2, 3	Automatic; can manually add missing accounts	Yes	Yes	Retirement age; job change; salary change		Yes		No	Yes		Retirement income planner for 54+; appoint power of attorney
UK	Pensions Dashboard	1, 2	Automatic; can manually add missing	Yes	Current entitle- -ments and if contribu-	No			No			Yes	Can export information to financial advisor

			accounts		-tions continue								

Notes

[1] Digital platforms that provide individuals with information on their accumulated pensions are commonly referred to as 'pension dashboards' or 'pension tracking systems'. The latter term was coined by EIOPA and is commonly used in Europe. However, this report will refer to these platforms as 'individual pension dashboards', or more briefly as 'dashboards'.

[2] The scope of the report only includes dashboards that incorporate information on asset-backed pensions.

[3] The author gratefully acknowledges the contributions of the following individuals, who generously took the time to share their information and experiences with digital platforms in their respective jurisdictions: Myriam Lanotte, Sigedis (Belgium); Cynthia Hui, MPFA (Hong Kong, China); Đorđe Nižetić, Damir Bilić and Zoran Protega, REGOS (Croatia); Michael Rasch, Insurance and Pension Denmark (Denmark); Trond Tørstad, Norsk Pensjon (Norway); Manuel Alvarez, Ministry of Inclusion, Social Security and Migration (Spain); Anders Lundström, Min Pension (Sweden); Matt Burrell, Standard Life (United Kingdom); Lucy Hemsley, DWP (United Kingdom).

[4] In Belgium there is also limited involvement of members in decisions relating to their occupational pensions, and therefore less of a need to support decision making.

[5] Annex 7.A provides the details of the elements included in the various dashboards discussed in this section.

[6] All sources to finance retirement refers to those sources solely intended to finance retirement, and not all financial assets that individuals may own.

[7] This compares to around EUR 5 million required to set up the Norsk Pensjon platform in Norway, which has a more limited scope of functionality.

www.ingramcontent.com/pod-product-compliance
Lightning Source LLC
Chambersburg PA
CBHW061211240926
51846CB00006B/1190